Basics & Beyond

An Educator's Reference

2nd Edition

TABLE OF CONTENTS

CHAPTERS

ACKNOWLEDGMENTS

The Emergency Nurses Association (ENA) would like to extend its appreciation to the following people who reviewed and revised the second edition of *Basics & Beyond–An Educator's Reference*.

SECOND EDITION EDITOR

Steven A. Weinman, RN, BSN, CEN
Emergency Department Instructor
New York Weill Cornell Medical Center at
New York-Presbyterian Hospital
New York, New York

SECOND EDITION REVIEWERS & CONTRIBUTING AUTHORS

Barrie Friedenberg, RN, MSN
Nursing Instructor
New York Weill Cornell Medical Center at
New York-Presbyterian Hospital
New York, New York

Robert Kneis, RN, MSN, CEN
Clinical Nurse Specialist
Emergency Services
Healthsystem Minnesota
St. Louis Park, Minnesota

Donna Massey, RN
Associate Director, Educational Services
Emergency Nurses Association
Des Plaines, IL

Dianne M. Ryan, RN, C, MA, CNA
Director, Department of Nursing Education
New York Weill Cornell Medical Center
and Columbia Presbyterian Medical Center at
New York-Presbyterian Hospital
New York, New York

Linda Saal, RN, MSN
Associate Director
School of Continuing Education for Nurses
New York Weill Cornell Medical Center at
New York-Presbyterian Hospital
New York, New York

Tom Trimble, RN
Emergency Nurse
San Rafael, CA

STAFF SUPPORT

Jennifer Heidenreich
Desktop Publisher
Emergency Nurses Association
Des Plaines, IL

PREFACE

The primary goal of the Emergency Nurses Association (ENA) is advancement of emergency nursing. Support of emergency nursing education and promulgation of requisite resource material are inherent to the attainment of this goal. The Scientific Assembly (annual education program sponsored by ENA) and *Orientation to Emergency Nursing: Concepts, Competencies, and Critical Thiking* (ENA, 2000) are just two examples of ENA's efforts to provide this educational support. Periodic membership surveys identify specific membership needs relative to education programs and resource materials.

A multitude of excellent resources exists for nursing education and emergency nursing. Analysis of recent surveys identified the need for a resource manual particularly for the emergency nurse educator. In 1995, the ENA Board of Directors charged a task force of emergency nurse educators with development of a resource manual specifically for the emergency nurse educator. The result was the first edition of *Basics & Beyond–An Educator's Reference*. Now in it's second edition *Basics and Beyond* is based on the premise that every emergency room, regardless of size, location, or patient population, faces the challenge of providing quality education.

In the wake of escalating health care costs and shrinking education dollars, emergency nurse educators must pursue new avenues to minimize costs and maximize efficiency of traditional education programs. Ironically, an increasingly complex and culturally diverse workforce has led to considerable scrutiny of traditional education programs. These challenges and constraints significantly impact the ability of emergency nurse educators to provide meaningful education at reasonable costs. *Basics and Beyond* is designed to support the emergency nurse educator in this endeavor. Novice emergency nurse educators will find *Basics and Beyond* provides a comprehensive view of emergency nursing education. Experienced emergency nurse educators will receive a new perspective on essential information.

The ability to provide creative, quality education requires knowledge of fundamental principles of education and integration of these tenets into the dynamic world of emergency nursing. To prosper in today's health care arena, the emergency nurse educator should be well versed in quality improvement, productivity analysis, marketing, and organizational concepts. Other fundamental principles the emergency nurse educator must be aware of include:

- Adult learning theories and teaching methodologies.
- Developmental steps for various educational programs.
- Creation and procurement of effective audiovisuals.
- Use of multimedia equipment.

Effective communication strategies and aggressive pursuit of professional development also play a significant role in growth of the emergency nurse educator.

The importance of clinical expertise to the emergency nurse educator cannot be overstated. Successful emergency nursing education programs are built on a solid foundation of strong clinical knowledge. Educators are encouraged to utilize hands-on experience and available resources to establish clinical credibility.

Basics and Beyond is designed to work in concert with existing resources. It should not be viewed as a substitute for definitive clinical and instructional texts. Each section identifies a specific body of essential knowledge for the emergency nurse educator, then elucidates key elements within the respective topic. The content of *Basics and Beyond* provides the emergency nurse educator, regardless of experience, with information to survive and thrive in today's changing health care arena.

REFERENCES

Emergency Nurses Association. (2000). <u>Orientation to emergency nursing: *Concepts, Competencies, and Critical Thiking*</u>. Des Plaines, IL: Author.

Introduction

OBJECTIVES

Upon completion of this manual, the emergency nurse educator will be able to:

1. State ENA's position on nursing education.

2. Discuss practical approaches to emergency nursing education.

3. Integrate key elements of emergency nursing practice and nursing education.

Emergency nursing education may be provided by staff nurses, designated educators, clinical nurse specialists, trauma nurse coordinators, or nurse managers. Experience and preparation for the educator role vary significantly for each. This manual is designed to provide pertinent information for development and implementation of emergency nursing education programs, regardless of the emergency nurse educator's experience, location, organizational position, or fiscal limitations.

FORMAT

The 11 chapters in this edition provide information across the spectrum of emergency nursing education. Each chapter lists behavioral objectives followed by a brief description of general information. Practical tips in concept application and troubleshooting for particular situations are included. Pertinent graphs, charts, and diagrams enhance the presentation of essential information. References and recommended readings have also been included and are provided for each chapter.

The number of chapters in the second edition has been condensed and each topic area has been reviewed and updated as necessary to assure current educational concepts, strategies, available technologies, and resources.

RESOURCE ANALYSIS

The Emergency Nurses Association (ENA) recognizes the importance of continuing education and has made it a high organizational priority. The need for education is an integral part of virtually every ENA position statement. Position statements specifically address trauma nursing education, education for emergency nurses caring for pediatric patients, education of prehospital providers, and integration of emergency nursing into basic nursing curricula. *Standards of Emergency Nursing Practice* (ENA, 1998) clarifies criteria for orientation and continuing education. Education of the emergency nurse also is addressed in *Emergency Nursing Core Curriculum, 5th edition* (ENA, 2000). A comprehensive, competency-based orientation program specifically for emergency nursing is recommended and available from the association. Other ENA resources center around trauma care, pediatric emergencies, nursing diagnoses, triage, and continuous quality improvement (CQI). Several of these resources are computer-based. Texts on adult learning theories, program development, and quality improvement are available through the association, other professional organizations, reference libraries, and publishing companies. The Internet has flourished in the number of interactive websites that emphasize emergency care; these sites are excellent teaching tools (Chapter 11).

Resources enhance the practice of the emergency nurse educator; however, the value of such resources may be limited by availability, content, and presentation. Geographic and economic constraints limit availability of some materials. Specialized programs, such as computer-assisted instruction (despite its widespread availability) may not be feasible for all educators. Recognition of potential barriers to resource utilization is essential for the emergency nurse educator to maximize available resources and gain access to additional resources.

In addition to resources available from ENA, the emergency nurse educator should be familiar with documents from regulatory agencies such as the Joint Commission on Accreditation of Healthcare Organizations (JCAHO), National Highway Traffic Safety Administration (NHTSA), Health Care Financing Administration (HCFA), Occupational Safety and Health Administration (OSHA), and other professional organizations such as the Society of Trauma Nurses (STN), American Association of Critical Care Nurses (AACN), American College of Emergency Physicians (ACEP), Society of Academic Emergency Medicine (SAEM), American Trauma Society (ATS), and the National Association of EMS Educators (NAEMSE). Comprehensive review and discussion of all resources is beyond the scope of this text, but selected resources do merit additional review. The brief description provided should not supplant the content of the original resource.

POSITION STATEMENTS

ENA has position statements that highlight the organization's opinion on issues impacting the practice of emergency nursing. These position statements elucidate the nature of the problem, provide insight into areas of controversy, articulate ENA's position on the problem, provide rationale for the position, and site applicable resources. As previously mentioned, position statements are beneficial in rationalizing new education programs as well as preservation or expansion of existing programs. Position statements that highlight education for emergency care providers, ancillary services, and the public include:

- Minimal Trauma Nursing Education Recommendations (ENA, 1999).

  ▪ Regardless of size or location, all emergency departments care for injured patients.

  ▪ Trauma care is not limited to designated trauma centers; therefore, trauma education is germane to all emergency nurse educators.

  ▪ Emergency nurses provide initial assessment and ongoing care for the majority of trauma patients.

  ▪ Emergency nurse educators have a responsibility to provide appropriate trauma-related education within their respective institutions.

- Role of the Emergency Nurse in the Prehospital Environment (ENA, 1998).

  ▪ Emergency nurses traditionally provided education for prehospital providers.

  ▪ Some states now mandate emergency medical technician (EMT) or paramedic (EMT-P) certification for the emergency nurse who provides formal training for prehospital providers.

  ▪ ENA supports the position that the emergency nurse who provides prehospital provider education should demonstrate requisite knowledge and skills without additional certification or licensure as an EMT or EMT-P.

  ▪ The educational role of the emergency nurse includes participation in the education of patients, the community, and other health care providers. All nurses have a responsibility to acquire and maintain a level of knowledge and skills commensurate with their scopes of practice. Emergency nurses should continue to have a major role in the education and training of prehospital care providers.

- Integration of Emergency Nursing Concepts in Nursing Curricula (ENA, 1998).

  - Historically, nursing curricula provided limited theoretical and clinical exposure to emergency nursing practice.

  - Consequently, nurses may find themselves inadequately prepared to prioritize and manage diverse patient situations.

  - The emergency department provides an optimal setting for students to integrate the nursing process into clinical practice. The emergency nurse is a role model for students.

- Educational Recommendations for Nurses Providing Pediatric Emergency Care (ENA, 1999).

  - Emergency nurses must be knowledgeable of injury and disease prevention strategies, pediatric triage, and assessment with appropriate interventions.

  - ENA recommends that the Emergency Nursing Pediatric Course-Provider be the minimal educational standard for nurses providing emergency care to children.

- Hazardous Material Exposure (ENA, 1998).

  - ENA acknowledges the risk of hazardous materials to the public and emergency care personnel.

  - Emergency care personnel should be knowledgeable in the recognition, management, and personal protection required when treating patients exposed to hazardous materials.

  - Emergency nurses have the legal, moral, ethical, and professional responsibility to all patients to possess current, comprehensive knowledge and skills.

- The following position statements also include educational components:

  - Advanced Practice in Emergency Nursing (ENA, 1998)

  - Autonomous Emergency Nursing Practice (ENA, 1999)

  - Care of the Pediatric Patient During Intrafacility Transfer (ENA, 1999)

  - CEN Review Courses and Resource Material (ENA, 1998)

  - Collaborative and Interdisciplinary Research (ENA, 1999)

  - Conscious Sedation (ENA, 1998)

  - CISM (ENA, 1998)

  - Domestic Violence and Human Neglect (ENA, 1998)

  - Family Presence at the Bedside During Invasive Procedures and/or Resuscitation (ENA, 1998)

  - Injury Prevention (ENA, 1998)

  - Medical Evaluation of Suspected Intoxication and Psychiatric Patients (ENA, 1999)

  - Observation/Holding Areas (ENA, 1997)

  - Protection of Human Subjects' Rights (ENA, 1999)

  - Role of Delegation by the Emergency Nurse in Clinical Practice Setting (ENA, 1998)

  - Role of the Emergency Nurse in Tissue and Organ Donation (ENA, 1998)

  - Specialty Certification in Emergency Nursing (ENA, 1999)

  - Telephone Advice (ENA, 1998)

  - The Obstetrical Patient in the ED (ENA, 1998)

- The Use of the Newly Deceased Patient for Procedural Practice (ENA, 1998)

- The Use of Nonregistered Nurse Caregivers in Emergency Care (ENA, 1999)

- Violence in the Emergency Care Setting (ENA, 1999)

STANDARDS OF EMERGENCY NURSING PRACTICE

Standards are quantitative or qualitative measures of value for professional practice. Nursing standards establish requirements for competent clinical practice, describe specific professional responsibilities, and establish measurement criteria for each standard.

Standards of Emergency Nursing Practice (ENA, 1998) is the cornerstone of emergency nursing. These standards identify professional practice standards unique to emergency nursing. Two distinct groups of emergency nursing standards are delineated.

1. Standards of care.

    A. Describe essential processes and components of emergency patient care.

    B. Specific standards address:

    - Assessment.

    - Diagnosis.

    - Outcome identification.

    - Planning.

    - Implementation.

    - Evaluation.

    - Triage.

2. Standards of professional performance.

    A. Identify principles of emergency nursing practice essential for professional growth and development.

    B. Standards include:

    - Quality of care.

    - Performance appraisal.

    - Education.

    - Collegiality.

    - Ethics.

    - Collaboration.

    - Research.

    - Resource utilization.

3. Competent level.

    A. Identifies the performance level considered when setting goals for the nurse's professional practice.

    B. Emergency nursing at this level is demonstrated by sound clinical judgment in autonomous practice.

In addition to competent professional practice for the emergency nurse, the standards also describe content and measurement criteria for the next level of emergency nursing practice—the excellent level.

4. Excellent level.

    A. Identifies emergency nursing practice that surpasses the competent level.

    B. Contributes to the growth of emergency nursing practice.

Several standards make specific references to education and merit brief discussion.

5. Education – Comprehensive Standard X.

    A. Pertains to education of the emergency nurse.

    B. The emergency nurse is responsible for recognition of self-learning needs and essential professional development.

    C. Measurement criteria identify defined bodies of emergency nursing knowledge such as the Trauma Nursing Core Course (TNCC) and Emergency Nursing Pediatric Course (ENPC).

6. Collegiality – Comprehensive Standard XI.

    A. Addresses professional development of peers, colleagues, and others.

    B. The emergency nurse has a responsibility to facilitate learning experiences for these individuals.

    C. Measurement criteria identify the roles of teacher, preceptor, and mentor.

7. Research – Comprehensive Standard XIV.

    A. The emergency nurse has a responsibility to identify and utilize pertinent research findings.

    B. Research validates the body of knowledge on which emergency nursing practice is based.

    C. Measurement criteria include use of research to improve practice.

EMERGENCY NURSING CORE CURRICULUM

The *Emergency Nursing Core Curriculum, 5th edition* (ENA, 2000) (Core) provides the framework for emergency nursing practice. The text addresses all facets of emergency nursing divided into the following areas:

- Clinical practice.
- Research.
- Education.
- Professionalism.
- Emergency department management.
- Disaster preparedness.
- Legal issues.

Overall content is formatted according to the emergency nursing process. Age-related considerations for pediatric and geriatric populations are included. Nursing diagnoses, collaborative problems, and expected outcomes for specific interventions are identified for each clinical topic. The Core is an excellent resource for development of education programs with a clinical focus or for review courses in preparation for the Board of Certification for Emergency Nursing (CEN) examination. The emergency nurse educator will find the chapter on education of particular value as it:

- Discusses essential principles of emergency nursing education.
- Provides a brief overview of one adult learning theory.
- Lists emergency nursing education needs.
- Emphasizes the broad knowledge base required for the emergency nurse.
- Identifies various teaching strategies.

ORIENTATION TO EMERGENCY NURSING

Orientation to the complexities, intricacies, and diversity that comprise the practice emergency nursing requires organization, structure, and time. Factors that significantly affect the orientation process include:

- Budget.
- Staffing demands.
- Time constraints.
- Number of orientees.
- Previous professional experience of orientee.
- Population diversity and case mix.
- Regulatory agency requirements.

These and other aspects of emergency nursing orientation are addressed in *Orientation to Emergency Nursing: Concepts, Competencies, and Critical Thinking* (ENA, 2000), a comprehensive, competency-based, orientation program for emergency nursing. Please refer to chapter 5 for more information on orientation of emergency department staff.

REGULATORY/ACCREDITING ORGANIZATIONS

Regulatory and accrediting organizations have and will continue to significantly impact education of staff in the emergency department. The JCAHO, OSHA, and HCFA are three major organizations that mandate specific education requirements and documentation parameters.

JOINT COMMISSION ON ACCREDITATION OF HEALTHCARE ORGANIZATION (JCAHO)

Accreditation by JCAHO represents adherence to national standards. These standards address patient care, quality improvement, institutional safety, and education requirements. Specific standards include, but are not limited to, nursing care, multidisciplinary collaboration, patient/family education, infection control, orientation, and continuing education/competencies of staff. Standards are frequently revised; therefore, a comprehensive description of these standards cannot be provided. The emergency nurse educator should consult the most recent JCAHO standards to identify specific education and/or documentation requirements. The JCAHO can be accessed on the Internet at *www.jcaho.org*.

OCCUPATIONAL SAFETY AND HEALTH ADMINISTRATION (OSHA)

OSHA's primary focus is safety in the workplace. Occupational safety guidelines are established for various industries to assure worker safety. Guidelines address:

- Universal precautions.
- Hazardous material exposure education.
- Mandatory tuberculosis testing.
- Hepatitis immunization for high-risk employees.

The emergency nurse educator should be familiar with OSHA guidelines related to requisite education and mandatory documentation. OSHA can be accessed on the Internet at *www.osha.gov*.

HEALTH CARE FINANCING ADMINISTRATION (HCFA)

The Consolidated Omnibus Budget Reconciliation Act 1986 (COBRA) and the Omnibus Budget Reconciliation Act of 1990 (OBRA), specifically the Emergency Medical Treatment and Active Labor Act (EMTALA), were developed under the purview of HCFA. These acts address patient transfers and related issues. It is crucial that every emergency nurse be familiar with COBRA/OBRA; therefore, the emergency nurse educator plays a vital role in staff education related to COBRA/OBRA. HCFA can be accessed on the Internet at *www.hcfa.org*.

The Balanced Budget Act of 1997 provides authority for HCFA to implement a prospective payment system (PPS) under Medicare for hospital outpatient services (including emergency care). All services paid under the new PPS are classified into groups called Ambulatory Payment Classes or APCs. Critical to successful reimbursement under APCs will be evidence of the care provided by emergency nurses. Part of the amount of monies that hospitals will receive are directly related to whether or not nursing documentation supports the APC chosen by the institution. Effective August 1, 2000 emergency departments are subject to this PPS for Medicare reimbursement. Emergency nurses must be educated as to the impact that this new system will have on emergency department reimbursement for services rendered. Additional information can be obtained by visiting HCFA's web site at *www.hcfa.org*.

OTHER AGENCIES

Other agencies that impact the educational needs/requirements of the emergency nurse include local and state health organizations, e.g., State Boards of Nursing, state EMS, regional trauma administration, state health departments and professional organizations, e.g., ENA.

SUMMARY

Basics and Beyond presents information for development and implementation of successful education programs. The emergency nurse educator, regardless of experience level, should benefit from the depth and breadth of selected topics. Use of *Basics and Beyond* in concert with authoritative references on education and emergency nursing will enhance the practice of the emergency nurse educator and, ultimately, contribute to the growth of emergency nursing.

REFERENCES

Emergency Nurses Association. (1999). <u>ENA position statements.</u> Des Plaines, IL: Author.

Emergency Nurses Association. (2000). <u>Orientation to emergency nursing: Concepts, Competencies, and Critical Thinking</u>. Des Plaines, IL: Author.

Emergency Nurses Association. (1998). <u>Standards of emergency nursing practice</u> (4th ed.). Park Ridge, IL: Author.

HCFA. (2000). Hospital Outpatient Prospective Payment System. <u>www.hcfa.gov.</u>

Joint Commission on Accreditation of Healthcare Organizations. (1999). <u>2000 Comprehensive manual for hospitals</u>. Chicago: Author.

Jordan, K. (Ed.). (2000). <u>Emergency nursing core curriculum</u> (5th ed.). Philadelphia: W.B. Saunders.

Occupational Safety and Health Administration, 29 C.F.R. § 1910.1030 (1992).

CHAPTER 1

Concepts of Emergency Department Organization & Structure

OBJECTIVES

Upon completion of this chapter, the emergency nurse educator will be able to:

1. Identify five organizational models.

2. Describe two types of organizational culture.

3. Define four types of organizational power.

4. Identify four levels of care recognized by the JCAHO.

5. Name two organizational relationships that may exist between the emergency nurse educator and the nurse manager.

6. Describe two locations where the emergency department (ED) may appear on the organizational chart.

INTRODUCTION

To function successfully in today's complex organizations, the emergency nurse educator must have a broad knowledge of organizational concepts. As an emergency nurse educator, you will be a key player in many organizational initiatives. A clear understanding of your role, your department's mission and goals, and the overall structure of your organization (institution) is imperative. Health care today is a plethora of corporate mergers and future unknowns that only intensify one's need to understand and possess functionality in organizations.

There is no single organizational structure in health care. This section highlights five structures and your organization may fit into one...or it may be structured to include properties of two, three, or all five. These structures typically are shared by the organization and the ED as it would be counterproductive for each department to have divergent structures. Typically administrators and upper level managers will guide the organizational as a whole, but as an emergency nurse educator, your job is not only to support the direction your department is going, but help steer it.

ORGANIZATIONAL STRUCTURE/CONFIGURATIONS

Every organized human activity from baking a loaf of bread to guiding a rover on the surface of Mars requires two fundamental and opposing properties: the <u>division of labor</u> into various tasks to be performed, and the <u>coordination</u> of those tasks to bring the project into fruition. The structure of an organization can be defined simply as the total of the ways in which its labor is divided into distinct tasks and then its coordination achieved among those tasks (Mintzberg, 1989).

ENTREPRENEURIAL ORGANIZATIONS

These are small, free-standing clinics or rural hospitals.

Structure: simple; informal; flexible; with little staff or middle line hierarchy; activities revolve around the chief executive who controls through direct supervision.

Context: simple and dynamic environment; strong leadership; sometimes charismatic; autocratic; "local producers."

Strategy: often visionary in process; broadly deliberate but emergent and flexible in details.

Issues: responsive; sense of mission; BUT vulnerable; restrictive; danger of imbalance toward strategy or operations.

These organizations are explained simply; they are not elaborate. Numbers of staff are small, the division of labor is loose, and there is a small managerial hierarchy. Its activity can be formalized but there may not be many policies or procedures. There is no formalized training program for new employees; there is expectation of previous knowledge and self-motivation.

The problem with organizations of this type is that the chief executive officer needs to have an in-depth understanding of operations and the role each employee plays in the organization. Frequently, leaders in this structure can become bogged down in operations and lose sight of strategy, or vice versa. The organization also may be limited by its location to advancements and improvements; therefore the employees also need to be creative and be able to explain problems and proposed solutions to the leader. These staff members need to be more cost conscious than very large organizations as they see the end product more personally.

THE MACHINE ORGANIZATION

These are the multifacility (either several hospitals or clinics) or multilocation provider group practices.

Structure: centralized bureaucracy; formal procedures; specialized work; sharp divisions of labor; usually functional groupings; extensive hierarchy; extensive support staff to reduce uncertainty.

Context: simple; stable environment; larger more mature organization; rationalized work; nonautomated technical system; can have external control via consumers but can be closed system.

Strategy: strategic programming; difficult to perform strategic change; long periods of stability interrupted by occasional bursts of strategic revolution.

Issues: efficient; reliable; precise; but obsession with control leads to human problems in operating core; leads to problems in administrative core; leads to adaptation problems at strategic apex.

Machine organizations have had analysis from some of the most respected theorists in the business and leadership world, including Michael Crozier and Max Weber (who coined the term machine organization). These organizations are precise, reliable, efficient, and easy to control. These are some of the reasons many organizations are structured as machine bureaucracies, but these same advantages are the disadvantages of this configuration. Machines consist of mechanical parts; organizational structures also include human beings, which is where the analogy breaks down.

DIVERSIFIED ORGANIZATIONS

These are organizations which are formed from mergers, first to combine businesses into larger entities, then to add activities at either end of the production chain under the label "vertical integration" (though always, for some unknown reason, displayed horizontally) (Mintzberg, 1989). These giant corporations form conglomerates, like the combining of Kentucky Fried Chicken®, Pizza Hut®, and Taco Bell®, or RJR Nabisco®. These organizations are thought not to care much about relationships between the various components except financial, but that is changing, especially when the idea is used in health care. There are many health care organizations that have formed mergers and have added activities to both ends. Typical examples are those that have started with hospitals and added EMS and transportation services at one end and long-term care facilities and home care at the other end.

Structure: market-based "divisions" loosely coupled together under central administrative headquarters; divisions run businesses autonomously.

Context: market diversity, especially of products and services; by-product, and related-product diversification encourages intermediate forms; typically found in the largest and most mature organizations.

Strategy: headquarters manages "corporate" strategy as portfolio of businesses; divisions manage individual business strategies.

Issues: tendency to drive structures of divisions toward machine configuration as instruments of headquarters; diversification is costly and discouraging of innovations; performance control system risks driving organization toward socially unresponsive or irresponsible behavior.

The way these organizations are formed affects their futures. They are at the will of their divisions: one section or product line can take the rest of the organization down and out or up to prosperity and expansion. Good leaders will only allow mergers with product lines that are safe or those that have a specialty that cannot easily be repeated. When it comes to health care organizations of this magnitude, the ED is just one player or product line in the big scheme of things. But because of its customers the ED has "branches" in multiple parts of the corporation (especially one that is well diversified); therefore understanding and having input to these other "branches" is key to the functioning of the educator, who will be asked to provide that input or even educate the leaders of the other "branches" of the ED customer needs (internal and external customers).

PROFESSIONAL ORGANIZATIONS

These are unique organizations. When it comes to organizations, many texts describe professional organizations as those that are bureaucratic without being centralized. An organization whose work is complex and needs to be carried out and controlled by professionals, yet at the same time remains stable so that the skills of those professionals can be perfected through standardized operating programs—sound familiar? Another definition of this group is *professional bureaucracy.* These definitions come from well recognized authors (Mintzberg, 1989, Bennis, 1964), and being active in today's health care environment allows us to really question their accuracy. Our environment is constantly changing, and considering that the staff necessary to keep a hospital operating is not totally professional, complicates any definition.

Structure: bureaucratic yet decentralized; dependent on training to standardize the skills of its many operating professionals; key to functioning is the creation of specialties in which individual professionals work autonomously subject to professional standards; large support staff.

Context: complex yet stable; simple technical system to professionals, yet high tech to general public.

Strategy: many strategies; often fragmented; overall strategy very stable.

Issues: problems of coordination between the specialties; misuse of professional discretion; reluctance to innovate; unionization exacerbates all problems.

The issues with this type of organization really relate to the identification of who is the "professional."

INNOVATIVE ORGANIZATION

These may be the most confusing types of organizations to observe because they are the ones that are viewed as inefficient, avant-garde, or high tech. Sophisticated innovation requires an ability to fuse experts from various disciplines into smoothly functioning ad hoc project teams.

Structure: selectively decentralized; functional experts deployed in multidisciplinary teams of staff; managers to carry out innovative projects.

Context: complex and dynamic environment; typically young due to bureaucratic pressure with aging; common in young industries.

Strategy: "grassroots" process; bottom-up processes; cycles of convergence and divergence.

Issues: effectiveness achieved at the price of inefficiency; ambiguity.

The typical example of this type of organization is the new upstart Internet or computer design companies. They find a niche in the market and build to that need. They are very effective initially, but when it comes to expansion they are the first to be bought up by the big diversified conglomerates. The key is they need to hire people who can constantly innovate, to keep the company moving in this format. These types of organizations are great to work for, but there is always a chance that it will be swallowed up by big business.

ORGANIZATIONAL MAKEUP

PEOPLE

When you talk about the people in an organization, <u>all</u> the people must be included. That includes the leaders within and without the organization, such as the president, chief executive officer, all the vice presidents, the board of directors, and other governmental influences (county commissioners, city council, department of veteran affairs, etc.). Involve staff members of all levels, professional and support as well as the community (as customers and influences change within your organization). We must remember that any decision not only affects our direct reports but many others that we do not even think of.

PARTS

This refers not only to the diversified organization that has multiple independent parts, but also to the organization that has many "feeders," or affiliated organizations (usually smaller than the receiving one) that bring customers to the larger or more specialized organization. If you examine a typical community hospital, there are many departments that function independently and interdependently within that hospital. Nursing needs respiratory therapy; respiratory therapy needs housekeeping; housekeeping needs engineering; and each needs each other. Again we must remember that we need each other; even the innovative organizations need suppliers to make the parts that they use to design that special service/product.

POLITICS

Most participants in an organization do not want to consider or believe that politics are ingrained in their organization. But we all know they are! Politics take on many forms, from covering shifts for a colleague to knowing the right person to go to for a new product to use to help yourself and your customers. Politics are prevalent everywhere, in the workplace, the community organization, the church, and even your home.

The ideal is learning to work with politics to your and your organization's benefits. This ideal will take time, however; you really learn though error, by asking the wrong people and obtaining ineffective results. You will make mistakes, but it is important to learn from them. That is how we grow. The old phrase, "Burn me once laugh at me, burn me twice laugh at you!" really applies.

HIERARCHY

The hierarchy promotes rigidity and timidity. Subordinates are afraid of passing bad news up the ladder or of suggesting changes. The hierarchy promotes delays and sluggishness. Everything must have approval from the "higher-ups."

We all know that there is hierarchy in every situation, not only at work, and hierarchy is a functional part of politics. To function in a group we need to work within the hierarchy to make our political actions effective. We learn to function within the hierarchies of our families, but in the work world we take different positions, and our hierarchical roles can be influenced by our actions (move up the ladder) if we so desire. Ultimately, we also will have official and unofficial hierarchical tracks. The trick is to learn both tracks and know when to use either or both, to obtain the objectives that are desired.

ECONOMICS

This term is almost as bad as politics, but the educator must be aware of the economic implications of his or her actions. No matter how large or small an organization is, every decision maker must recognize how his or her actions will affect the "bottom line."

As educators in health care settings we should be "in touch" with the bottom line information. Financial boundaries of departments within organizations affect how we design and implement projects. We may have great and fantastic plans for programs, but if the dollars are not there, neither will the project.

There are also hidden economics that the educator must consider, such as staff coverage time and overtime so staff can attend education programs, compensation for self-learning packets, and many others. New educators must learn their (financial) limits and work with department leaders to decide how to accomplish the educational needs.

SPAN OF CONTROL

Leaders in an organization (educators included) must recognize their span of control. As an educator, your span of control will often extend beyond the ED; take advantage of that. Use colleagues in program planning and development and be prepared to reciprocate. Use other emergency nurses or educators/clinical nurse specialists. They can economically spice up your programs by giving your participants different faces to look at and different teaching styles to learn from.

As your reputation builds so will your span of control; take advantage of it and use it to your advantage in any way possible. Also, do not expect your span of control to be complete within your department—someone was there before you, someone will be there after you. You will not have a positive influence on every department member and should not expect to, but don't give up—you will have to prove yourself to gain that influence.

PROFESSIONALISM AND DISCIPLINE

Organizations of all types and sizes employ professionals. The interaction and personalities of those professionals are what make organizations work. When at "work" the professional is expected to act in a professional manner, to uphold the standards of his or her profession, make every attempt to interact professionally, and carry out the mission of the institution. Leaders have these expectations of their staff and the professional will meet these expectations. Leaders provide opportunities for professionals and support their actions. It should be remembered that in today's medical center, the manager of professionals often is not as much an expert in the clinical care of patients as their highly educated and trained subordinates. Leaders today are hired for their leadership ability, not their expertise in an area or specialty.

Discipline is very complex in organizations of any type or size. When dealing with professionals, there are expectations of practice that necessitate disciplinary protocols or policies. Remember, even though there are professional expectations, organizational members are human and many will not follow all the rules. In many organizations this "rule breaking" is encouraged or supported; however, these are usually the smaller or innovative organizations. The larger or more complex the organization, the more rules there are with discipline associated with them. Even as an educator you will be confronted with "rule breakers." As with other leaders you must be consistent in dealing with these people. You must be clear with your expectations and a mutual understanding of the consequences is necessary. An emergency nurse educator will be dealing with all levels of staff, not only professionals but semi- and nonprofessionals, and the same standards and expectations must be kept at all levels, or your credibility and effectiveness will fail.

ESSENTIALS OF AN ORGANIZATION'S STRUCTURE

AGE AND SIZE

The age of an organization often affects its design and ideology. Older organizations often have ideologies that "have been around forever" and are "steeped in their history." Newer organizations often are designed to reflect modern health care and have a definite business structure and ideology. This new philosophy also is evident as hospital design has shifted from that of functionality to one of artistic design.

The age of an organization can be a double-edged sword; on one side because it has been in existence for an extended period of time, it becomes set in its ways and is resistant to change. On the other side, the organization may clearly see the need to be at the forefront of issues and recognize that is how it has been in existence for an extended period of time.

Organizational mergers are the norm today and smaller, private institutions are being usurped into larger, diversified organizations.

In the smaller organization structure everyone knows each other and communication between administrative levels is direct, as is most decision making. Larger conglomerations have organizations within themselves, making the decision process more laborious.

TECHNICAL SYSTEM

In today's high-tech world the discussion of the technical systems within and without an organization cannot be dismissed. No matter how large or small, how old or new, the type of organization design, the ability to adapt and use of technology for the benefit of the organization is a necessity. Technology is moving at a rapid pace. In the past five years, we have seen the mandate for basic computer literacy by staff usurped by the need to be familiar with increasingly complex programs (productivity, patient management, data retrieval, etc.) beyond the "basics." The ability to keep current with the technology is a must or the outcomes of the organization will be affected. There are several ways to meet this need, including recruiting personnel who have advanced computer skills, development of an internal information department to provide 24-hour technical support to all staff and to maintain and improve the equipment as well as staff competencies (in collaboration with the educator).

ENVIRONMENT

The environment in which an organization functions will have multiple effects on the current and future functioning of the organization. Some issues to consider include:

- How much and what quality is the competition?
- How long has the competition been in business and what is their coverage area?
- How acceptable is the local environment or community to change and competition?
- Who is setting the community standards?
- What does the community expect?

And many others. Remember, nothing drives change stronger and faster than competition and community expectations.

POWER

Power, as with politics, has positional and personal influences. There are people within organizations who have power based on their position, and others who have power due to their ability to complete projects or influence other people (indirect power). It is rare that these are the same person. Those who wish to be "players" within an organization will need to know both these groups and learn how to work with them if the player wishes to accomplish objectives. One of the potential outcomes of working effectively with these power people is that the "player" is often imparted a certain amount of power. That power may affect the person's position within the organization and will in turn affect future projects and objectives. Increased power has the untoward side effect of changing a person's vision and possibly creating enemies. The educator role has some form of power within it; however, to accomplish tasks you will have to obtain the support of positional powers and indirect powers. Learning how to obtain support from the indirects may require effort and time.

CHANGE WITHIN ORGANIZATIONS

WHY CHANGE?

Change is another necessity within the work/organizational environment. Change keeps the organization moving, keeps its workers current and forward-thinking, and keeps its customers happy. Educators are key change agents; they are given assignments from leaders to affect change. Educators are not the only change agents. Another key change agent in the clinical setting is the clinical nurse specialist. There are many texts and articles about change, which the educator can access. It is important for the educator to understand the theories and formats for change.

HOW?

There are many ways to affect change. As with the other issues in this chapter, there are numerous texts available to assist educators and other change agents to accomplish their goals. Besides texts there are journals, Internet sites, and seminars available to assist in the change process. Some keys in the "how" of change are adapting to the goal; adapting to the audience; measuring the current knowledge, ability, pattern, process, etc.; evaluating the outcomes; and planning for alternatives when the outcome is not reached or there is opposition.

WHEN?

When to do a "change" can be important. Many things must be considered, such as:

- When was the last change done?
- How big is the planned change?
- How many people will be affected by the change?
- Who else (other parts of the organization) will be affected or is participating in this change process?

To create an effective change process, these and many other considerations must be understood. Change is not easy, and it does not make friends. Human nature is to keep with something we are accustomed to, not to learn, do, or make something new. There is no easy way to learn how to perform change. As with other things, if you have a good understanding of the theories and techniques, you will have the tools. The rest is through experience.

ORGANIZATIONAL CULTURE

Organizational culture is a blend of symbols, language, assumptions, and behaviors overtly manifested in a particular setting. Culture shapes individual and group behavior within an organization. The entire organization and individual departments develop and exhibit their own unique culture. Recognition and understanding of cultural aspects within an organization facilitates performance within the confines of a specific culture.

The cultural orientation of an organization is based on power, role, task, or person (Fleeger, 1993). Power-oriented cultures tend to be competitive or autocratic; role-oriented cultures are more orderly and rational. A task-oriented culture values goal achievement, whereas, a person-oriented culture focuses on commitment to member needs. Clues to an organization's culture may be explicit, implicit, or both. Explicit clues include mission statements, policies, procedures, organizational charts, and formal communication channels (Fleeger, 1993). Informal, unwritten rules and unstated expectations constitute implicit clues. Dress, communication, and other aspects of day-to-day operations represent implicit clues.

The melding of cultures within an organization plays an important role in organizational success. Intradepartmental conflict limits department function and, ultimately, impacts organizational effectiveness. Harmonious relationships between distinct department cultures is called consonance. Conflict between professional cultures is known as dissonance. The presence of dissonance impairs organizational and professional productivity. Consonance is desirable for any organization. When necessary, the movement from dissonance to consonance requires time and commitment from all levels of the organization. Recognition of distinguishing characteristics for consonant and dissonant organizational cultures enables the emergency nurse educator to function more effectively in the organization.

- Consonant organization culture.
  - The golden rule is the norm.
  - Goals are the same from department to department.
  - There is a high degree of cooperation between departments.
  - Conflicts are addressed by formal and informal networks and systems.
  - Professional and organizational goals are similar.
  - Behavior norms are the same for everyone.
- Dissonant organization culture.
  - Affiliations are stronger with the union than with the organization (Fleeger, 1993).
  - There is minimal staff representation on various organizational and departmental committees.

- Organizational values do not match organizational outcomes.
- A double standard exists with regard to behavior.
- Stories, myths, and symbols are negative and do not project a caring spirit.

ORGANIZATIONAL POLITICS

Organizational politics is a reality in any organization—regardless of size, location, and purpose. Politics refers to actions and interactions between the people who determine policies (Schoolcraft, 1994). Essential constructs include power and influence. Success within a specific organization mandates recognition and understanding of organizational politics. Organizational politics dictate the elements of success, recognition, and promotion. In an organization where promotion is determined by who you know rather than what you know, success and recognition will be short-lived for anyone out of favor with the right people.

ORGANIZATIONAL CHARTS

The organizational chart is a schematic representation of the organization. It depicts placement of various departments, divisions, and positions. Respective lines of authority are clearly delineated. Individuals with authority for each division are usually identified by position and/or name. Figure 1 presents an organizational chart for a large hospital which is a member of a multihospital health care system.

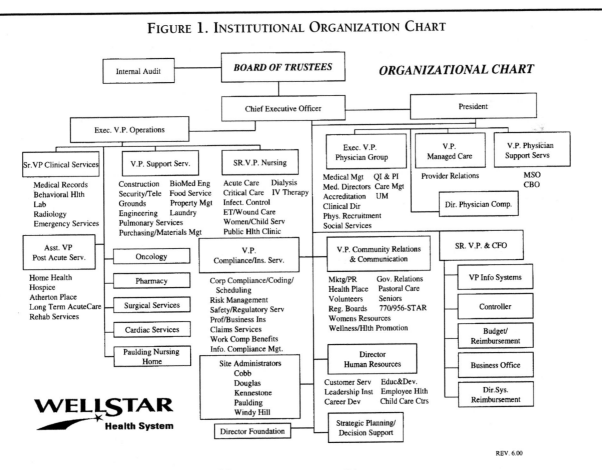

FIGURE 1. INSTITUTIONAL ORGANIZATION CHART

Used with permission from Wellstar Health System, Marietta, GA.

Department Organization Chart

The organizational chart for a specific department includes individual positions, regardless of authority within the organization. Figure 2 presents an organizational chart for an ED operating as a separate department within the division of nursing.

FIGURE 2. DEPARTMENT ORGANIZATION CHART

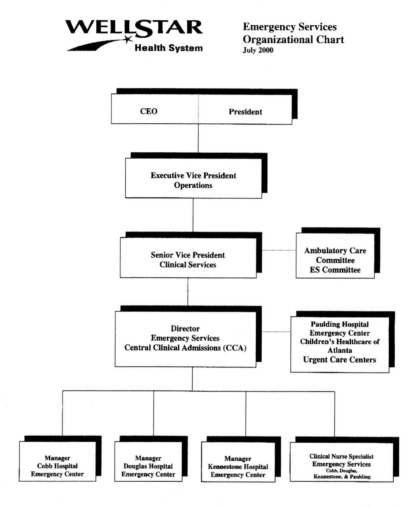

Used with permission from Wellstar Health System, Marietta, GA.

ED ORGANIZATIONAL STRUCTURES

INTRODUCTION

EDs come in all shapes and sizes—from one-room treatment bays to the ED with multiple treatment zones and a large number of beds. Despite obvious differences, all EDs share key organizational themes (Buschiazzo, 1987). A comprehensive review of every organizational construct pertinent to the ED is beyond the scope of this text; however, a brief overview of level of care, organizational placement, and job descriptions is provided. Knowledge and understanding of these constructs is essential for the emergency nurse educator to function effectively within organizational confines.

ORGANIZATIONAL STRUCTURE

Organizational structure refers to the organization of various departments, divisions, and positions within the institution. This structure determines lines of authority, chain of command, and supervisory responsibility. To function effectively within organizational confines, the emergency nurse educator must understand placement of the ED on the organizational chart, as well as location of the educator position.

Departmental Location

The ED may operate as a unit in the nursing department or as a separate department in the division of nursing, ambulatory services, or other division. Each structure has unique communication channels and lines of authority. Figure 3 depicts the ED as a nursing unit within the department of critical care, in the division of nursing. Within this structure, the ED manager answers to the director of critical care, who answers to the director of nursing. Advantages include staff support and shared services such as education and orientation programs. Disadvantages relate to distance from the administrative decision maker and application of critical care unit policies and procedures in the outpatient setting.

FIGURE 3. ED AS A NURSING UNIT WITHIN DEPARTMENT OF CRITICAL CARE

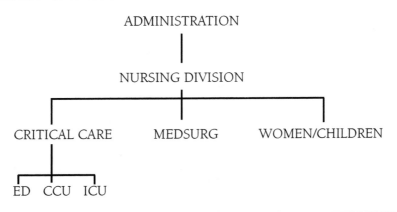

Figure 4 presents the ED as a separate department in the nursing division, and Figure 5 shows the ED as a separate department in the ambulatory care division. These structures provide managerial autonomy for decision making, clarify nursing identity, and minimize organizational layers between the ED manager and the administrator. Isolation from the nursing division, lack of available resources, and limited staff resources are disadvantages related to these structures.

FIGURE 4. ED as a Separate Department in the Nursing Division

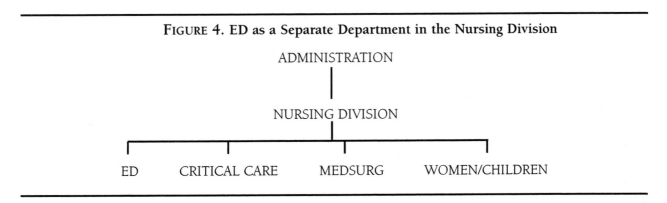

FIGURE 5. ED AS A SEPARATE DEPARTMENT

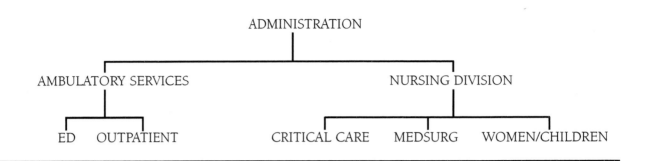

Emergency Nurse Educator Location

The emergency nurse educator must clearly understand the location of the educator position—organizationally and departmentally. Organizationally, the emergency nurse educator may be found in the ED, the staff development department, or a separate resource department. Each situation has distinct advantages and disadvantages. Emergency nurse educators should study the organizational chart carefully to identify lines of authority and channels of communication for their specific situation.

The relationship between the emergency nurse educator and the nurse manager may be vertical or horizontal. Figure 6 illustrates both relationships for an emergency nurse educator placed in the ED. Each relationship demonstrates unique interpersonal dynamics and organizational expectations. In a vertical relationship, the nurse manager is directly responsible for the emergency nurse educator. A horizontal relationship places the nurse manager and the emergency nurse educator on the same organizational level.

FIGURE 6. RELATIONSHIP BETWEEN EDUCATOR AND MANAGER

VERTICAL

NURSING DIRECTOR

ED MANAGER

EDUCATOR   ED STAFF

HORIZONTAL

NURSING DIRECTOR

EDUCATOR   ED MANAGER

ED STAFF

Hierarchy and the Emergency Nurse Educator

The role of an educator in the ED can vary from a staff nurse who has special talent in teaching new employees or current staff on new products and equipment, to the nurse who has education experience and is placed in a dedicated education position, or the clinical nurse specialist/nurse practitioner. The position on the organizational structure will undoubtedly vary depending on the role.

The educator can report to the nurse manager, the department director, or the education department (CNS/NP may report to senior nursing leadership or may even be free-standing positions).

The location of the educator on the organizational chart is not as important as the relationships that are developed and cultivated by the educator. Each relationship demonstrates unique interpersonal dynamics and organizational expectations. It is important for educators to keep a big picture view of the organization and department. This view is mandatory for the effectiveness of changes that will be planned, carried out, and evaluated. Only looking at the department in which you function is almost guaranteed to lead to failure and will create a disturbing view of you by administration.

Customers

Within an organization of any size there are customers, internal and external, superior and inferior. As with life, it is important to accept all for who and what they are and learn how you and they can benefit from each other. The ability to prevent the "we versus they" phenomenon is key to effective functioning and leadership. Who are our customers?

- Administration.
- Nursing staff (both in the ED as well as other areas of the institution).
- Support staff.
- Physician staff.
- Departments within the organization that facilitate ED function, lab, radiology, respiratory therapy, pharmacy, admissions, etc.
- "Hidden departments" within the organization: housekeeping, maintenance and engineering, bio-medical, dietary, social services, etc.
- EMS/fire/police.
- Community and its leaders (elected and nonelected).
- Other health care organizations within the surrounding environment, nursing homes, other hospitals, urgent care centers, etc.

Customer relations can make or break an organization. As an educator you must have excellent customer relation skills and portray them at all times.

SUMMARY

Every section of this chapter could be a book unto itself. The purpose was to enlighten and encourage you to seek more information on areas of interest or need. Please take advantage of the texts or authors which follow and do some further reading. They are considered experts and you will find the information presented in these texts greatly expanded in these references. You may have fun doing it.

REFERENCES

Austin, N. (1993, September). Reorganizing the organization chart. Working Woman, pp. 23-26.

Bennis, W.G. & Slater, P.L. (1964). The temporary society. New York: Harper & Row.

Crozier, M. (1964). The bureaucratic phenomenon. Chicago: University of Chicago Press.

Fleeger, M. (1993). Assessing organizational culture: A planning strategy. Nursing Management, 24(2), 39-41.

Garner, J., Howard, L., & Piland, N. (1990). Strategic nursing management. Rockville, MD: Aspen.

Joint Commission on Accreditation of Healthcare Organizations. (1999). 2000 Comprehensive manual for hospitals. Chicago: Author.

Mintzberg, H. (1989). Mintzberg on management: Inside our strange world of organizations. New York: The Free Press.

Perrow, C. (1986). Complex organizations: A critical essay, 3rd edition. New York: Random House.

Schoolcraft, V. (1994). A down-to-earth approach to being a nurse educator. New York: Springer.

Sterling Consulting Group. (1992). Building a winning quality service strategy. Seminar Proceedings.

Webster's II new Riverside University dictionary. (1984). Boston: Houghton Mifflin/Riverside.

RECOMMENDED READINGS

Alberta Multicultural Commission. (1989). Understanding seniors and culture. Edmonton, Alberta: Author.

Dernocoeur, K., & Taigman, M. (1991, January). Kaizen: Continuous improvement is a lifelong challenge. Journal of Emergency Medical Services, pp. 105-107.

Drucker, P. (1992). Managing for the future. New York: Truman Talley Books/Dutton.

Holmes, B.H. (1993, June). The lenient evaluator is hurting your organization. Human Resources Magazine, pp. 75-78.

Kouzes, J., & Posner, B. (1990). The leadership challenge. San Francisco: Jossey-Bass.

Malone, B.L. (1993). Caring for culturally diverse racial groups: An administrative matter. Nursing Administrative Quarterly, 17(2), 21-29.

Overman, S. (1991, April). Managing the diverse workforce. Human Resources Magazine, pp. 32-36, 40-41.

Payson, M.F., & Rosen, P.B. (1991, April). Playing by fair rules. Human Resources Magazine, pp. 42-43.

Robbins, S. (1990). Organizational theory. Englewood Cliffs, NJ: Prentice-Hall.

Salluzzo, R. F., Mayer, T. A., Strauss, R. W., et al. (1997). Emergency department management: Principles and applications. St. Louis: Mosby.

Schorr, T.M., & Zimmerman, A. (1988). Making choices, taking chances. St. Louis: Mosby.

Schuler, R., & Huber, V. (1990). Personnel and human resource management (4th ed.), St. Paul, MN: West Publishing.

Swansburg, R.C. (1993). Introductory management and leadership for clinical nurses: A text-workbook. Boston: Jones and Bartlett.

Williams, J., & Rogers, S. (1993). The multicultural workplace: Preparing preceptors. Journal of Continuing Education in Nursing, 24(3), 101-104.

C H A P T E R 2

Determining the Role of the Emergency Nurse Educator

OBJECTIVES

Upon completion of this chapter, the emergency nurse educator will be able to:

1. Distinguish Benner's five levels of proficiency and specific implications for the developing educator.

2. Differentiate five roles of the nurse educator.

3. Identify three methods to facilitate research application to clinical practice.

ROLE DEVELOPMENT

Benner (1984) critically evaluated development of knowledge and clinical proficiency utilizing the Dryfus model of skill acquisition. This analysis led to delineation of five widely recognized levels of clinical proficiency—novice, advanced beginner, competent, proficient, and expert. Movement from one level to the next reflects change in three general aspects of skill performance:

- Movement from abstract principles to concrete experiences.
- Learner views the situation as a whole rather than a compilation of bits of information.
- The detached observer becomes an involved performer.

Benner's work specifically addressed clinical proficiency; however, the model has been successfully applied to staff development instructors and clinical nurse specialists (Simpson, 1990; Hamric & Spross, 1989). Skill progression also is relevant for the emergency nurse educator.

Novice/Advanced Beginner

Transition from expert clinician to novice educator represents a major role change. Loss of clinical expert status and peer group support creates a sense of loss for the educator (Roach & Tremblay, 1993). There is a strong need for structure and guidance at this stage of skill proficiency. Novac (1993) offers the following suggestions for skill enhancement of the beginning nurse educator:

- Review available literature.
- Attend conferences related to teaching the adult learner.
- Keep initial presentations small. Prepare well. Develop a feeling of comfort with material.
- Spend time on the unit to determine ways to meet staff learning needs.
- Participate in unit/departmental committees.
- Seek a mentor.

- Network with other educators.

- Participate in professional organizations such as ENA.

- Get a feel for what is happening in the unit as well as in the institution.

COMPETENT

Conscious, deliberate planning to achieve long-range goals typifies the competent level. Thorough planning creates effective organizational skills and enhances educator efficiency. Ironically, this level also is noted for a lack of flexibility. Techniques for skill enhancement at the competent level include:

- Focus on development of larger educational programs.

- Submit programs for continuing education credit.

- Assess staff learning needs in a more formal manner.

- Develop competency-based assessment tools and self-learning packets.

- Obtain additional clinical credentials such as CEN, TNCC, and ENPC Provider status.

- Obtain additional educator credentials such as TNCC Instructor and ENPC Instructor.

- Utilize research in teaching and practice.

PROFICIENT

The proficient nurse is characterized by the ability to see the big picture. Past experiences rather than concurrent thinking guide performance. The educator focuses on aspects of a situation that are most important. Methods to enhance skill proficiency of the proficient nurse educator include:

- Participate and/or coordinate workshops and conferences.

- Chair or co-chair departmental committees.

- Develop additional contacts inside and outside the institution.

- Remain current on local, regional, state, and national trends in emergency nursing.

- Establish patient care performance standards.

- Participate in hospital-wide research.

EXPERT

Rules do not govern expert practice. The expert operates from an intuitive grasp of various situations. The expert emergency nurse educator should consider the following actions to enhance skill proficiency at this level:

- Identify topics for research in the clinical arena.

- Mentor a new educator.

- Develop community outreach programs.

- Act as a consultant for the institution and the community.

ROLE PREPARATION

Few programs exist to prepare nurse educators for their role. Ideally the nurse fulfilling the role of an educator in the ED will have a solid foundation of knowledge in emergency nursing. While typically not a requirement, attainment of Board Certification in Emergency Nursing will confirm the nurse's base of knowledge. Additional knowledge proficiency for the educator role can be demonstrated by attainment of provider and instructor verification from the Trauma Nursing Core Course (TNCC) and Advanced Cardiac Life Support (ACLS) course. If the ED treats pediatric patients, additional verifications from the Emergency Nursing Pediatric Course (ENPC) or Pediatric Advanced Life Support (PALS) course will serve to provide both cognitive and psychomotor competence.

Mentoring can be another method of role preparation for the new educator. The mentoring educator can be a nurse educator in another specialty area in the same institution or another emergency nurse educator in a neighboring medical center.

The emergency nurse also can prepare for the educator role by taking college level courses in education, leadership, fiscal responsibility, research, and assessment. If a graduate level program geared towards the role of the clinical nurse specialist or staff development specialist is available, this is certainly another method for role preparation.

Formal education is not the only method available to the emergency nurse educator to expand knowledge related to teaching. Continuing education opportunities and personal reading are also useful (Kelly, 1992). Suggested content areas for formal course work or continuing education include:

- Adult learning theory.
- Teaching/learning strategies.
- Needs assessment methods.
- Program development.
- Educational evaluation.
- Administration of adult education programs.
- Organizational behavior.
- Educational research.

Ideally, the new nurse educator should receive a formal orientation to the educator role that emphasizes principles of adult learning, program design, needs assessment, and essential communication/negotiation skills (Gordon & Franklin, 1993). In reality, this rarely occurs. The value of formal education and structured orientation experiences is widely recognized; however, few nurse educators receive formal preparation for these activities. Most educators learn through trial and error—on-the-job training (Warmuth, 1992; Roach & Tremblay, 1993).

SELF-ASSESSMENT FOR THE EDUCATOR ROLE

The novice educator should begin with a critical assessment of personal knowledge and skills. Through this candid assessment, the emergency nurse educator can focus on personal learning needs, enhance existing strengths, and attack specific weaknesses. Holmes (1992) recommends the following questions as the basis for this self-assessment.

- What do I know about the educational design process?
- Can I write an objective that is specific and measurable?

- Do I get nervous speaking in front of groups?

- What do I know about the principles of adult learning?

- Am I flexible and creative?

- Have I taught in any courses or program? If so, how were the evaluations?

- What am I good at?

- What do I like doing?

Education credentials for individuals assuming the nurse educator role vary. Graduates of diploma programs, associate degree programs, and baccalaureate programs may all function well as an educator in a variety of organizational settings. Nurses wishing to teach at the university level will find that the minimal requirements are either a master's degree (nursing or education) and/or an earned doctorate degree (PhD, DNS, or Education).

ROLE EXPECTATIONS

Growth as an emergency nurse educator requires identification of applicable role expectations. The nurse educator is challenged by expectations from the staff and the organization. Ironically, the nurse educator may also be limited by personal expectations. Conscious, readily verbalized expectations generally have little potential for conflict. Unconscious expectations that come to light only when proved wrong hold greater potential for conflict (Schoolcraft, 1994). This is particularly true when the educator's unspoken expectations are not congruent with organizational expectations. Potential areas of conflict between personal and organizational expectations include:

- Access to resources.

- Workload.

- Appropriate attire.

- Orientation process.

- Mentor availability.

- Committee responsibilities.

- Employee benefits.

- Involvement in decision making.

- Office size and amenities.

- Advancement opportunities.

- Relationship with schools or universities.

- Release time for library work.

- Secretarial support.

Clarification of organizational expectations prior to assumption of the emergency nurse educator position minimizes the potential for conflict and reduces reality shock. This dialogue may also clarify areas for negotiation such as clinical responsibilities, resource allocation, and support personnel.

ROLE TRANSITION

Recognized clinical expertise and interpersonal communication skills are two reasons nurses may be promoted into an educator position. Typically, the nurse has a strong clinical background and excellent emergency nursing skills. Historically, this background combined with a desire to learn were sufficient for success as an emergency nurse educator. Recent changes in health care delivery systems have altered existing expectations of the nurse educator and highlighted increased accountability for noneducational functions. Clinical expertise and interpersonal communication skills remain an essential requirement for the nurse educator; however, increasing complexity of the emergency nurse educator role demands broader knowledge of other aspects.

The staff nurse may transition to the educator role with few difficulties. Familiarity with staff enhances communication channels. Awareness of workplace pressures and demands enables the nurse educator to realistically appraise education needs and identify practical methods to meet these needs. Conversely, disadvantages related to changing role perceptions may be encountered. Staff may be apprehensive about loss or change in existing relationships. Jealousy and resentment may also occur. Don't panic. Try not to be discouraged. Staff acceptance does not happen overnight. Just as the educator must adjust to a new role, the staff needs time to adjust.

ROLE INTEGRATION

Integration and socialization to the emergency nurse educator role is affected by experience level and tenure in the department or organization. An emergency nurse educator new to the department or organization must first learn values and norms related to the work setting. Identification and familiarity with key staff enhances this socialization process. Schoolcraft (1994) suggests looking for a mentor within the department or institution who is:

- Assured and confident of his or her own position.
- Available to help in the way you need help.
- Aware and knowledgeable about what you need to know.
- Capable of providing the kind of support you need.
- Considerate and understanding of newcomers.
- Respected by others.
- Not threatened by the new educator or is nonthreatening to the new educator.

The mentor eases the transition period through knowledge of organizational politics and the key players. The mentor should also provide pertinent historical information and details related to current conflicts. Access to this information minimizes feelings of isolation and facilitates the socialization process. Refer to Chapter 3 for further discussion of mentoring concepts.

Other aspects of role integration relate to organizational culture, past emergency nurse educators, and communication norms. The emergency nurse educator's unique personality is also a significant factor in role integration (Fain, 1987). The emergency nurse educator must understand these various forces to assure successful role integration.

Roles and responsibilities are often ambiguous and ill-defined. The self-directed emergency nurse educator may find this ambiguity encourages creativity and promotes autonomy. Educators who require more structure may experience additional stress as a result of this ambiguity. Expected roles, requisite functions, and various expectations should be articulated in behavioral terms in the job description. See Chapter 9 for a discussion of job descriptions.

Understanding various organizational relationships is essential for organizational fit. The emergency nurse educator should have a clear understanding of organizational accountability, chain of command, and position responsibilities. If the nurse manager has direct supervisory responsibility for the emergency nurse educator, the relationship is vertical. If the nurse manager and emergency nurse educator are on the same organizational level, the relationship is horizontal. Regardless of type, the relationship between the emergency nurse educator and the nurse manager exhibits unique interpersonal dynamics and requires the utmost attention. Ideally, the emergency nurse educator and nurse manager work collaboratively for staff development and improved patient care. To accomplish this, the emergency nurse educator and nurse manager must have a relationship based on mutual trust, respect, and appreciation for these different yet complementary roles.

ROLE DIMENSIONS

The emergency nurse educator role has dimensions beyond emergency nurse education. Primary responsibility may be staff education; however, an organization may require additional functions such as research and consultant. Leadership dimensions of the emergency nurse educator role include performance evaluation, role model, and change agent.

EDUCATOR

The emergency nurse educator identifies professionally as an emergency nurse. Assumption of the emergency nurse educator role does not obliterate the nursing role. The educator is in an excellent position to define strategies and identify methods for continued improvement in nursing care.

The emergency nurse educator focuses primarily on learning opportunities for the ED staff; therefore, familiarity with various teaching and learning methodologies is essential. Other considerations include adult learning theory, teaching and learning styles, motivational and cultural issues, factors that influence learning, and personal values/beliefs. See Chapter 3 for further discussion of teaching and learning concepts.

The emergency nurse educator also is responsible for orientation. Completion of orientation does not signal the end of these responsibilities. Staff competency in clinical practice creates new challenges for the emergency nurse educator. Development of staff must be intentional, continuous, lead to increased professionalism, and expand responsibilities in more complex patient care situations. Understanding emergency nursing practice enables the emergency nurse educator to apply sound educational principles and facilitate learning in this unique environment.

ROLE MODEL/CONSULTANT

The roles of clinical consultant and role model are inherent to the emergency nurse educator role. Role modeling and consulting establish clinical credibility and facilitate professional relationships with staff. Clinical proficiency also promotes socialization and supports desired professional behavior in the staff. Without clinical competence, the emergency nurse educator loses effectiveness as an educator.

Time at the bedside affords the emergency nurse educator an opportunity to identify potential learning needs. Assisting with delivery of expert care in complex clinical situations enhances learning through exchange of information and application of knowledge on a personal and professional level. Mutual exploration of a complex clinical situation by the educator and staff facilitates exchange of pertinent data and focuses staff on key issues. Gradual increase of staff responsibility for patient care in concert with gentle withdrawal by the nurse educator encourages the learner to assume total responsibility for the patient. The educator then becomes a consultant, acting as a resource rather than a primary care provider (Gianella, 1992).

One of the benefits of the consultant role is promotion of problem-solving skills in the learner. This occurs as a result of the consultant:

- Assessing the nature of the problem.

- Prioritizing components.

- Planning problem solving strategies.

- Implementing the planned solution.

- Evaluating outcomes.

In addition to clinical excellence, emergency nurse educators should consciously identify those professional characteristics they wish to exhibit and those they wish others to emulate. These behaviors include ethical behavior, empathy, respect for others, and willingness to admit errors.

RESEARCH

Nursing research and its relationship to nursing practice has changed in recent years. The quantity of nursing research has increased and research quality has improved. Researchers are now exploring areas of nursing practice not previously studied. Unfortunately, a gap still remains between research and practice. Utilization of research results in the clinical arena remains low (Funk, Champagne, Wiese, & Tornquist, 1991). Application of research in clinical practice is significantly affected by a nurse's time on the job as well as lack of administrative and physician support (Funk et al., 1991). Factors that impede nurse involvement in research include lack of research knowledge and inaccessibility of research reports (Thomas, 1985).

Emergency nurse educators have an obligation to incorporate research into practice, stimulate peer interest, and promote departmental interest in research. The emphasis now and into the future is on evidence-based clinical practice. Promoting and actively participating in research will help to establish the evidence needed to enhance patient care. Factors that affect research participation include level of education and experience, role expectations, available resources, and organizational goals and priorities. Limited research has been conducted in emergency nursing. Scientific study, as well as awareness and application of research findings to practice, will advance emergency nursing. Suggestions to promote research by the emergency nurse include:

- Provide research-related articles for the staff. Assist the staff in interpretation of articles.

- Subscribe to newsletters that summarize research findings.

- Summarize and distribute relevant research to staff.

- Integrate research into in-service education.

- Include research reports in journal clubs.

- Promote staff involvement in multidisciplinary patient care conferences (discussion of the literature is common place in this forum).

- Serve on a research committee. Encourage staff nurses to participate on similar committees.

CHANGE AGENT

Learning represents change in behavior; therefore, the role of change agent is inherent to the role of educator. Organizational change occurs in all settings at all levels. The educator may be expected to implement change or assist staff/management responding to change. The ability of the educator to influence change should not be underestimated. See Chapter 9 for a discussion of job descriptions.

There is no right way to introduce change. The successful strategy for change must develop from recognition and understanding of all forces present in the situation. Early work done by Lewin (1951) identified three stages of change.

- Unfreezing.

    I Readiness or preparatory stage.

    I Motivation to create change is determined by how much unfreezing has occurred.

    I Motivation for change occurs when a stressor or conflict occurs within the system.

    I If success and satisfaction exist with the status quo, a longer time will be required for this stage.

- Changing.

    I The second stage of change is the actual changing or moving.

    I Marked by development of new responses based on new learning.

    I Successful change occurs when there is change in the way individuals think about things, not just the way things are done.

- Refreezing.

    I Refers to permanence of the change.

    I Change is stabilized and integrated into the existing culture.

    I Without refreezing, the change does not become a part of normal behavior.

To effect change, the nurse educator must understand organizational culture. Culture is the way things are done. It is a distinct pattern of group behaviors based on what group members believe is necessary for group survival. This belief makes it difficult to implement change (Coeling & Simms, 1993). Culture is a subtle, yet powerful force unconsciously passed to new employees. Change must be adapted to each work group, depending on culture and specific needs of that group. Cultural assessment prior to change involves understanding and predicting resistance which is likely to occur, and then developing methods to overcome or minimize the negative effect of this resistance on the desired change (Coeling & Simms, 1993).

The change process must be carefully designed, receive managerial support, and involve the staff. Strategies used to decrease resistance to change include:

- Identify positive and negative informal leaders, then involve them in the change.

- Establish a healthy group process based on open communication, mutual respect, and trust.

- Assure that the group has authority to make decisions regarding matters within group control, i.e., how the work is handled.

- Establish formal communication networks to assure information is passed to all staff. Each staff member needs access to available information and the decision-making process.

The threat of change may be reduced by providing pertinent information and involving staff in decisions regarding implementation of the change. Clark (1979) suggests the following questions be answered prior to introducing change:

- What is the change? Why is it being introduced now?

- What are the advantages and disadvantages of this change?

- What methods will be used to introduce the change?

- How does the staff regard their work?

- How will this change affect staff work habits?

- What are the operating factors that might serve to inhibit or enhance the change?

- What new teaching/learning will need to take place as a result of the change?

- How aware are staff members of the need for change?

It is essential that individuals effecting the change believe that those who perform the work are the right people to make decisions regarding how the work should be done. The more staff involvement in the process, the less resistance there will be (Clark, 1979). For example, a unit-level committee or task force may be used to guide implementation of a significant change.

Foster staff willingness to break the status quo. Promote staff confidence in individual autonomy and ability to change. Be patient. Change takes time and some resistance is inevitable. Be prepared. Change begets change, so prepare for the domino effect (Tobin, Wise, & Hull, 1979).

REFERENCES

American Nurses Association. (1979). Study of credentialing in nursing: A new approach. Kansas City: Author.

Benner, P. (1984). From novice to expert: Excellence and power in clinical nursing practice. Menlo Park, CA: Addison-Wesley.

Clark, C.C. (1979). The nurse as continuing educator. New York: Springer.

Coeling, H., & Simms, K. (1993). Facilitating innovation at the nursing unit level through cultural assessment: 1. How to keep management ideas from falling on deaf ears. Journal of Nursing Administration, 23(4), 46-53.

Fain, J.A. (1987). Perceived role conflict, job ambiguity, and job satisfaction among nurse educators. Journal of Nursing Education, 26(6), 233-238.

Funk, S., Champagne, M., Wiese, R., & Tornquist, E. (1991). Barriers to using research: Findings in practice—The clinician's perspective. Applied Nursing Research, 4(2), 90-95.

Gianella, A. (1992). Effective teaching and learning strategies for adults. In R.S. Abruzzese, Nursing staff development: Strategies for success (pp. 215-233). St. Louis: Mosby.

Gordon, B., & Franklin, E. (1993). An orientation for inexperienced educators. Journal of Nursing Staff Development, 9(2), 75-77.

Hamric, A., & Spross, J. (1989). The clinical nurse specialist in theory and practice (2nd ed.). Philadelphia: Saunders.

Holmes, S.A. (1992). Orienting yourself to a staff development role. Journal of Nursing Staff Development, 8(4), 189-191.

Kelly, K. (1992). Nursing staff development: Current competence, future focus. Philadelphia: Lippincott.

Lewin, K. (1951). Field theories in social science. New York: Harper & Row.

Novac, A. (1993). Tips for the new nurse educator: Thoughts one year after being in the role. Journal of Emergency Nursing, 19(1), 63-4.

Roach, J., & Tremblay, L. (1993). Socialization transformation: The passage from caregiver to educator. Journal of Nursing Staff Development, 9(3), 155-157.

Schoolcraft, V. (1994). A down-to-earth approach to being a nurse educator. New York: Springer.

Simpson, M. (1990, February). Development of the staff development specialist: From orientation to peek performance. Paper presented at Nursing Continuing Education Program, Orlando, FL. In K. Kelly, Nursing staff development: Current competence, future focus (pp. 22-23). Philadelphia: Lippincott.

Thomas, E. (1985). Attitudes toward nursing research among trained nurses—survey. Nursing Education Today, 15(1), 18-21.

Tobin, H.M., Yoder, L., Wise, P.S., & Hull, P.K. (1979). The process of staff development: Components for change (2nd ed.). St. Louis: Mosby.

Warmuth, J. (1992). Implementing the staff development program: Organizing to meet the institution's needs. In K. Kelly, Nursing staff development: Current competence, future focus (pp. 155-182). Philadelphia: Lippincott.

RECOMMENDED READINGS

Bhola, H.S. (1994). The CLER Model: Thinking through change. Nursing Management, 25(5), 59-63.

Bostrom, J., & Wise, L. (1994). Closing the gap between research and practice. Journal of Nursing Administration, 24(5), 22-27.

Chisholm, M. (1991). Use and abuse of power. Clinical Nurse Specialist, 5(1), 57.

Chop, R.M., & Silva, M.C. (1991). Scientific fraud: Definitions, policies, and implications for nursing research. Journal of Professional Nursing, 7(3), 166-171.

Cornell, D. (1993). Say the words: Communication techniques. Nursing Management, 24(3), 42-46.

DeMong, N. C., & Aussie-Lussier, L. L.(1999, January/February). Continuing education: An aspect of staff development related to the nurse manager's role. Journal of Nurse Staff Development, 15(1), 19-22.

Glazer, H.R., Stein, D.S., & Schafer, D.S. (1994). How do health care education and training professionals learn about the environment? Journal of Healthcare Education and Training, 8(1), 8-11.

Klinefelter, G. (1993). Role efficacy and job satisfaction of hospital nurses. Journal of Nursing Staff Development, 9(4), 179-183.

Kopala, B. (1994). Conflicts in nurse educators' role obligations. Journal of Professional Nursing, 10(4), 236-243.

Mateo, M., & Fahje, C. J. (1998, July/August). The nurse educator role in the clinical setting. Journal of Nurse Staff Development. July-Aug; 14(4), 169-175.

Nayak, S. (1991). Strategies to support the new nurse in practice. Journal of Nursing Staff Development, 7(2), 64-66.

Nierenberg, G. (1981). The art of negotiating. New York: Pocket Books.

Schwartz, K., & Tiffany, C.R. (1994). Evaluating Bhola's configurations theory of planned change. Nursing Management, 25(6), 56-61.

Sheridan, D., & O'Grady, T. (1992). Nursing staff development in the 1990's. In R.S. Abruzzese's, Nursing staff development: Strategies for success (pp. 15-27). St. Louis: Mosby.

Smeltzer, C.H. (1991). The art of negotiation: An every day experience. Journal of Nursing Administration, 21(7/8), 26-30.

Sneed, N.V. (1991). Power: Its use and potential for misuse by nurse consultants. Clinical Nurse Specialist, 5(1), 58-62.

CHAPTER 3

"See one, do one, teach one?" Teaching, Learning, and Mentoring

OBJECTIVES

Upon completion of this chapter, the emergency nurse educator will be able to:

1. Describe the principles of adult learning.

2. Discuss multicultural issues in education.

3. Utilize appropriate teaching methodologies for specific educational activities.

4. Discuss teaching challenges and ways to overcome them.

5. Define mentoring.

6. Describe four models of mentoring.

7. Identify four phases of a mentoring relationship.

INTRODUCTION

Learning is defined as "acquiring of knowledge or skill" (Pocket Webster School and Office Dictionary, 1990, p. 804). From an educator's standpoint, this definition has inherent limitations. One cannot observe knowing or understanding. The educator can only observe the learner exhibit certain behaviors from which inference can be made that the student knows or understands. Consequently, instruction focuses on learner behavior. Operationally, learning is defined as a planned change in behavior that has some degree of permanence.

Teaching and learning methodologies form the framework for much of an educator's activities. This chapter provides an overview of basic adult learning principles and practical suggestions for effective teaching strategies. New educators will gain a basic understanding of the needs of adult learners. Experienced educators are provided a resource that may be beneficial when planning new educational activities.

ADULT LEARNING THEORIES

Educators may subscribe to one learning theory or incorporate aspects of many learning theories into their practice. The new educator is encouraged to study various learning theories and develop their own personal philosophy of teaching and learning. Five popular adult learning theories are summarized in this section. For more information on these and other theories, consult the references at the end of this chapter.

ERIC LINDEMAN

Lindeman (1926) was one of the first educators to theorize about adult education. He was a major influence on future theorists with his key assumptions about adult learners:

- Experience should be the starting point for organizing adult learning activities.

- Experience is the richest resource for adult learners.

- Adult orientation to learning is life-centered.

- "Adults have a deep need to be self-directed; therefore, the role of the teacher is to engage in a process of mutual inquiry with them rather than to transmit his or her knowledge to them and evaluate their conformity to it" (pp. 118-119).

MALCOLM S. KNOWLES: THEORY OF ANDRAGOGY

Malcolm Knowles is perhaps the most often quoted theorist in adult education. Knowles (1987) stated that "at its best, an adult-learning experience should be a process of self-directed inquiry, with the resources of the teacher, fellow students, and materials being available to the learners, but not imposed on them." His theories are based on the differences between teaching children—Pedagogy, and teaching adults—Andragogy. Knowles believed the primary mission of every adult educator should be to assist adults in meeting their learning needs and achieve their goals.

Critical Assumptions

Knowles (1970) articulated four critical assumptions based on differences between pedagogy and andragogy. As a person matures and moves from child to adult:

- Self-concept moves from that of a dependent person toward one of a self-directed human being.

- A growing reservoir of experience is accumulated that becomes an increasing resource for learning.

- Readiness to learn becomes increasingly oriented to developmental tasks for social roles.

- Time perspective changes from postponed knowledge application to immediacy of knowledge application. Consequently, orientation toward learning shifts from subject-centeredness to one of problem-centeredness (p. 39).

Andragogy Assumptions

Knowles (1970) identified three additional assumptions related to teaching and learning within the adragogical approach.

- Adults need to know the reason they should learn something.

- Learning is an internal process.

- Superior conditions of learning and principles of teaching exist.

Ideal Conditions for Learning

Adult learning occurs under ideal learning conditions (Knowles, 1970). Absence of one of these ideal conditions significantly affects the learning process. Learning occurs when the adult learner:

- Feels a need to learn.

- Experiences an environment characterized by physical comfort, helpfulness, freedom of expression, acceptance of differences, and mutual trust and respect.

- Perceives goals of the learning experience as their goals.

- Accepts some responsibility for planning and operating the learning experience; therefore, the learner feels a commitment to the experience.
- Participates in the learning process.
- Feels the learning process relates to and utilizes the learner's experiences.
- Feels a sense of progress toward their goals (pp. 52-53).

Gordon G. Darkenwald and Sharan B. Merriam

Darkenwald and Merriam (1982) agree that teaching adults differs from teaching school children; however, commonalties do exist between adult learning and childhood learning. Their research into adult learning included exploration of behaviorists, Gestaltists, cognitive theorists, and theorists dealing with aging. Based on this research, Darkenwald and Merriam identified guidelines for adult education.

Guidelines for Educational Practice

1. An adult's readiness to learn depends on previous learning.
   - The more knowledge a person has accumulated the better he or she will absorb new information and engage in critical thinking.
   - The variety of past educational experiences influences the educational learning activity.
2. Intrinsic and extrinsic motivation produces pervasive and permanent learning.
   - Building an educational activity around needs of the adult learner ensures more permanent learning.
3. Positive reinforcement of learning is more effective than negative reinforcement.
   - Many adults are insecure and fearful because of negative educational experiences as a child.
   - Feelings of success in adult learning are essential for continued learning and participation.
4. Information should be presented in an organized fashion to maximize learning.
   - Material should be arranged from simple to complex or organized around related concepts.
   - The starting point for organizing adult learning material is related to the adults' past experiences and knowledge.
5. Learning is enhanced by repetition, spaced over a period of time.
   - This is particularly true for skill development.
6. Educational material that is meaningful to the learner is valued more than meaningless or insignificant material.
   - This is particularly true for older adult learners.
   - Any information or task has the potential to be meaningful or meaningless.
   - The facilitator of adult learning must relate the material to the learner's experiences and needs.
7. Active participation in the learning activity enhances learning.
   - Adults who are personally involved will discover relationships, concepts, and meanings on their own. The reward is the actual learning.
8. Internal and external factors affect learning.
   - Tangible stimuli such as noise, crowded seating, temperature, lighting, etc., interfere with the learning process.
   - Factors such as tension, derision, pressure, fatigue, and poor health also impede learning.

W.B. James

James (1983) identified nine basic principles of adult learning, based on findings from extensive review of collected articles, research reports, textbooks, and dissertations on adult learning principles.

Basic Principles of Adult Learning

- Adults maintain the ability to learn.
- Adults are a highly diversified group of individuals with widely differing preferences, needs, backgrounds, and skills.
- Adults experience a gradual decline in physical/sensory capabilities.
- Learner experience is a major resource in learning situations.
- Self-concept moves from dependence to independence as individuals grow in responsibilities, experience, and confidence.
- Adults tend to be life-centered in their orientation to learning.
- Adults are motivated to learn by a variety of factors.
- Active learner participation in the learning process contributes to learning.
- A comfortable, supportive environment is a key to successful learning (p. 132).

Stephen D. Brookfield

Brookfield writes extensively on self-directed learning. Self-directed learning is defined as "assisting adults to free themselves from externally imposed direction in their learning and encouraging them to become proactive, initiating individuals in reshaping their personal, work, political, and recreational lives" (Brookfield, 1986, p. 60).

Central Themes of Self-Directed Learning in the Adult

From his review of various studies on self-directed learning, Brookfield (1986) articulated five central themes related to adult learning and self-directed learning.

1. Learning contract.
   - Chief mechanism used for enhancement of self-direction.
2. Preparation for self-directed learning.
   - Most adult learners are familiar with more traditional methods of education.
   - Facilitators and students face ambiguity, uncertainty, and problems with planning and directing learning if they are not adequately prepared for self-directed learning.
   - Facilitators should attend a workshop on self-directed learning before attempting this mode of learning.
3. Peer learning groups.
   - Self-directed learners rely heavily on peer learning groups for support, information exchange, stimulus through new ideas, and location of relevant resources.
   - Facilitators should encourage learners to form peer learning groups as soon as possible.
4. Time commitment.
   - Altered time requirements are usually necessary when using this nontraditional learning mode.
   - A period of adjustment is required for the learner and the facilitator.

- Fewer assignments can be given with this mode compared to the traditional lecture-style class.
- The institution as a whole must support self-directed learning for it to be successful.

5. Perceived benefits.
- Despite initial frustration with self-directed learning, most learners recognize the benefits.
- Learners see learning as more personally significant (pp. 81-84).

FACILITATING LEARNING

Learning has been defined as a change in behavior which has some degree of permanence. To affect learner growth, facilitators of learning must focus on ways to change learner behavior. Educators do not utilize the same teaching method for every situation or every learner. Despite this individuality, there are certain key elements and processes common to all successful educators.

1. Secure and maintain attention.
- This is the first step to teaching.
- During a presentation, the average adult pays attention 25% of the time.
- Inform the learner of the objectives for the presentation.
- Repeat key points and reinforce each one with visual material to maintain learner attention.

2. Present the task.
- Keep the presentation brief and to the point.
- Relate the material directly to the objectives.

3. Secure a response.
- Learning is enhanced through active responses.
- The more you engage the audience with questions and activities the more opportunity they will have to respond and learn.
- Opportunities for participation increase audience attention!

4. Provide feedback.
- When participants respond, provide feedback concerning the correctness of their response.
- Feedback should be as immediate and specific as possible.

5. Provide opportunities for practice.
- New behaviors must be practiced if they are to achieve any degree of permanence.
- Identify relevant and meaningful ways learners can use their new knowledge or skill.
- Provide opportunity for participants to receive feedback on their practice.
- Unsupervised practice may lead participants to practice their mistakes.

CHARACTERISTICS OF VALUED TEACHERS

Teachers have had a profound effect on the lives of many. Good teachers must be able to communicate effectively with the students they teach. Eason and Corbett (1991) identified teacher attributes valued by adult learners (see Table 1).

TABLE 1. TEACHER ATTRIBUTES VALUED BY ADULT LEARNERS

Professional Characteristics	Personal Characteristics
Answered questions	Energetic
Informative	Easy to listen to
Knowledgeable	Entertaining
Clear, concise	Enthusiastic
Realistic content	Fascinating
Well-prepared, organized	Helpful
Used audiovisuals, handouts	Interesting
Used examples, case studies	Friendly
Shared their experiences	Good sense of humor
Dynamic	

Demonstrating these basic attributes does not prevent emergency nurse educators from exercising their own personal style. Rather, these attributes should enhance personal style and increase effectiveness. New and experienced educators should periodically evaluate their professional and personal characteristics as a way to monitor their effectiveness.

MULTICULTURAL CONSIDERATIONS

Culture can be defined as "the total way of life a people creates during the course of its history. It is the way its members think and behave, the values and beliefs they hold, the social practices and structures influencing their conduct and the languages they speak" (Alberta Multiculturalism Commission, 1989, p. 21). Culture has a great influence on the way individuals think, act, and feel. Cultural differences may interfere with communication and impede understanding between individuals from different cultures.

The world is indeed becoming a smaller place. As geographic barriers are broken, cultural diversity increases. Many countries around the world are becoming more heterogeneous. In the health care world, patients and staff form a radically diverse group. Agreements and governing bodies such as the North American Free Trade Agreement and the European Economic Community have changed the workforce considerably. In the past 20 years, many hospitals have experienced an influx of nurses educated in other countries.

Foreign-educated nurses may have many cultural and language differences that can affect staff and patient interaction, despite the nurses' level of professional training (Thiederman, 1989). Cultural differences include beliefs about health and illness, religion, politics, and gender roles. Health practices include folk medicine, spiritual healing, and conventional medical practices. Emergency nurse educators must be aware of and sensitive to cultural differences among participants in an educational activity.

Strategies for Multicultural Issues in Education

- Identify the cultural mix that exists in your population.
    - Obtain information about the cultures represented.
    - Become familiar with pertinent cultural beliefs before the educational activity.
    - Cultural information often focuses on what is strange or different about a particular culture.
        - ♦ Avoid stereotypes based on this information.
- Use visual techniques and instructional media to support your presentation.
    - Pictures and diagrams help overcome a language barrier.
    - Choose colors carefully. In some cultures, white is the color for mourning and red symbolizes good luck and happiness.
- If a significant number of participants have a language barrier, consider translation of essential materials.
    - Translation can be expensive and time-consuming.
    - It is important that the overall message is conveyed in the translated materials.
    - Often word-for-word translation does not convey the overall message. Be sure to field test the translated material prior to use.
    - If a written test is used and translation is not feasible, consider use of a translator during the test.
        - ♦ Make sure the translator knows that providing test answers is not acceptable.
- When time permits, have participants introduce themselves and share their beliefs about health and illness.
    - Ask foreign-educated nurses to share the similarities and differences in health care.
    - Participants learn from this exchange and gain a greater appreciation for health care on a global level.
- Enjoyable, effective teaching methods for multicultural groups include role-playing, certain games, story-telling, and songs.
    - Assess the audience. Participants may be uneasy or shy about participating and need encouragement.
    - Teaching methods are covered in more detail later in this chapter.
- A preceptor program that includes specific preparation on multicultural issues reduces culture shock that occurs three to nine months after the new nurse arrives.
    - Williams and Rogers (1993) developed a program at the Texas Medical Center in Houston "to help preceptors, who are likely to be orienting nurses from cultural backgrounds different from their own, to step out of their traditional views and to become more open-minded, accepting, and effective in their preceptorship" (p. 102).
        - ♦ Topics covered in the two-day program include communication, dealing with difficult people, values clarification, and multicultural interaction.

Staff Resources for Multicultural Clients

As an educator, you will assist with the provision of resources in your department. In addition to books and journal articles on clinical topics, access to information on the various cultures of clients will also benefit the staff. Resources include:

- Current list of institution translators posted in a convenient location.
- Information about local language courses.
    - Encourage staff to learn a second language that will help with patient and staff interactions.

- Texts, pamphlets, and guides on medical terminology for the languages served by your institution.
  - ▎ A list of resources is provided in the recommended readings section for this chapter.
- Information on health and illness beliefs and practices for the cultures served by your institution.
  - ▎ Beliefs and practices related to death are particularly germane to the emergency department.
    - ♦ Local funeral homes are a good source of information.

TEACHING AND LEARNING STRATEGIES

Teaching and learning strategies enhance the outcomes of educational activities and the learner's understanding of the content. Educators often find experimenting with and perfecting teaching strategies as one of the most exciting aspects of teaching. Novice educators usually begin with more traditional teaching methods, i.e., lecture, discussion, and demonstration. As comfort and experience in teaching increase, innovative strategies such as games, role-playing, case studies, and story-telling are used.

1. The appropriate teaching strategy should be based on an assessment of the content, audience, resource allocation, and time constraints.

2. Variety is the spice of life.

   - Teachers who use a variety of teaching methods maintain participant interest and usually enjoy the teaching experience themselves.

3. Audiotapes, videos, and computer-assisted instruction are both a medium and a strategy.

   - These are discussed in Chapter 8 along with other instructional media.

This section provides a brief overview of selected teaching strategies. Additional information on these and other strategies can be found in the references and recommended readings section for this chapter.

Lecture

- Provides new information in a short time to a large group of people.
- Formal setting.

Advantages:

- Time-efficient.
- Useful for presentations to large groups.
- Presenter has control over the learning situation.

Disadvantages:

- Learners become passive observers.
- Little interaction between presenter and participant.
- Retention of information is generally short-term.

Tips for lecture enhancement:

- Combine lectures with discussion, questioning, and visual aids.
- Relate new information to the learner's past experiences.
- Provide examples and illustrations to stimulate retention of the material.

- Use audiovisual aids to illustrate main points and maintain participant attention. See Chapter 8 for more information on specific instructional media.

- Provide handout materials.

- Summarize information presented.

- Provide supplemental information.

Major Elements of a Lecture

- Introduction.
  - State the objectives of the lecture, i.e., what you will tell them.
  - Identify the importance of the topic to the overall course or to participant practice, i.e., why they should pay attention.
- Presentation of the topic.
  - Limit major points to no more than five.
  - Speak less than one hour whenever possible.
  - Repeat major points.
  - Use appropriate language at the audience's level of understanding.
  - Engage the audience, involve participants in the topic.
- Summary.
  - Review purpose of the presentation.
  - Review key points, i.e., what you have just told them.
  - Tell the audience how they can use the new information.

Lecture Preparation

- Ensure the lecture format is appropriate for the content and the audience.

- Know the time frame for the lecture and stick to it.

- Formulate objectives.

- Develop an outline.

- Identify lecture content and make sure it flows logically.

- Formulate notes.
  - Index cards are helpful.
- Obtain audiovisual aids appropriate for the content.
  - If audiovisual aids are not available, develop materials to support the content (see Chapter 8).
- Practice, Practice, Practice!
  - Coordinate lecture with audiovisual aides.
- Present the lecture to your friends and/or coworkers. Ask for feedback.
  - Evaluate
- The learner should evaluate the educator and the content.

- The educator should do a self-evaluation.

Tips for improving lectures:

- Attend lectures by experienced presenters and analyze their style.

- Join groups such as Toastmasters to improve general public speaking skills.

- Attend classes in dramatic techniques and voice training.

- Audiotape or videotape your presentations. Analyze tapes with other educators for constructive feedback.

Group Discussion

- Stimulates participant interaction.

- Informal.

- Encourages solutions to problems.

Advantages:

- Promotes participant involvement.

- Stimulates individual thinking and introduces different points of view.

- Allows individuals to share knowledge

- Encourages in-depth review of a topic.

Disadvantages:

- Students may not participate.

- Group may stray from the main subject.

- Not suited for large groups.

  ▎ Large group may break into many smaller groups to the detriment of the overall purpose.

- Time-consuming.

- Irrelevant information may be generated.

Major Elements of Group Discussion

- Introduction.

  ▎ State the purpose of the discussion.

  ▎ Set a time limit for discussion.

  ▎ Create an open and informal atmosphere.

- Leading the discussion.

  ▎ Maintain control without inhibiting discussion.

  ▎ Listen and paraphrase ideas.

  ▎ Record ideas on a chalkboard, flipchart, or white board.

  ▎ Keep participants on track. Minimize distraction with statements such as:

  ◆ "That's an important thought. Let's discuss it later. Right now we need to get back to the problem, which is . . . ."

  ▎ Provide input as necessary.

- If important points are left out of the discussion, add them at the end.
- Don't allow one person to dominate the discussion. Use phrases such as:
  - "You have offered several good ideas. I wonder what others might think about that."
- Closure.
  - Restate the problem.
  - Review major points presented.
  - Suggest ways to apply the information.

Tips for group discussion:

- Prepare for the discussion.
- Don't dwell on lack of participation by some individuals.
  - More may be lost by putting them on the spot for a response.
  - Most people will join in a discussion when they feel comfortable and ready.

Tips for improving group discussion:

- Attend courses or read literature on group dynamics and group facilitation.

Role-play

- Increases self-awareness toward an issue or problem.
- Enhances attitudinal change.
- Acts out a situation.
- Assists participants in developing skills such as problem-solving, counseling, and interviewing.

Advantages:

- Promotes participant involvement as players or observers.
- Enables participants to take on different roles and act out the roles in a nonthreatening environment.
  - Participants gain an appreciation for how people interact by taking on a variety of roles.
- Participants often describe this method as fun and realistic.

Disadvantages:

- Adults may initially feel awkward and uncomfortable about role-playing; therefore, it is important to develop trust and camaraderie within the group.

Major Elements of Role-Playing

- Setting the scene.
  - Prepare the group for role-play by providing valid reasons for its use.
    - Questions raised during group discussion can be dealt with through role-playing.
    - Lead into role-playing with a short lecture or vignette.
    - Use a film. Stop at a point where role-playing takes over problem-solving.
    - Use a case study as background information.

- Role-playing
  - Be short and specific with instructions.
    - Don't dwell on describing the technique of role-playing or participants lose interest.
  - Assign specific roles to participants.
    - Ask for volunteers first.
    - If no one steps forward, ask individuals to participate.
  - Short, written descriptions of the situation and the individual roles are very helpful.
  - Instruct those not involved in the role-play to act as observers.
    - Give observers clear instructions related to observations to make and notes to take.
  - Specify the length of the role-play.
    - Role-play can be as short as 10 minutes or as long as 30 minutes.
  - Stop the role-play after the stated duration with a closing statement such as "You have reached a point where we can break."
    - Role-play should not drag on to the point of boredom or heated discussion.
- Debriefing
  - Ask players to report.
    - A quick summary from each player is all that is needed at this point.
  - Assist players to step out of their roles.
    - Asking them to physically move away from the playing space and change chairs is sometimes needed for the player to rejoin the group.
  - Ask observers to report their observations.
- Closure
  - Assist participants to integrate role-playing results into previously covered materials.
  - Avoid direct comments about the acting skills of the role players.
    - Role-playing in this setting is not intended as an exercise in drama.

Brainstorming

- Unstructured participant responses to a given problem or issue.
- Generates ideas in an atmosphere where suggestions are not criticized.

Advantages:

- Nonjudgmental.
  - All ideas are recorded.
- Encourages involvement of all participants.

Disadvantages:

- Provides a large quantity of information that must be processed by the group and/or the instructor.

Major Elements of Brainstorming

- Introduction.
  - Explain the rules.
    - ♦ Participants must not criticize or reject any idea.
    - ♦ All suggestions are acceptable.
    - ♦ The more creative the suggestion the better.
  - Choose a recorder for all suggestions.
    - ♦ Write each suggestion or idea on a flipchart, white board, or chalkboard.
    - ♦ The instructor can serve as the recorder.
    - ♦ Define the task using very specific terms.
    - ♦ Clarify time allowed for the session.

Brainstorming Session

- Get started quickly.
- Stop the session when the allotted time has passed.
  - Suggested time frames are five minutes for most topics, up to 20 minutes for larger problems or tasks.
  - During longer brainstorming sessions, give the group a 5-minute warning of session closure.
  - Monitor the group to identify when ideas have been exhausted.
- Closure
  - Reconvene the group.
  - Summarize ideas.
    - ♦ If a problem was discussed that needs solution, ask the group to choose a solution from the generated list.
  - State the original problem and solutions that have been identified.

Tips for brainstorming:

- Difficult for a large group.
  - The technique works best for groups of eight to 15 people.
  - Divide a large class into smaller groups.
    - ♦ Give each group the same problem/task to discuss.
    - ♦ A large problem can be divided into sections for each group.
  - Keep the session short.
    - ♦ Criticism can surface in longer sessions.
  - Can be difficult in groups with large differences in age and backgrounds.

Case Study

- An in-depth discussion on a patient and related clinical problem.

- Opportunity for the instructor to share real experiences that relate to the content discussed.

- Popular teaching method for experienced practitioners.

Advantages:

- Develops analytical skills.

- Encourages originality and creativity.

- Can be assigned to individuals or small groups.

- Captures and maintains participant interest.

- Patient care can be the focus.

- Establishes the instructor's credibility as a knowledgeable clinician.

- Reality-based method for applying theory to practice.

- Very flexible technique.

Disadvantages:

- Instructor may use routinely without considering purpose.

- Requires careful processing and closure.

Types of Case Studies

- Interactive case study.

  - Case may be presented using computer multimedia.

  - Instructor presents the case using slides or overheads.

  - Patient care information is provided on a limited or incomplete basis.

  - Participants fill in these information gaps on patient care.

- Lead-in case study.

  - Instructor presents the case, often using slides or overheads. All details of the case are included.

  - At the end of the case presentation, participants discuss issues or problems related to the case.

- Written case study.

  - Given as an assignment.

  - Each participant receives a copy of the case with a list of questions to be answered.

  - Used as a classroom assignment or a take-home examination.

  - Some written case studies provide a lot of information, much of which is a red herring.

    - Shows participant perception and their ability to sort information.

Major Elements of a Case Study

- Process required to present a case study depends on the type of case study used.

- General process.

- Introduction.
    - Demographic data for the patient.
    - Presenting chief complaint.
    - History of present signs and symptoms.
    - Past medical history.
- Objective data.
    - Clinical presentation.
    - Clinical course of patient care.
    - Caregivers involved.
    - Laboratory and radiology findings.
- Identification of problems or issues.
    - Discuss any controversial treatments.
    - Focus teaching on one aspect of patient condition.
- Summary.
    - Review outcomes and best practices.

Tips for case study presentation:

- Use multidisciplinary approach for the presentation.
- Include psychosocial aspects of care.

Skills Demonstration and Practice

- Teach motor skills or procedures.

Advantages:

- Hands-on practice helps facilitate the learner to perform a skill.
- Mistakes can be quickly corrected.
- Participants proceed at their own pace.
- Procedure can be repeated as often as needed.
- Creates and holds participant interest.

Disadvantages:

- Can be challenging in a large group.
- Large number of supplies required to minimize waiting time and maintain participant interest.

Major Elements of a Demonstration and Practice Session

- Introduction.
    - Review skill or procedure.
- Instructor demonstration.
    - Demonstration of the skill in a sequential, logical manner.

- Whole-part-whole demonstration is most effective (complete demonstration followed by a step-by-step presentation followed by another complete demonstration).

- Return demonstration.

  - Each student returns the demonstration in a step-by-step approach.

    - The instructor acts as a coach.

  - Participant should not proceed to the next step until the first step is performed correctly.

  - Correct mistakes as they occur.

- Practice.

  - Participant proceeds at his or her own pace.

  - Practice sessions should be closely supervised.

Tips for skill demonstration and practice:

- The instructor must practice the skill before demonstration to ensure 100% proficiency.

- Visual aids enhance the demonstration and practice session.

- A poster outlining each step of the skill can be placed in the practice area for participant referral.

- If the instructor notices a trend in participant mistakes, the practice session should be stopped to review the appropriate steps for the entire group.

- When the skill involves unfamiliar equipment, it is beneficial for the participants to use and troubleshoot the equipment before they practice the entire procedure.

- Use of a skills checklist can reinforce learning and verify performance.

Panel Format

- Exposes participants to outside experts.

- Provides debating experience to the participants.

- Provides structured interaction between panel and audience.

- Discusses the issue from a multidisciplinary point of view.

- Issue can be discussed or debated.

Advantages:

- Takes spotlight off the instructor.

- Interactive teaching method.

- Maintains participant interest.

Disadvantages:

- Requires orchestration by the instructor.

- Some issues are so controversial that arguments between panel members occur.

Major Elements of a Panel Format

- Planning stage.

  - Select panel members.

- Decide on topic, issue, or specific questions.
- Select a moderator.
    - ♦ The instructor is often the moderator.
- Ensure that each panel member is familiar with his or her role and the role of other panel members.
- Provide member names and phone numbers to the entire panel so they can communicate with each other before the session.
- Meet with panel members as a group at least once before the session to review questions and procedures.
- Prepare participants for the session by providing advanced readings and discussion on the topic.

- Panel debate.
    - The moderator introduces the topic, then each panel member.
    - Each panel member is allotted time to present his or her view and opinions.
    - After each panel member has spoken, the moderator initiates and directs questions and discussion between the panel and the audience.

- Panel discussion.
    - The moderator introduces the topic, then each panel member.
    - Each panel member is allotted time to present his or her aspect of the chosen topic.
    - Topics usually are not as controversial as those used for a panel debate.
    - After each panel member has spoken, the moderator initiates and directs discussion between the panel and the audience.

- Closure.
    - Summarize interactions between panel members and the audience.
    - Suggest follow-up discussion or readings as appropriate.

Games

- Icebreaker or opening exercise.
- Acquisition or practice of knowledge or skills.
- New approach to an old topic, e.g., fire safety, CPR review, policies, and procedures.
- Challenges experienced nurses.
- Problem-solving.

Advantages:

- Motivates participants.
- Can be very realistic.
- Requires participant interaction.
- Provides a change of pace.
- Encourages summarization and synthesis of material.
- Aids knowledge and skill retention.
- Provides immediate feedback.

Disadvantages:

- Adults may not be comfortable playing games.
- Competition in games may seem threatening.
- Requires significant amount of time.
- Often requires specific space and equipment that may not be available.
- Can be expensive to develop or purchase.
- May have limited reuse value.

Choosing a Suitable Game

- Does the game meet the educational objectives?
- Can the game be completed within the time allotted?
- Is the physical environment conducive to the game?
- Are a minimum or maximum number of participants required?
- Is extra time required for preparation beforehand and cleanup afterwards?
- Does the game require special equipment or supplies? If so, are resources available to purchase or design these materials?
- Do staff members have the time and interest to design or adapt games?
- Are the participants known to be negative toward games?
- Is the game reusable? (Lewis, Saydak, Mierzwa, & Robinson, 1989).

Tips for games:

- Educators interested in using games as a teaching method should refer to the literature as a rich source of ideas for designing games or adapting existing games.
- Within an institution, challenges can be established between nursing units or different shifts in one unit.
  - For example, night shift challenges day shift to a game of Emergency Pursuit, a review of emergency nursing knowledge.
  - Before initiating any competition, the educator should know the participants':
    - ♦ Comfort level with other participants.
    - ♦ Attitude towards games and friendly competition.

Clinical Teaching at the Bedside

- Teaches physical assessment skills.
- Teaches interviewing skills.
- Observe new practitioners or experienced practitioners in a new environment.

Advantages:

- Realistic setting.
- Provides hands-on experience.
- Enhances instructor's credibility as a knowledgeable clinician.

- Participants can see the big picture.
- Case studies can be discussed with the actual patient present.

Disadvantages:

- Limited to small groups.
- Activity within the unit or department impedes opportunities for learning.
  - On a very busy day, crises in the emergency department do provide a good learning opportunity; however, staff may not be receptive to students, observers, or new practitioners during this time.
- Individual patient permission is often required for a group of learners to observe or perform procedures.
- There are many distractions to learning in a busy department, i.e., noises, smells, sights, etc.

Major Elements of Clinical Teaching at the Bedside

- Design basic objectives for the clinical experience.
  - Objectives may focus on a single clinical experience or spread over an orientation period of a few weeks.
  - Educators involved in teaching clinical courses should write objectives for an entire semester.
- Develop guidelines for clinical activities.
  - If written assignments are given, provide guidelines on what is expected.
  - For observation activities, provide guidelines for what is to be observed and reported.
  - Provide a skills checklist.
- Preconference and postconference.
  - Meet briefly with the clinical group before the actual clinical activity as well as after the activity.
    - ◆ Review expectations for the experience.
    - ◆ Summarize the activities of the day.
    - ◆ Clarify concerns and answer questions.
- Supervised practice.
  - Base the need for direct supervision on the experience level of the individual or group.
  - Use preceptors for practice supervision in patient care areas.

Tips for clinical teaching at the bedside:

- If you are an educator new to a department or unit, orient yourself to the area.
  - New educators may have the option of going through the staff orientation program to familiarize themselves with the staff, the equipment, policies, and procedures.
- Inform staff before bringing participants into the clinical area for experience or observation.
  - Acquaint staff with planned activities and obtain approval from necessary personnel prior to the session.

Self-Learning Modules

- Self-contained learning activity.
- Useful for a variety of educational activities, i.e. orientation, mandatory education programs, inservices.

Advantages:

- Cost-effective.
- Self-paced.
- Consistent delivery of information.
- Provides immediate feedback.
- Portable.
  ▎ Module can be completed anywhere.
- Promotes the facilitator role of the emergency nurse educator.
- Provides a method to document employee knowledge.

Disadvantages:

- Not compatible with all adult learning styles.
- Requires constant motivation by the learner to complete the module.
- Not effective for teaching complex motor skills.
- Time required to develop the module.
- Little interaction between educator and participant.

Major Elements of Self-Learning Modules

- Overall purpose
- Objectives.
- Written instructions for use.
- Deadline for completion of modules.
- Appropriate background reading for completing the modules, i.e., policies and procedures, procedure steps, current literature.
- Adjunct audiovisual materials if available, i.e., videotapes.
- Pretests and posttests.
- Bibliography or reference list.
- Evaluation form for the learning method and module.
- Educator needs to follow-up with learner at regular intervals to check on progress and answer questions.
- Telephone number and/or beeper number for the emergency nurse educator should questions arise.

Tips for self-learning modules:

- Update self-learning modules with current materials.
- Educator should be available for questions, if not, ask participants to make a list questions for the emergency nurse educator.
- Space should be available for use.
- Time should be provided for the learning activity.
- Reinforcement of knowledge should be acquired through classroom or clinical activities.

ROOM SETUP

The physical setting for an educational session influences participant learning. Educators should be aware of the power seating arrangements have on learning. A variety of seating arrangements can be used for a presentation depending on the:

- Size of the room.

- Number of participants.

- Need for group discussion during the lecture.

- Use of instructional media.

- Formality of the presentation.

- Flexibility of the room furniture.

STANDARD SEATING ARRANGEMENTS

- Theater style.

    ▎Accommodates the greatest number of participants in the smallest space.

    ▎More than 50 individuals seated in a small space benefit from this style.

    ▎Utilizes rows of chairs.

    ▎Does not provide tables for notetaking.

    ▎Instructor should be raised on a platform or stage to enhance visibility.

- Classroom style.

    ▎Commonly used seating arrangement for groups of 30 to 50.

    ▎Tables are provided for notetaking.

    ◆ Refreshments are easily managed on a table.

    ▎Promotes instructor-participant discussion, but does limit group discussion.

SAMPLE ROOM SETUPS

Suggestions for room setups are provided for each teaching method discussed in the previous section.

Lecture

- Slide projector, flipchart, or blackboard can be substituted for the overhead projector in these diagrams.

- Some rooms have a slide projector permanently mounted at the back of the room or in a separate projection room.

- When using an overhead projector, arrange the room so the audience's view of the screen is not obstructed.

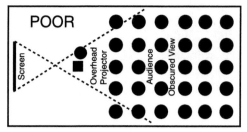

Note poor screen visibility caused by presenter and overhead projector.

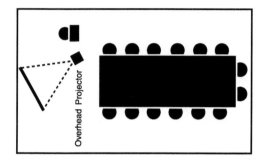

When using an overhead projector, arrange the room so the audience's view of the screen is not obstructed.

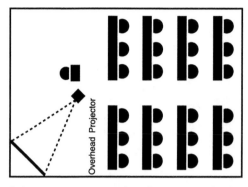

Classroom arrangement. This is a standard arrangement suitable for any size group.

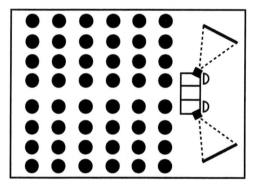

Center table arrangement. Suitable for under 20 people. This setup promotes discussion and is best for long meetings.

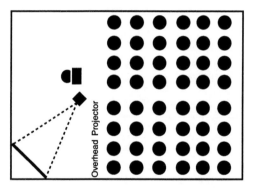

Auditorium/theater arrangement (single projector). Suitable for any size audience, but most efficient for large groups.

Auditorium/theater arrangement (dual projectors). As above, this arrangement works well with large groups. Two projectors and screens give the presenter more latitude in his or her presentation.

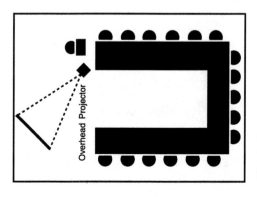

U-table arrangement. Suitable for 30 people or fewer. This arrangement is ideal for group discussion and interaction.

Group Discussion and Brainstorming

- Seating arrangement depends on the size of the group and use of instructional media.

- The following seating arrangements are suitable for smaller groups.

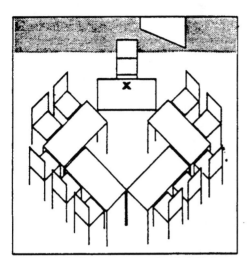

Renner, P. (1983), *The Instructor's Survival Kit (2nd ed.). Training Associates, Ltd: Vancouver, B.C., Canada. Used with permission.*

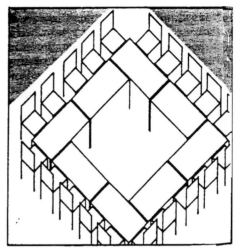

Renner, P. (1983), *The Instructor's Survival Kit (2nd ed.). Training Associates, Ltd: Vancouver, B.C., Canada. Used with permission.*

Everyone can look at everyone else while speaking and listening. The X is your spot and behind you is a flipchart or chalkboard. Most of the comments will probably flow towards you at the "head of the table." Watch who sits at the other end of the table, because the person(s) there may have a similar power position. This arrangement makes it awkward to use the overhead projector. This format enhances group discussion, but may limit use of audiovisual materials.

The closest thing to a round table using rectangular tables. The more distance between tables the more formal the interactions tend to be at the beginning. Here, almost everyone is in view but it is probably impractical for more than 25 people.

Role-play

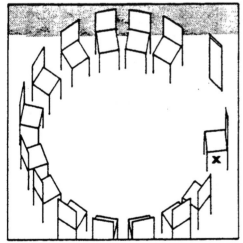

Renner, P. (1983), *The Instructor's Survival Kit (2nd ed.). Training Associates, Ltd: Vancouver, B.C., Canada. Used with permission.*

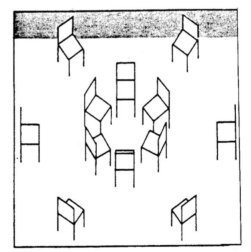

Renner, P. (1983), *The Instructor's Survival Kit (2nd ed.). Training Associates, Ltd: Vancouver, B.C., Canada. Used with permission.*

Circular arrangements are preferable in attitudinal learning situations. X is your spot and indicates that all contributions will be given equal value. The traditional "up front" power position would not encourage personal statements and learning.

This one is called group-on-group or "fishbowl." The inner group is working on some problem-solving talk or discussing an issue or concern. The outer group is instructed to watch for certain behaviors in the inner group, and will later act as consultant and process-evaluator to it. To avoid one-upmanship, groups should be switched around. The instructor floats to give instructions, observe, and keep time.

Case Study

- For interactive case studies involving slides or overhead transparencies, choose a seating arrangement that facilitates the best view of the instructional media.

- For case studies involving group discussion, choose a seating arrangement appropriate for group size and the instructional media used.

Skills Demonstration and Practice

- Seating arrangements can be modified for skills performed on the floor, e.g., CPR.

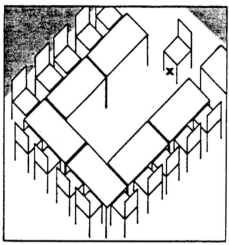

X marks the spot where you either sit or stand to give your demonstration. If imitation or practice by the students follows, this arrangement allows you to move in and out of their work areas, give individual attention, and keep an eye on all.

Renner, P. (1983), The Instructor's Survival Kit (2nd ed.). Training Associates, Ltd: Vancouver, B.C., Canada. Used with permission.

Panel Format

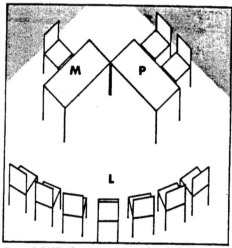

Renner, P. (1983), The Instructor's Survival Kit (2nd ed.). Training Associates, Ltd: Vancouver, B.C., Canada. Used with permission.

- Panel Discussion.

  ▮ M–moderator (either instructor or student)

  ▮ P–panel members

  ▮ L–learners

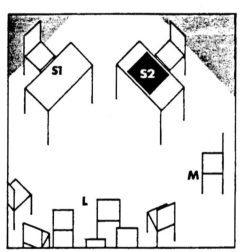

Renner, P. (1983), The Instructor's Survival Kit (2nd ed.). Training Associates, Ltd: Vancouver, B.C., Canada. Used with permission.

- Panel Debate.

  ▮ S1 & S2–opposing sides, opinions, viewpoints

  ♦ (may be separated for effect)

  ▮ M–moderator (you or a student)

  ▮ L–learners

Games

- The most effective seating arrangement for a game depends on the game itself.
- Many games require a specific physical setting.
- When designing your own game, always identify the seating arrangements.

TEACHING CHALLENGES

PARTICIPANT QUESTIONS

Questioning is an expression of genuine interest in a presentation. Participant questions should be considered compliments to the presenter. Tips for handling various participant questions are provided.

When the Presenter Does Not Know the Answer:

Do

- Redirect the question to the audience.
- State that you don't know the answer, indicate your willingness to find the information and get back to them.
  - I If possible, obtain a business card and then forward the information.
  - I For a local participant, offer to give the information to him or her later.

Do not

- Bluff or fabricate an answer.
- Offer an answer that is irrelevant to the question.
- Put down the questioner.
- Say "I don't know" and move on to the next question.

Hostile or Challenging Questions

- Remain calm and poised.
- Repeat the question to ensure all participants have heard the question and to gain extra time to think of an appropriate response.
- Paraphrase the question to include the essence of the question but not the anger.
- If the question includes information contradictory to the presentation, answer carefully to avoid agreeing with the contradictory information.
- Do not argue with the questioner. Your credibility will suffer.

Rambling Questions

- Once the questioner has finished, clarify the main question the questioner would like addressed.
- Restate what you think the question was, then ask the questioner for clarification.

No Questions

- If the audience asks no questions, this does not mean everything was crystal clear. The audience may not ask questions if the presenter:

  I Spoke too long.

    ♦ The audience may be anxious for a break.

  I Offended the audience in some way.

  I Did not connect with the audience.

    ♦ The language may have been too heavy or scientific and the audience lost interest.

General Tips for Question Sessions

- Allow time for questions in the educational activity.

- Decide at the beginning of the activity if questions will be accepted throughout or saved until the end.

- If there will be a general question period at the end of the presentation, encourage participants to write down their questions when they think of them.

- For large groups, place microphones in select locations to facilitate questions from participants.

- Repeat each question to be sure the entire audience understood the question.

- For large groups with a question session at the end, distribute index cards or pieces of paper at the beginning of the session for questions. Ask volunteers to collect the questions and give them to the presenter.

- When there is a large number of questions, the presenter may select which ones to answer.

- If the question period has expired, offer to remain during a break or after the class to answer further questions.

- Anticipate questions that may be asked and be prepared to answer.

  I Some educators start the question period with what they think is a commonly asked question.

  I This technique may get the audience involved.

Questioning Techniques for the Presenter to the Audience

- Ask questions of the entire audience, then select participants at random to answer.

- Allow time for participants to answer the question.

- Do not answer your own question.

- If one participant cannot answer a question, select another participant.

- Ask one question at a time.

Characteristics of a Good Question

- Indicates clearly the points to which the participants are expected to respond.

- Purposeful and thought provoking.

- Asked in a logical sequence.

- Brief.

- Phrased in simple language with vocabulary familiar to the audience.

Participant Learning Curves

Adults learn at their own pace. This variability in learning curves can be particularly challenging for the educator, since there is often a specific time frame in which objectives must be met. This can be especially true with teaching psychomotor skills. Suggestions to maximize learning is listed below.

Tips for Psychomotor Skill Sessions

- Ensure a practice session that allows the instructor one-on-one time with each participant.
- If the instructor identifies participants that need extra time to master the skill, offer to stay after the class or invite the participant to return for a future session.
  - Be careful not to embarrass the participant.
- When a participant masters the skill before the majority of the class, encourage him or her to help other participants who have not yet mastered the skill.
  - This prevents the advanced learner from becoming bored and disruptive to the rest of the class.
- If the educational session is longer than one class, encourage participants to practice skills outside the class with their peers or at home.
  - Provide specific instructions to assure correct technique.
- Be available to participants. Provide your telephone number or pager number so you can be reached outside class.
  - Some participants are embarrassed to ask for help in front of their peers, but will call for individual coaching.

Participant Attitudes that Interfere with Learning

Attitudes are formed through experience. Participants come to educational sessions with an array of attitudes towards both the subject matter and, often, the instructor. Positive and negative attitudes are contagious; therefore, it is essential that the instructor convey a positive attitude toward the participants and the topic at hand.

How to Handle Negative Attitudes

1. Remain positive and enthusiastic about the subject matter.
   - Your tone and body gestures should be positive throughout the class.
2. Recognize that participant attendance is mandated for many educational sessions, e.g., CPR.
   - Mandatory educational sessions are greeted with a less-than-enthusiastic response from participants.
   - Acknowledge this fact to the participants, while assuring them they can still learn and enjoy themselves.
   - Relate learning to the work setting and the home setting. For example, fire and safety knowledge and techniques are very useful if a home fire occurs.
3 If an individual participant or group of participants disrupts the class with negative comments, announce a refreshment or bathroom break for the entire class.
   - Speak to the involved individual(s) in private.
   - Acknowledge their negative comments and the disruption they are causing (give examples).
   - Provide the choice to refrain from disrupting the entire class or leave.
   - Participants may then express the rationale for their comments and their suggestions for improving the situation.

- Individuals with negative attitudes may be helped by involving them in the class discussion.

  ▮ This is particularly pertinent when individuals feel their opinions are not valued.

  ▮ Include these individuals in activities.

MENTORING

The term "mentor" is derived from Greek mythology. When Odysseus left to fight the Trojan War, he left his son with Mentor, an older gentleman friend (Fitzgerald, 1961). Mentor acted as a helper, teacher, advisor, tutor, protector, and guide. He inspired the son to meet life's challenges and accomplish his goals.

Modern texts on interpersonal relationships and professional development kindled interest in the mentoring phenomenon (Sheehy, 1976; Levinson, 1978; Roche, 1979). A mentor is officially defined as a "wise and trusted teacher or counselor" (Webster's II New Riverside University Dictionary, 1984). Kelly (1978) discussed mentoring from a nursing perspective in Power Guide-The Mentor Relationship. In recent years, a large number of articles on mentors and mentoring in nursing have appeared in nursing literature.

The purpose of the mentor relationship is to foster the protégé's growth and development. Ultimately, the protégé acquires and applies the mentor's wisdom. From this reference point, mentoring should benefit the emergency nurse educator.

MENTORS

A mentor is an individual who is insightful and nurturing. Nursing literature describes a mentor as a nurse who:

- Is older, wiser (Kinsey, 1990).

- Has specific career status and takes an active interest in the career development of another person (Bova & Phillips, 1989).

- Is a seasoned leader with a personal interest in molding the career of a young practitioner (O'Connor, 1988).

MENTOR TYPES

Effective mentor utilization requires understanding of the mentor role, types, functions, and process. Business and management literature identify six mentor types.

- Traditional mentor:

  ▮ Older authority figure.

- Supportive boss:

  ▮ Coach.

- Organizational sponsor:

  ▮ Top-level manager without close contact.

- Professional mentor:

  ▮ Paid career counselor.

  ▮ Paid advisor.

- Patron:
  - Supporter with status and financial resources.
- Invisible godparent:
  - Behind-the-scenes provider of recommendations and arrangements (Anderson & Shannon, 1988).

FUNCTIONS AND BEHAVIORS

Regardless of type, mentors generally exhibit similar behaviors and perform similar functions. Anderson and Shannon (1988) described five functions and requisite behaviors for the successful mentor.

- Teach.
  - Model, inform, confirm, prescribe, and question.
- Sponsor.
  - Protect, support, and promote.
- Encourage.
  - Affirm, inspire, and challenge.
- Counsel.
  - Listen, probe, clarify, and advise.
- Befriend.
  - Accept and relate.

MENTORING RELATIONSHIPS

Mentoring is the process of providing information, advice, and emotional support in a relationship marked by significant emotional attachment between the participants (Bowen, 1985). Mentoring relationships are long term, lasting three to 10 years.

A mentoring relationship exhibits two functional dimensions that reflect the innate complexity inherent to the mentoring relationship (Kram, 1985).

- Instrumental functions enhance career development.
  - Includes coaching, protection, sponsorship, and exposure/visibility.
- Psychosocial functions promote a sense of competence, clarity of identity, and effectiveness in role acquisition.
  - Includes counseling, acceptance, confirmation, role modeling, and friendship.

Mentoring relationships are not born, they evolve over time and pass through distinct developmental phases.

- Initiation phase.
  - Period when the relationship is established.
- Cultivation phase.
  - Time when instrumental and psychosocial functions are at maximum capacity.
- Separation phase.

- Occurs when the relationship alters in response to structural changes in the organization or psychological changes in the participants.
- Redefinition phase.
  - The relationship evolves into a new form or ends completely (Ross, 1984; Kram, 1985; Pillette, 1980; Urbano, 1986).

CONCEPTUAL PERSPECTIVES OF MENTORING

Authors have described mentoring as a structural role, organizational phenomenon, or interpersonal relationship (Yoder, 1990).

- Structural perspective.
  - Targets the novice within an organization or discipline. Within this context, mentoring is described as a:
    - ◆ Role phenomenon – promotes career progression and achievement (Noe, 1988).
    - ◆ Role development strategy – facilitates role clarification, role rehearsal, and role modeling (May, Meleis, & Winstead-Fry, 1982).
- Organizational perspective.
  - Conceptualization of mentoring as an organizational phenomenon leads to development of formal mentorships for junior executives.
  - Mentorships encourage organizational stability and continuity by:
    - ◆ Introducing culture and operations of the corporate world.
    - ◆ Promoting career advancement through organizational visibility.
    - ◆ Establishing beneficial organizational alignments.
- Interpersonal perspective.
  - Described as a complex love relationship that often ends in stormy conflict (Levinson, 1978). Descriptions of nursing mentoring from an interpersonal context include:
    - ◆ Intense, emotional, exclusionary, and transitional as seen in a parent-child relationship (Vance, 1982).
    - ◆ Hierarchical, intense, exclusionary, and not democratic (Hamilton, 1981).

MODELS FOR MENTORING

Successful mentoring programs are based on distinct structures and relationship concepts. Several models of mentoring are described in the literature. Utilization of these models requires understanding the concepts and applications unique to each model.

- Grooming-mentoring.
  - Special assistance by an older, more experienced professional.
  - The mentor grooms the protégé during a transition period and helps shape the protégé's professional development (Levinson, 1978).
- Diffuse-mentoring.
  - Guidance from several influential persons (Fagan & Fagan, 1983).

- Networking-mentoring.

  I Series of contacts between two or more people.

  I Each person plays the role of mentor and protégé at different times, with varying degrees of intensity.

- Patron-mentoring.

  I Development of mentor from a same-level peer pal to guide, sponsor, influential patron, and finally, a paternalistic mentor (Merriam, 1983).

MENTORING PROCESSES

Mentoring may be formal or informal, depending on the individual, profession, and the organizational setting.

- Formal mentoring:

  I Formalized mentorships provide organizational management opportunity.

- Informal mentoring:

  I Initiated by the mentor or the protégé.

  I The emotional bond between participants may be stronger in informal mentoring because of the process of personal selection.

MENTORING CHARACTERISTICS

Darling (1984) identified three elements essential for an informal mentoring relationship—attraction, action, and affect. Informal mentoring is an intense, highly emotional relationship driven by chemistry and sustained by mutually beneficial affect. Chemistry is the result of personality congruence related to present and future work and life goals (Yoder, 1990).

NURSE MENTOR CHARACTERISTICS

Nurses seek a mentor who is knowledgeable, respected by the profession, and open to the mentoring relationship. General characteristics include:

- Performs job well.
- Judged well by the organization.
- Good teacher and motivator.
- Secure in his or her position.
- Possesses power and influence in the organization.
- Exercises discipline to facilitate upward mobility.
- Increases responsibilities by providing challenging assignments.
- Serves as a role model, counselor, and friend.
- Offers encouragement, acceptance, and confirmation when mistakes occur.

PROTÉGÉ CHARACTERISTICS

Nurse mentors seek a protégé who is intelligent and displays teachable attitudes. Desirable protégé characteristics include:

- Intelligence.
- Ambition.
- Desire and ability to accept power and risks.
- Loyalty.
- Ability to eventually perform the mentor's job.
- Similar perceptions of work and organization.
- Commitment to the organization or discipline.
- Organizational savvy.
- Capacity to be perceived in a positive light by the organization.
- Ability to establish alliances (Zey, 1984).

RELATED CONCEPTS

Mentoring has been described as role modeling, sponsorship, precepting, and peer strategizing (Vance, 1982; Atwood, 1979; Bidwell & Brasler, 1989; Darling, 1984; Darling, 1985). Many authors feel these concepts relate to mentoring, but should not be considered the same process.

- Role modeling:
  - One-sided relationship based on identification and internalization of another person's standards (Hamilton, 1981; Bidwell & Brasler, 1989).
  - The role model is passive.
  - Role modeling is thought to be a small part of mentoring (Yoder, 1990).
- Sponsorship:
  - Demonstrates all the properties of mentoring with the additional requirement of protégé promotion (May et al., 1982).
  - Protégé promotion includes name dropping at the right time and in the right spot.
- Preceptorships:
  - Also called internships.
  - Form of staff orientation.
  - The relationship focuses on task accomplishment with a small psychological component (Kelly, 1987).
  - Preceptorships take place over a short period of time, whereas mentoring relationships occur over years.
- Peer strategizing:
  - Refers to comentoring or mentoring by peers (Darling, 1984).
  - Relationship is based on reciprocal or mutual guidance and assistance.

REFERENCES

Alberta Multicultural Commission. (1989). Understanding seniors and culture. Edmonton, Alberta: Author.

Abbruzzese, R. S. (1996). Nursing Staff Development: Strategies for Success. St. Louis: Mosby Year Book, Inc.

Anderson, E., & Shannon, A. (1988). Toward a conceptualization of mentoring. Journal of Teacher Education, 39(1), 38-42.

Atwood, A. (1979). The mentor in clinical practice. Nursing Outlook, 26(11), 714-717.

Bidwell, A., & Brasler, M. (1989). Role modeling versus mentoring in nursing. Image, 21(1), 23-25.

Bova, B.M., & Phillips, R.R. (1989). Cited in Weekes, D.P. "Mentor-protégé relationships." Nursing Outlook, 37(40), 156-57.

Bowen, D. (1985). Were men meant to mentor women? Training and Development Journal, 39(1), 30-34.

Brookfield, S. (1986). Understanding and facilitating adult learning. San Francisco: Jossey-Bass.

Darkenwald, G., & Merriam, S. (1982). Adult education: Foundations of practice. New York: Harper & Row.

Darling, L. (1984). Mentor types and life cycles. Journal of Nursing Administration, 14(11), 43-44.

Darling, L. (1985). Mentors and mentoring. Journal of Nursing Administration, 15(3), 42-43.

Eason, F., & Corbett, R. (1991). Effective teacher characteristics identified by adult learners in nursing. Journal of Continuing Education in Nursing, 22(1), 21-23.

Fagan, M., & Fagan, P. (1983). Mentoring among nurses. Nursing and Health Care, 4(2), 80-82.

Fitzgerald, R. (1961). The odyssey. (Homer, Trans.). Garden City, NY: Doubleday.

Hamilton, M. (1981). Mentorhood: A key to nursing leadership. Nursing Leadership, 4(1), 4-13.

James, W. (1983). An analysis of perceptions of the practices of adult educators from five different settings. Proceedings of the Adult Education Research Conference, no. 24. Montreal, Quebec: Concordia University/University of Montreal.

Kelly, L. (1978). Power guide: The mentor relationship. Nursing Outlook, 26(6), 339.

Kinsey, D. (1990). Mentorship and influence in nursing. Nursing Management, 21(5), 45-46.

Knowles, M.S. (1970). The modern practice of adult education. New York: Association Press.

Kram, K. (1985). Mentoring at work: Developmental relationships in organizational life. Glenview, IL: Scott Foresman.

Levinson, D. (1978). The seasons of a man's life. New York: Knopf.

Lewis, D., Saydak, S., Mierzwa, I., & Robinson, J. (1989). Gaming: A teaching strategy for adult learners. Journal of Continuing Education in Nursing, 20(2), 80-84.

Lindeman, E. (1926). The meaning of adult education. New York: New Republic.

May, K., Meleis, A., & Winstead-Fry, P. (1982). Mentorship for scholarliness: Opportunities and dilemmas. Nursing Outlook, 30(1), 22-28.

Merriam, S. (1983). Mentors and protégés: A critical review of the literature. Adult Education Quarterly, 33(3), 163-170.

Noe, R. (1988). Women and mentoring: A review and research agenda. Academy of Management Review, 13(1), 64-78.

O'Connor, K. (1988). "For want of a mentor. . ." <u>Nursing Outlook</u>, <u>36</u>(1), 38.

Pillette, P. (1980). Mentoring: An encounter of the leadership kind. <u>Nursing Leadership</u>, <u>3</u>(2), 22-26.

<u>Pocket Webster school and office dictionary</u>. (1990). New York: Pocket Books.

Renner, P. (1983). <u>The instructor's survival kit</u> (2nd ed.). Vancouver, British Columbia: Training Associates, Ltd.

Roche, G. (1979). Much ado about mentors. <u>Harvard Business Review</u>, <u>57</u>(1), 14-28.

Ross, A. (1984). The mentor's role in developing new leaders. <u>Hospital and Health Care Administration</u>, <u>29</u>(5), 21-29.

Sheehy, G. (1976). <u>Passages: Predictable crises of adult life</u>. New York: E.P. Dutton.

Thiederman, S. (1989). Managing the foreign-born nurse. <u>Nursing Management</u>, <u>20</u>(7), 13.

Urbano, M. (1986). A developmental approach to doctoral education. <u>Journal of Nursing Education</u>, <u>25</u>(2), 76-78.

Vance, C.N. (1982). The mentor connection. <u>Journal of Nursing Administration</u>, <u>12</u>(4), 7-13.

<u>Webster's II New Riverside University Dictionary</u>. (1985). Boston: Houghton Mifflin/Riverside.

Williams, J., & Rogers, S. (1993) . The multicultural workplace: Preparing preceptors. <u>Journal of Continuing Education in Nursing</u>, <u>24</u>(3), 101-104.

Yoder, L. (1990). Mentoring: A concept analysis. <u>Nursing Administration Quarterly</u>, <u>15</u>(1), 9-19.

Zey, M.C. (1984). <u>The mentor connection</u>. Homewood, IL: Dow-Jones & Irwin.

RECOMMENDED READINGS

ADULT LEARNING THEORIES

Houle, C. (1989). <u>Continuing learning in the professions</u>. San Francisco: Jossey-Bass.

Knox, A. (1977). <u>Adult development and learning</u>. San Francisco: Jossey-Bass.

Lumsden, B. (1985). <u>The older adult as learner</u>. New York: Hemisphere.

Nielsen, B. (1992). Applying andragogy in nursing continuing education. <u>Journal of Continuing Education in Nursing</u>, <u>23</u>(4), 148-151.

MULTICULTURALISM/LANGUAGES

Beunker, J.D., & Ratner, L.A. (1992). <u>Multiculturalism in the United States</u>. New York: Greenwood.

Bodiwala, G., McCaskie, H., & Thompson, M. (1993). <u>International translation guide for emergency medicine</u>. Oxford, Great Britain: Butterworth-Heinemann.

Gonen, A. (Ed.). (1993). <u>The encyclopedia of the people of the world</u>. New York: Henry Holt.

Kastenbaum, R., & Kastenbaum, B. (Eds.). (1989). <u>Encyclopedia of death</u>. Phoenix: Oryx Press.

Kelland, B., & Jordan, L. (1994). <u>Committed multilingual patient assessment manual</u>, (3rd ed.) St. Louis: Mosby.

Nasr, I., Cordero, M. (2000). <u>Medical Spanish in pediatrics: An instant translator</u>. St. Louis: Mosby.

Nasr, I., Cordero, M. (1996). <u>Medical Spanish: An instant translator</u>. St. Louis: Mosby.

Teed, C., Raley, H., Barber, J., & Harcourt, B. (1983). <u>Conversational Spanish for the medical & health professions</u>. Philadelphia: Jonanovich.

PUBLIC SPEAKING

Hoff, R. (1988). <u>"I can see you naked." A fearless guide to making great presentations</u>. New York: Andres and McMeel.

Schloff, L., & Yudkin, M. (1991). <u>Smart speaking</u>. New York: Henry Holt.

Smith, T. (1991). <u>Making successful presentations</u> (2nd ed.). New York: John Wiley & Sons.

Valentine, N. (1993). <u>Speaking in public</u>. New York: Penguin Books.

GAMES

Gruending, D., Fenty, D., & Hogan, T. (1991). Fun and games in nursing staff development. <u>Journal of Continuing Education in Nursing</u>, <u>22</u>(6), 259-262.

Gucciardo, J., & Matera, R. (1991). A teaching method that makes nurses ask for more. <u>RN</u>, <u>55</u>(7), 18-Z(missing #).

Hitchcock, D. (1988, March). Building instructional games. <u>Training</u>, pp. 33-38.

Karrei, I. (1992). Fun & games. <u>Canadian Nurse</u>, <u>88</u>(6), 28-30.

Resko, D., & Chorba, M. (1992). Enhancing learning through the use of games. <u>Dimensions of Critical Care Nursing</u>, <u>11</u>(3), 173-177.

Schmitz, B., MacLean, S., & Shidler, H. (1991). An emergency pursuit game: A method for teaching emergency decision-making skills. <u>Journal of Continuing Education in Nursing</u>, <u>22</u>(4), 152-158.

Speers, A. (1993). Crossword puzzles: A teaching strategy for critical care nursing. <u>Dimensions of Critical Care Nursing</u>, <u>12</u>(6), 52-55.

Terenzi, C. (2000). The triage game. <u>Journal of Emergency Nursing</u>, <u>26</u>(1):66-69.

Wright, D. (1993). "The princess and the chemo spill" ? A policy magically turned into a fairy tale. <u>Journal of Continuing Education in Nursing</u>, <u>24</u>(1), 37-38.

OTHER TEACHING METHODS

Cherry B., & Howard, J. (1987). CPR by blitz: An intense campaign for annual recertification. <u>Focus on Critical Care</u>, <u>14</u>(1), 30-34.

Cochenour, C. (1992). Self-learning packages in staff development. <u>Journal of Nursing Staff Development</u>, (May/June), 123-127.

Cooper, S. (1986). Self-directed learning. <u>Journal of Continuing Education in Nursing</u>, <u>17</u>(3), 104-105.

Fuszard, B. (1989). <u>Innovative teaching strategies in nursing</u>. Gaithersburg, MD: Aspen.

Kozole, A., & Andrea, J. (1990). Mock delivery: An educational tool for the emergency department. Part 1. <u>Journal of Emergency Nursing</u>, <u>16</u>(3), 162-165.

Novak, A. (1993). Tips for the new nurse educator: Thoughts one year after beginning the role. <u>Journal of Emergency Nursing</u>, <u>19</u>(1), 63-64.

Schoolcraft, V. (1989). <u>A nuts-and-bolts approach to teaching nursing</u>. New York: Springer.

Schoolcraft, V. (1994). <u>A down-to-earth approach to being a nurse educator</u>. New York: Springer.

Sheehy, S. (1987). Teaching as an art and a science: One philosophy and method of continuing education for the new nurse educator. <u>Journal of Emergency Nursing, 13</u>(5), 314-316.

Somes, J. (1990). Skill day: A method of reviewing and verifying ED skills for nurses. <u>Journal of Emergency Nursing, 16</u>(2), 111-115.

MENTORING

Arnoldussen, B., & White, L. (1990). The mentoring experience. <u>Nursing Administration Quarterly, 15</u>(1), 28-35.

Boyle, C., & James, S. (1990). Nursing leaders as mentors: How are we doing? <u>Nursing Administration Quarterly, 15</u>(1), 44-48.

Chisholm, M. (1991). Use and abuse of power. <u>Clinical Nurse Specialist, 5</u>(1), 57.

Collins, N.N. (1983). <u>Professional women and their mentors</u>. Englewood Cliffs, NJ: Prentice-Hall.

Darling, L. (1985). Becoming a mentoring manager. <u>Journal of Nursing Administration, 15</u>(6), 43-44.

Darling, L. (1985). "Can a non-bonder be an effective mentor?" <u>Journal of Nursing Administration, 15</u>(2), 30-31.

Darling, L. (1985). Cultivating minor mentors. <u>Journal of Nursing Administration, 15</u>(9), 41-42.

Darling, L. (1985). Endings in mentor relationships. <u>Journal of Nursing Administration, 15</u>(11), 40-41.

Darling, L. (1985). Mentor matching. <u>Journal of Nursing Administration, 15</u>(1), 45-46.

Darling, L. (1985). Self-mentoring strategies. <u>Journal of Nursing Administration, 15</u>(4), 42-43.

Darling, L. (1985). The case for mentor moderation. <u>Journal of Nursing Administration, 15</u>(7/8), 42-43.

Darling, L. (1985). What to do about toxic mentors? <u>Journal of Nursing Administration, 15</u>(5), 43-44.

Haas, S. (1992). Coaching ? Developing key players. <u>Journal of Nursing Administration, 22</u>(6), 54-58.

Hamilton, E.M., Murray, M.K., Lindholm, L.H., & Myers, R.E. (1989). Effects of mentoring on job satisfaction, leadership behaviors, and job retention of new graduate nurses. <u>Journal of Nursing Staff Development, 5</u>(4), 159-165.

Kram, K. (1985). Improving the mentoring process. <u>Training and Development Journal, 39</u>(4), 40.

Prestholdt, C. (1990). Modern mentoring: Strategies for developing contemporary nursing leadership. <u>Nursing Administration Quarterly, 15</u>(1), 20-27.

Rogers, B. (1992, August). Mentoring takes a new twist. <u>Human Resources Magazine</u>, pp. 48-51.

Taylor, L.J. (1992). A survey of mentor relationships in academe. <u>Journal of Professional Nursing, 8</u>(1), 48-55.

Wilbur, J. (1987). Does mentoring breed success? <u>Training and Development Journal, 41</u>(11), 38-41.

Better Teaching Through the Use of Effective Communication Techniques

OBJECTIVES

Upon completion of this chapter, the emergency nurse educator will be able to:

1. Recognize distinguishing characteristics of effective communication.

2. Define constructive criticism.

3. Identify characteristics of successful public speaking.

4. List three elements of effective writing.

INTRODUCTION

Communication is the "exchange of ideas, messages, or information, as by speech, signals, or writing" (Webster's II New Riverside University Dictionary, 1984, p. 284). The importance of communication to the emergency nurse educator cannot be overstated. This chapter provides an overview of three communication concepts germane to the emergency nurse educator, i.e., communication style, spoken communication, and written communication.

COMMUNICATION PATTERNS

Recognition of communication patterns in oneself and others facilitates selection of an effective approach for a specific situation and a specific individual. A number of communication patterns have received attention from various investigators. In reality, each person utilizes several patterns at any given time. A brief overview of two patterns is provided. The emergency nurse educator is encouraged to review literature on additional communication patterns (Keirsey & Bates, 1978; Myers & Myers, 1988; Myers & McCaulley, 1989).

MYERS-BRIGGS TYPE INDICATOR

The Myers-Briggs Type Indicator (MBTI) categorizes communication patterns with regard to how the individual communicates, obtains information, makes decisions, and orients his or her life (Hirsch, 1985). Four unique pairs of communication patterns or preferences are identified by the MBTI. Each pair represents diametric extremes of behavior. Individuals may appear anywhere along the continuum of the specific behavior. Recognition of these behavior patterns strengthens the emergency nurse educator's ability to communicate.

- Extroversion-introversion.
  - Refers to personal energy source.
    - ◆ Extrovert.
      - Talkative, charged up.
      - Expends more energy.
      - Acting out an idea is more appealing than thinking about it.
      - Open in their communications.
    - ◆ Introvert.
      - Discloses personal information slowly.
      - Keeps thoughts to themselves.
      - Tends to conserve energy.
- Sensing-intuitive.
  - Relates to how the individual becomes aware of facts or ideas.
  - Sensor.
    - ◆ Uses the five senses.
    - ◆ Lives very much in the present.
    - ◆ Practical.
    - ◆ Good with facts.
    - ◆ Very literal.
  - Intuitive individual.
    - ◆ Goes with their instincts.
    - ◆ Very creative.
    - ◆ Generates a lot of ideas.
    - ◆ Bored and restless with routine.
- Thinker-feeler.
  - Refers to decision-making patterns.
    - ◆ Thinker.
      - Logical, brief, and business-like.
      - Bases decisions on cause and effect.
      - Prioritizes tasks over relationships.
    - ◆ Feeler.
      - Bases decisions on personal values.
      - Concerned with harmony and effect a decision will have on others.

- Judgment-perception.

  I Concerns how the person organizes his or her world.

  I Individual who prefers judgment.

    ♦ Plans ahead, responds well to deadlines.

    ♦ Controlling and regulating workflow is very appealing.

  I Perceiver.

    ♦ Open and spontaneous.

    ♦ Views deadline as a signal to start.

Brain Lateralization

Early twentieth century physiologists suggested the existence of two separate brains, each capable of independent thought (Fincher, 1984; Corballis, 1991). Since that time, brain lateralization has received considerable attention from a variety of disciplines.

Each cerebral hemisphere manifests unique behaviors and communication patterns. Individuals may operate exclusively from one side of the brain or exhibit a synchronous blend of characteristics from both sides (Wonder & Donovan, 1984).

- The left hemisphere utilizes sequential, analytical thinking. An individual who lateralizes to the left hemisphere tends to be unemotional, logical, and rational.

- The individual who lateralizes to the right hemisphere is emotional, intuitive, and creative.

Understanding manifestations of lateralization toward a specific side enhances interpersonal communications. For example, the individual who lateralizes strongly to the left side requires facts and figures. This is important information to consider when presenting a request for a new program. Characteristics unique to each hemisphere are summarized below (Veehoff, 1992).

- Left brain characteristics.

  I Rational, sequential, and analytical.

  I Enjoys step-by-step instructions.

  I Expresses thoughts and ideas verbally.

  I Detached and unemotional.

  I Thinks logically and evaluates critically.

  I Likes facts, figures, and data.

- Right brain characteristics.

  I Spontaneous and playful.

  I Grasps the big picture.

  I Imaginative and inventive.

  I Sees patterns in events.

  I Craves variety and change.

CONSTRUCTIVE CRITICISM

Feedback is inherent to the education process. Positive, sincere information is the basis of constructive criticism. Criticism delivered without personal bias or misuse of power enables the individual to improve performance. Harsh, negative feedback decreases morale, self-esteem, and self-respect. Regrettably, the result is often lasting resentment. The ability to present criticism constructively requires forethought and conscious effort. Criticism must focus on the behavior rather than the person.

Tips for providing constructive feedback:

- Speak directly to the person. Avoid venting frustrations to a third party.

- Consider the magnitude of the event in terms of intention and outcome. Don't make a mountain of a mole hill.

- Avoid contaminating the discussion with personal bias.

- Cool off. Words spoken in anger or without adequate forethought may create lasting ill will.

- Time the discussion. Consider events that may be directly and indirectly affected, i.e., current assignments, future deadlines.

- Speak privately. Never criticize in the presence of others. Privacy means visual and verbal privacy.

- Ask questions first. Get the facts. Don't accuse or assume.

- Focus on behavior. Present specific, objective information.

- Appreciate, then criticize. In almost all instances, some type of sincere, appreciative comment can be made about the person's performance. Avoid personal flattery.

- Avoid emotional exchanges. Don't be unpleasant (Economics Press, 1975).

PUBLIC SPEAKING

Public speaking is an essential skill for the emergency nurse educator. Formal and informal education offerings, meetings, professional association functions, and community events challenge the emergency nurse educator to demonstrate effective public speaking skills. Some people are better speakers than others; however, effective speaking is an acquired skill and does not depend on an innate ability.

General guidelines and tips on public speaking are provided. The educator is encouraged to fine tune speaking skills through exploration of other resources, i.e., books, videos, drama classes, voice classes, and clubs such as Toastmasters.

TYPES OF PUBLIC SPEAKING

Speech

A speech may be given to entertain, inform, or persuade. Speech delivery usually occurs at social and political gatherings. The speech topic may be chosen by the speaker or assigned by the sponsoring agency or organization. A speech may be written word for word and read directly to the audience. A successful speech has distinct opening and closing remarks that bracket strong delivery of the body of the speech, which contains the main content.

- Opening remarks.
  - Rhetorical questions or a series of questions.
  - Story or humorous anecdote related to speech content.
  - Needs and beliefs of the audience.
  - Quotation related to speech content.
- Body of the speech.
  - Clear, concise.
  - Makes a strong statement on the subject.
- Closing remarks.
  - Summary, repetition, or review of speech theme.
  - Repetition of opening story or anecdote with a new or different twist.
  - Appeal to the audience for action or belief.

Presentation

A presentation is associated with education and business environments rather than entertainment. Nurse educators are more likely to make a presentation than a speech. Hoff (1988) describes a presentation as a "commitment by the presenter to help the audience do something—and a constant, simultaneous evaluation of the worth of that commitment by the audience" (p. 7).

A presentation is designed to inform, instruct, persuade, arouse interest, initiate action, or make recommendations. It should be vital and compelling. The entertainment factor should be suitable to the environment. For example, a board of directors meeting may require a more serious presentation than an education presentation to a civic group.

- Opening remarks.
  - Dynamic statement of purpose.
  - Clear plan of intent.
  - Sequence of presentation for main points.
- Closing remarks.
  - Summary of main points.
  - Recommendation, challenge, or other dynamic concluding statement.
  - Never introduce new material in the conclusion.

QUALITIES OF A GOOD SPEAKER

There are many essential qualities of a good speaker. All can be gained through practice. Valentine (1993) compiled a list of qualities essential for an effective speaker.

- Voice that carries.
- Fine use of language.
- Clarity of speech.
- Smile.

- Confident appearance.

- Well-researched subject.

- Ability to appeal to an audience.

- Power of persuasion.

- Knack of speaking to listeners, not at them.

- Precise timing.

- Self-control.

- Attention-gaining manner.

- Easy progression of ideas.

- Sense of audience reaction.

- Knowledge of how to adapt to a particular occasion.

- Vitality in presentation of ideas.

- Genuine desire to communicate.

The novice speaker may find this list intimidating; however, the list is an excellent way for this speaker to complete a self-assessment. Recognition of strengths and identification of areas for improvement is the first step in developing effective speaking skills.

Voice

The voice, like fingerprints, is unique. It is the most powerful tool available for public speaking. You do not hear the same voice the audience hears. When speaking, you hear your own voice through bone, your audience hears it through air. Listen to your voice on a tape recorder for a realistic impression of your speaking voice. Evaluate the tone, pitch, clarity, projection, and speed. Note use of distracting words or sounds, incorrect grammar, or inappropriate pronunciation.

The voice cannot be changed, but it can be improved. Voice exercises are utilized by many speakers to improve delivery. Description of these exercises is beyond the scope of this text; however, the following suggestions are offered for consideration:

- Speaking too slowly or too quickly can irritate an audience. Most people listen to speech at a rate of 150 words per minute. Tape yourself to determine how quickly you speak.

- Use pauses when you speak. Well-placed pauses emphasize important points and prevent distracting phrases such as "and um . . . ."

- Add variety to your tone. Practice reading children's stories aloud. Most people project enthusiasm when reading aloud to children.

- Practice speaking in front of a mirror. Visualize the movements of mouth and larynx. This exercise usually improves posture, which in turn increases lung capacity and the ability to project.

- Do not smoke or expose yourself to smoke before a presentation. Smoke and other fumes cause hoarseness.

- A moderate amount of saliva is necessary for a fluid voice. It is acceptable to pause for water when you speak.

- Practice difficult or unfamiliar terms in advance.

- Do not chew gum during a speech.

Habits and Gestures

Whereas the voice is a presenter's most powerful tool, nonverbal body language also plays an important role in speech delivery. Some psychologists argue that body language is 95% of the message!

Hand and Arm Position

- Hold arms and hands at the side in a relaxed position.

- When using a microphone, hold it in one hand.

- Avoid standing with both hands over the groin. This fig leaf position presents a weak, ineffectual image.

- Holding the hands behind the back in a reverse fig leaf position is restrictive and limits gestures.

- Crossing the arms in front of the body presents a defensive position.

- Putting the hands on the hips presents an authoritative position.

- Thrusting hands into pockets makes it difficult to gesture without appearing awkward. Some speakers do place one hand lightly in a pocket without appearing awkward.

- When speaking behind a podium, rest hands lightly on the surface. Do not lean heavily.

- Jingling coins and keys in pockets conveys nervousness. Empty pockets before a presentation unless you have a prop you wish to pull out as part of the presentation.

- Do not rifle through your notes. Place notes in sequence on the podium or table.

- Hand gestures should not distract from the overall presentation. Gestures should appear natural. Distracting gestures such as playing with hair, adjusting clothing, and blinking eyes frequently should be eliminated.

- Practice in front of a mirror or use a videotape to identify annoying gestures.

Stance

- Stand well balanced on both feet.

- Stiff posture conveys nervousness and inexperience.

- Change position discreetly on the ball of the foot, not the heel.

- If a podium is too high, stand to one side and adjust the microphone to the appropriate level. Do not allow the podium to block your view of the audience.

- Maintain good posture. Stand with the spine straight, shoulders relaxed, and chin parallel to the floor.

- Moving adds variety to the presentation and may encourage audience participation. Move naturally, do not pace. Some speakers move up and down a central aisle or across the room.

Appearance

When you make a presentation, you project a personal image as well as an image of your institution. Comfort and personal style should be incorporated into overall appearance for the best effect.

Outfit Selection

Clothes are a form of nonverbal communication. Hoff (1988) observed that "Clothes don't just cover, they communicate . . . . We tend to like people, who, on special occasions, get a little bit dressed up for us. Nothing splashy. Nothing flashy. Just a little bit dressed up" (p. 153).

- Consider the audience. What will they be wearing? Is the event formal or informal? If you are not sure, err on the side of formality.

- Accentuate your strengths.

- You should appear comfortable and confident. Avoid wearing a new outfit for a presentation. Buy the outfit well in advance and wear it a few times before you speak.

- The presenter's appearance should fit the audience, but the presenter should be memorable.

  I Choose colors that are personally flattering and contrast with the background of the presentation area.

  I Beige fades into the background of a presentation and drains color from faces.

- If the outfit has not been worn recently, check for cleanliness, wrinkles, and fit. The morning of your presentation is not the time to discover it no longer fits or has missing buttons.

- If your skin tends to flush when speaking, avoid clothing with open or low necklines.

Accessories

Jewelry, scarves, ties, hats, and shoes make statements about the wearer. Choose accessories that coordinate with the outfit, but do not distract from overall appearance. You don't want the audience to focus on your jewelry rather than the presentation.

- Wear comfortable shoes, particularly if you will stand for a long period of time for the presentation. Shoe style should be appropriate to the outfit.

- Check stockings for damage. You may wish to carry an extra pair.

- Remove objects from clothing that make noise when you move.

Audience

Presentations are more effective when the presenter has some background information about the audience. Consider the following basic facts when preparing a speech or presentation:

- Demographic information.

  I Age, sex, occupation, and educational background.

- Estimated size.

- Is attendance voluntary or mandatory?

- What does the audience already know about the topic?

- What does the audience want to know?

- What does the audience need to know?

- What doesn't the audience need to know?

- What subjects should not be discussed, i.e., sensitive or political subjects?

Tips on age considerations:

- Consider your age and language. If you are much younger than your audience, avoid trendy phrases.

- If you are older than the audience, refrain from nostalgically referring to how long you have been in the business. The audience is not interested.

- Speak the language of the audience without appearing uncomfortable or unfamiliar with the terms.

- What you wear will make an impression.

  I When you are much younger than your audience dress conservatively.

- When you are much older, your outfit should be lively and contemporary.

- Ask for a second opinion from someone you trust to avoid looking ridiculous.

• Don't patronize the audience. There is no need to mention age in most presentations.

Humor

Humor can add to or detract from a presentation. Most people like to be entertained; however, the humor must be appropriate to the setting, the audience, and the subject matter. Humor should be natural and contribute to the presentation. It should be avoided if it distracts the audience from the content of the presentation.

• Few people tell jokes well. Avoid them if you cannot deliver them.

• Humor should not be offensive in language or subject matter.

• Practice jokes or anecdotes many times in front of a mirror.

• Use war stories sparingly. Real experiences lend credibility to the speaker; however too many stories distract the audience from the main points of the presentation.

• Slides or transparencies of popular cartoons can be used to add humor. Follow appropriate copyright laws.

WORKING WITH THE MEDIA

Public events often attract the media. As a nurse educator, you may be responsible for a press release on an education event. The public relations department of your institution is a good resource for assistance with media relations. Many public relations or marketing departments provide a media kit for staff. It is always advisable to have public relations representatives present when interacting with the media. Most institutions have specific guidelines for media interaction.

Tips related to media interactions:

• Listen carefully to questions from the press. Your answer may appear in print or during a broadcast without the question as a frame of reference.

- Do not repeat a bad choice of words from the question in your answer.

• Remember that the real audience is not the reporter.

• If you wish your comment to be off the record, make this clear before you make a statement.

- It is important to remember that nothing is truly off the record.

• If you are challenged about a controversial subject, do not say "No comment." Alternatives include:

- "This is outside my area of expertise."

- "I don't know the answer to that question."

- "It's being studied and the report is due on . . . ."

- Refer the reporter to a person or agency who may be able to answer their question.

• Don't ramble. Keep answers clear and concise. The reporter wants quotes 15 to 20 seconds long.

• Silence provides you an opportunity to gather your thoughts before you respond to a question.

• Give reporters time to digest your comments.

• Know in advance what your newsworthy story is and tell this story no matter what questions you are asked.

• Do not lose your temper or allow yourself to be pressured into an argument.

FINAL CHECKLIST FOR SPEAKERS

Dunckel and Parnham (1984) compiled helpful suggestions for public speakers, similar to last minute advice from a coach before a big game.

- Eat lightly. No matter what time of day you speak you want your blood focused on your brain not your digestion.

- Do not drink alcohol. It gives you false courage, impaired articulation, and scrambled ideas.

- Do not drink milk. It causes mucous.

- Do not drink carbonated beverages. Stifling a burp can undermine confidence.

- Keep your body alert.

- When seated at the head table, you are on stage before you speak. The audience is looking at you in anticipation.

- Don't cross your legs. It stops circulation.

- When you are introduced, listen. You must acknowledge the comments.

- Walk with confidence and purpose when you get up to speak.

- Take your time before you begin to speak. Count 1-2-3. Look at your audience. Smile. Establish your presence. Center your breathing.

- Remain flexible. The unexpected can happen. You might need to update your speech or presentation on short notice.

- There are always three speeches for one speaking opportunity—the speech you are going to give, the one you give, and the one you wish you had given. When you are well organized and well rehearsed, they will probably be the same speech. Analyze these three speeches, learn the differences, and apply that knowledge the next time you speak (pp. 85-86).

- Finally, remember what Ralph Waldo Emerson said about great speakers. "All great speakers were bad speakers at first."

ORGANIZATIONAL WRITING SKILLS

Letters, memorandums, reports, speeches, evaluations, and articles challenge the writing skills of the emergency nurse educator. Effectiveness requires clear understanding of essential writing elements, the writing process, and the unique requirements for each writing task.

ESSENTIAL ELEMENTS

Effective writing is produced for a specific purpose, on a specific topic, and for a specific audience (Ferrara, 1989). The writer must clearly understand each element to write effectively.

- Reader/audience.

  ⚊ Who will read this? What is the reader's knowledge base and educational level? Does the reader have a unique need? An unusual attitude?

  ⚊ Reader-based prose that targets a specific audience is more effective for letters, memorandums, and other professional writing.

- Topic.
  - What is the topic?
  - If you are not clear on the topic, the writing will convey this.
- Purpose.
  - Why are you writing this? What is the logic behind the writing?
  - Clarify the goal of any writing. The key is to express, not impress. Most professional writing is written to inform, persuade, or both.

WRITING PROCESS

The written product is unique for each writer; however, the actual writing process has three generic steps (Ferrara, 1989). Understanding the purpose of each step enhances the process and the final product.

- **Predraft phase** is the time when the writer identifies and develops an understanding of the topic. Purpose, structure, format, audience, and organization are clarified during this phase.
- **Draft phase** refers to the time when the writer begins to write ideas and thoughts.
- **Postdraft phase** is characterized by change of focus from writer-centered to reader-centered.

PROCESS TYPES

Writers may utilize a single type of writing process or a combination of several types. Understanding various processes increases the number of options available to the writer. Hambrick (1991) identified eight types of processes.

- **Craftsmen** utilize a lengthy process that begins with jotting down ideas and establishing a repository for clippings and reference notes. The craftsman then does a rough draft, which is reviewed and edited before the final draft is completed.
- **Dash writing** involves a few mental notes with a single draft corrected for errors.
- **Brainstorming start** initiates the process and identifies specific content ideas through brainstorming. Ideas are generated then listed according to merit. This list becomes the outline for the project.
- **From impulse to order** begins with writing on impulse to create a source of ideas. The ideas are then ordered and organized to establish an outline for the project.
- **Incremental outline** refers to development of a comprehensive outline and draft for the project—one section at a time.
- **Boilerplate writing** utilizes prewritten information or boilerplate to present a specific idea.
- **Argument tree approach** identifies the audience needs as a problem. A decision tree is then utilized to outline the solution.
- **Throw away and restart** begins with a stream-of-consciousness draft, which is reviewed and discarded. A new draft is then completed.

WRITING CONSTRAINTS

Most professional writing must be accomplished within specific constraints. Awareness of these constraints allows the writer to work effectively within their boundaries.

- **Deadlines** are identified for many writing tasks. If the organization does not set a deadline, set personal deadlines to prevent procrastination.

- **Length** may be limited to a specific number of words or pages for such professional documents as job descriptions, research abstracts, and manuscripts. Clarity and brevity are essential.

- **Budget** applies to resource materials and supporting documents.

- **Resources** include writing instruments, library/research material, and time.

Tips to enhance the writing process:

- Establish a comfortable setting for writing. Minimize distractions, i.e., noise or visitors.

- Place resources such as dictionary, thesaurus, and phone numbers within easy reach.

- Utilize word processors and computers to enhance speed and quality of the writing process.

- Organize writing material with a box, file, shelf, or other system.

- Write so that revision is easy—then revise. Double spaced, one-sided documents are easier to revise.

- Ask for feedback early on specific items such as content, style, grammar, and graphics.

- Let it go.

WRITTEN PRODUCT

Each writer approaches writing from his or her own unique perspective; however, individuality should not preclude effective interpretation and application of essential elements. Appearance, substance, flow, readability, tone, and style are keys to a successful final product (Ferrara, 1989).

Appearance

Make it easy for the audience to use the product. Confirm content accuracy. Eliminate typos and misspelled words. Utilize subheadings, bullets, white spaces, visuals, and summaries.

- **Subheadings** help organize material and establish flow.

- **Bullets** simplify complex subjects, highlight main points of information, break the page visually, and give the reader a break. Bullets should be parallel in verbiage, syntax, and sentence structure.

- **White spaces and visuals** give the reader a break and highlight specific areas of information.

- **Summaries** provide a synopsis of the entire product. A summary should structurally parallel the report. Avoid research methodologies in the summary.

Style

In professional writing, style refers to the formality of the written product. The finished product should complement the audience, purpose, and topic of the written product.

- **Informal style** is personal, more reflective of spoken language. This style is appropriate for some letters and memorandums.

- **Semiformal style** is less personal than informal. This style is commonly used for certain letters, evaluations, and reports.

- **Formal style** is written in third person without personal references. This style is appropriate for all types of research and manuscripts.

Structure

Writing should have a beginning, a middle, and an end. Without these basic ingredients, the reader is left without a clear understanding of purpose or content.

- **Beginning** clarifies context, purpose, or theme.

- **Middle** asserts, demonstrates, tells, and shows. It should be coherent and flow from one point to the next.

- **End** summarizes major conclusions, reiterates significant information, calls for appropriate action, and directs attention to future action. It announces the job is done.

Content

Content is the essence of the written product, regardless of subject, audience, or purpose. Express yourself clearly and concisely. Roman and Raphaelson (1981) offer the following suggestions related to content:

- **Don't mumble**. Organize writing. Use specific, concrete language—active voice and action verbs. Keep writing vigorous and direct.

- **Be clear and direct**. Use short paragraphs, short sentences, and short words. Limit paragraphs to one idea. Use the right word—effect is a noun and a verb. Come to the point. Use clear references in sentences and paragraphs. Avoid cliches and stock phrases.

- **Omit needless words**. Use standard English. Delete words you do not need. Define abbreviations and punctuate carefully. Clarify thoughts with judicious use of commas. Use facts and numbers with restraint. Utilize analogies to make ideas tangible.

Review and Editing

Review and editing enhance the final product. In addition to spelling, grammar, and punctuation, consideration should be given to the following concepts (Mastrian & Birdsall, 1986; Sheridan & Dowdney, 1986; Mirin, 1981):

- **Personality/tone**. Does the product portray the right tone? Is the tone personal, abrupt, caustic, persuasive, respectful?

- **Jargon**. Is jargon included? Is it appropriate for the document? Is the meaning clear?

- **Sexist/stereotypic language**. Does the document eliminate unnecessary references to gender? Does it contain titles with inappropriate gender implications? Are there barbarisms such as "typical female logic" or "typical male brutality"? Are inappropriate stereotypes included?

- **Clarity and force**. Cut the deadwood, e.g., use "currently" rather than "at the present time." Attack flabby words, e.g., use "discuss" rather than "establish meaningful dialogue." Use action verbs; avoid passive verbs.

SPEED OF WRITING

The ability to write quickly without loss of clarity is an acquired skill. Impediments to rapid, skillful writing can be grouped into three areas—sloppy thinking, inadequate physical writing skills, and perfectionism/fear of criticism (Ferrara, 1989).

- **Sloppy thinking**. Fast writing correlates with fast thinking. Do essential research. You cannot write quickly about a subject you do not understand. Know your own chain of logic so you can lead the reader through it.

- **Inadequate physical writing skills**. Learn to use a word processor or computer. Speed writing is limited without one of these tools. Develop a big vocabulary. Identify specific areas of weakness and take steps to strengthen them.

- **Perfectionism/fear of criticism**. Accept the fact that not everyone will like what you write. Don't write to avoid criticism. Recognize constructive criticism and utilize it to your advantage.

WRITER'S BLOCK

Many writers—novelists, historians, and nurses—find themselves unable to write. Various techniques can be used to overcome writer's block (Mastrian & Birdsall, 1986; Sheridan & Dowdney, 1986).

- **Free writing**, also called automatic writing, is based on Freud's theory of the unconscious. Write whatever comes to mind without stopping. Keep writing for a full five minutes even when repeating a single word. Don't worry about spelling, punctuation, or grammar. When finished, review the material for ideas.

- **Lists** can be generated on any aspect of the project, e.g., words; concepts; topics; pro and con of the topic; who, what, when, where, how, and why of the project, etc.

- **R and R with percolation**. When all else fails, go do something else.

- **Other tricks**. Consider one of the following tricks to get started.

  - Turn off the display screen. Staring at a blank screen will sometimes get you started.

  - Just write something. Sometimes words on the screen get you started.

  - Bribe your brain. Promise yourself a reward after completing a specific task.

  - Turn off the screen while you write.

  - Consider writing from a different perspective, e.g., a child, a minister, or homeless person.

  - Admit when you have nothing to say or you have not really decided how to handle the project.

TYPES OF WRITING

The emergency nurse educator encounters a variety of writing tasks, e.g., memorandums, letters, and reports.

MEMORANDUMS

Memorandums, or memos, are the most frequent form of communication in any institution, used almost exclusively to communicate within an agency or institution. A memo contains clear, concise notes that provide information or direction, define a problem, relay instructions, describe a procedure, or justify actions. A memo is less complex than an informal report, usually no more than two pages long.

Format

Memos generally follow a specific format. In addition to the date, memos contain the following elements:

- **From**. Who is sending the memo? Formal and informal address may be utilized. Preprinted memorandums may lead with From or with To.

- **To**. Who will receive the memo? Department or office of the recipient may also be included.

- **Subject/Re**. Alerts the reader to the subject of the memo. Equivalent to the title of a report or a newspaper headline.

- **Body**. Content is usually written freestyle.

Tips for effective memo writing:

- The memo should always be reader-centered.

- Use appropriate grammar and punctuation.

- Remember titles, courtesy, and organizational chain of command.

- **Electronic memos**. Communication sent via electronic mail should be drafted with the same consideration that a handwritten or typed memo receives. Do not respond so quickly that you regret what you wrote. Angell and Heslop (1994) offer the following suggestions for effective electronic mail.

- Read the message twice before you send it to assure message clarity. Once you send it, you cannot get it back.

- Do not use obscene or abusive language.

- **Sensitive memos**. If the memo contains sensitive material, do not rush.

- Complete a rough draft then leave it in a drawer for a few days or even a few weeks. Reading the memo after time has passed may provide you with a different perspective on the contents.

- If you do not have the luxury of time, consider asking someone you trust to read the memo before you send it.

SHORT NOTES

Short notes are used to express appreciation, recognition, courtesy, and gratitude. These handwritten notes are less formal and more personal than a business letter or memo. They build and strengthen professional relationships. Short notes are usually mailed the same day as the event that led to the note. They may be sent to express pleasure at a recent meeting or event, thanks for meeting on a particular issue, or congratulations on an appointment or professional success.

LETTERS

Most letters are written for general business communication with individuals outside the organization. Certain organizational cultures dictate letters for internal communications. Professional business letters utilize a block or modified block style. Tone may be formal, semiformal, or informal depending on the purpose as well as the writer's relationship to the recipient. Letters should have a beginning, a middle, and an end (Mastrian & Birdsall, 1986).

- **Introduction** should get to the point. Make it short. Beginning with "you" or "thank you" focuses the letter on the reader.

- **Body** should contain coherent paragraphs that discuss a logical unit of information. Use long paragraphs cautiously. Match pronouns within the text. Transitional words and phrases should be used to link paragraphs.

- **Conclusion** should summarize contents and end on a positive note. Avoid overused formula closing statements.

INFORMAL REPORTS

Informal reports are usually longer and more complex than a memo. A title page, table of contents, and abstract are beneficial for reports more than four pages long. Bibliography, reference list, and index should be considered for extremely long reports.

FORMAL REPORTS

The degree of formality for a specific report depends on the purpose and stated audience. Formal reports include, but are not limited to, proposals, manpower analyses, and descriptions of new programs. A title page, table of contents, abstract, bibliography, reference page, and index should be utilized for formal reports.

PROPOSALS AND GRANTS

Proposals are utilized to create and implement change within an organization. Examples include service feasibility studies and product evaluation. A proposal should contain background information, recommendations, implementation plan, cost analysis, time line, evaluation methods, and pertinent supportive materials (Baillie, Trygstad, & Cordoni, 1989).

REFERENCES

Angell, D., & Heslop, B. (1994). The elements of E-mail style. Reading, MA: Addison-Wesley.

Baillie, V., Trygstad, L., & Cordoni, T. (1989). Effective nursing leadership. Rockville, MD: Aspen.

Corballis, M.C. (1991). The lopsided ape: Evolution of the generative mind. New York: Oxford.

Dunckel, J., & Parnham, E. (1984). The business guide to effective speaking. Toronto: International Self-Counsel Press Ltd.

Economics Press, Inc. (1975). The positive way to criticize. Frontline Management, (105).

Ferrara, C. (1989). Effective business writing in ten minutes a day. Radnor, PA: Chilton.

Fincher, J. (1984). The brain, mystery of matter and mind. New York: Torstar.

Hambrick, R. (1991). The management skills builder. New York: Praeger.

Hirsch, S.K. (1985). Using the Myers-Briggs Type Indicator in organizations. Palo Alto, CA: Consulting Psychologists Press.

Hoff, R. (1988). "I can see you naked." A fearless guide to making great presentations. Kansas City: Andrews and McNeel.

Keirsey, D., & Bates, M. (1978). Please understand me: Character and temperament types (3rd ed.). Del Mar, CA: Prometheus Nemesis Books.

Mastrian, K., & Birdsall, E. (1986). Writing on the job. New York: John Wiley & Sons.

Mirin, S.K. (1981). The nurse's guide to writing for publication. Wakefield, MA: Nursing Resources.

Myers, I.B., & McCaulley, M.H. (1989). Manual: A guide to the development and use of the Myers-Briggs Type Indicator. Palo Alto, CA: Consulting Psychologists Press.

Myers, I.B., & Myers, P.B. (1988). Gifts differing. Palo Alto, CA: Consulting Psychologists Press.

Roman, K., & Raphaelson, J. (1981). Writing that works. New York: Harper & Row.

Sheridan, D.R., & Dowdney, D.L. (1986). How to write and publish articles in nursing. New York: Springer.

Valentine, N. (1993). Speaking in public. New York: Penguin Books.

Veehoff, D. (1992). Whole brain thinking and the nurse manager. Nursing Management, 23(8), 33-34.

Webster's II new Riverside University dictionary. (1984). Boston: Houghton Mifflin/Riverside.

Wonder, J., & Donovan, P. (1984). Whole brain thinking. New York: William Morrow.

RECOMMENDED READINGS

Abramis, D.J. (1992, August). Humor in healthy organizations. Human Resources Magazine, pp. 72-74.

Agonito, R. (1994). All about grants workbook. Syracuse, NY: New Futures Enterprises.

American Journal of Nursing. (1990). Small doses: The well-read nurse. American Journal of Nursing, 90(1), 41.

American Psychological Association. (1994). Publication manual of the American Psychological Association (4th ed.). Washington, DC: Author.

Armstrong, M.A., & Kelly, A.E. (1993). Enhancing staff nurses' interpersonal skills: Theory to practice. Clinical Nurse Specialist, 7(6), 313-317.

Chisholm, M. (1991). Communication: Roots within nursing. <u>Clinical Nurse Specialist</u>, <u>5</u>(3), 169.

Costello, K. (1993). The Myers-Briggs Type Indicator—A management tool. <u>Nursing Management</u>, <u>24</u>(5), 46-51.

Dougal, J. & Gonterman, R. (1999). A comparison of three teaching methods on learning and retention. <u>Journal of Nurses Staff Development</u>, <u>15</u>(4), 152-158.

Edwards, J.B., & Lenz, C.L. (1990). The influence of gender on communication for nurse leaders. <u>Nursing Administration Quarterly</u>, <u>15</u>(1), 49-55.

Evans, M.L. (1986). Getting the message across: Nurses and the media. <u>Australian Nurses Journal</u>, <u>16</u>(5), 38-39.

Flanagin, A. (1994). Fraudulent publication. <u>Journal of Nursing Administration</u>, <u>24</u>(4), 60-61.

Freeland, D.B. (1993, September). Turning communication into influence. <u>Human Resources Magazine</u>, pp. 93-96.

Gabor, D. (1994, March/April). How to handle the conversations every manager dreads. <u>Executive Female</u>, pp. 33-37.

Genua, R.L. (1993, November/December). How well do you manage your mouth. <u>Executive Female</u>, pp. 72-73.

Hanson, S. (1988). Write on. <u>American Journal of Nursing</u>, <u>88</u>(4), 482-483.

Harary, K., & Weintraub, P. (1991). <u>Right brain learning in 30 days</u>. New York: St. Martin's Press.

Hobdell, E.F., Slusser, M., Patterson, J., & Burgess, E. (1991). Showcasing a profession: Getting nursing on the newsstand. <u>Clinical Nurse Specialist</u>, <u>5</u>(3), 174-177.

Jimenez, S.L.M. (1991). Consumer journalism: A unique nursing opportunity. <u>Image</u>, <u>23</u>(1), 47-49.

Jones, K. (1993). Confrontation: Methods and skills. <u>Nursing Management</u>, <u>24</u>(5), 68-70.

Kushner, M. (1996). Successful presentations for dumies. Foster City, CA: IDG Books.

Leeds, D. (1989, March). How to be sure your speech is a success. <u>Working Woman</u>, pp. 98-99.

Lindquist, R.A. (1993). Strategies for writing a competitive research abstract. <u>Dimensions of Critical Care Nursing</u>, <u>12</u>(1), 46-53.

Majorowicz, K. (1999). Eight strategies to stretch your educational resources. <u>Home Healthcare Nurse Managment</u>, <u>3</u>(5), 2-10.

Martinez, M.N. (1994, July). How to avoid accidents on the electronic highway. <u>Human Resources Magazine</u>, pp. 74-77.

McCaulley, M.H. (1983). <u>Applications of the Myers-Briggs Type Indicator to medicine and other health professions</u>. Gainesville, FL: Center for Applications of Psychological Type.

McCaulley, M.H. (1988). <u>The Myers-Briggs Type Indicator and leadership</u>. Gainesville, FL: Center for Applications of Psychological Type.

Mercer, M.W. (1993, March). How to make a fantastic impression. <u>Human Resources Magazine</u>, pp. 47-49.

Nativio, D. (1994). Authorship. <u>Journal of Nursing Administration</u>, <u>24</u>(4), 58-59.

Pollan, S., & Levine, M. (1993, December). Maximizing your performance review. <u>Working Woman</u>, pp. 74.

Quick, T. (1989). <u>Quick solutions: 500 people problems managers face and how to solve them</u>. New York: John Wiley & Sons.

Rideout, C., & Richardson, S. (1989). A team building model . . . appreciating the differences using the Myers-Briggs Type Indicator with developmental theory. <u>Journal of Counseling and Development</u>, <u>67</u>, 529.

Schloff, L., & Yudkin, M. (1991). <u>Smart speaking</u>. New York: Henry Holt.

Schuler, R., & Huber, V. (1990). <u>Personnel and human resource management</u> (4th ed.). St. Paul, MN: West Publishing.

Smith T. (1991). <u>Making successful presentations</u> (2nd ed.). New York: John Wiley & Sons.

Tornquist, E.M. (1986). <u>From proposal to publication: An informal guide to writing about nursing research</u>. Menlo Park, CA: Addison-Wesley.

Watson, W., Pardo, L., & Tomovic, V. (1978). <u>How to give an effective seminar</u>. Don Mills, Ontario: General Publishing.

Wise, P.S.Y. (1986). Developing the press release. <u>Journal of Continuing Education in Nursing, 17</u>(6), 217.

Wylie, P., & Grothe, M. (1993, November/December). [Let's pretend it never happened.] <u>Executive Female</u>, pp. 31-35, 77.

CHAPTER 5

Meeting the Needs of Orientation in the ED

OBJECTIVES

Upon completion of this chapter, the emergency nurse educator will be able to:

1. Identify the role of the emergency nurse educator in the orientation process.

2. Describe advantages and limitations of three orientation strategies.

3. State the role of evaluation in the orientation process.

INTRODUCTION

Orientation is one of the critical activities used to assure delivery of safe, quality care. It is also one of the most expensive activities. One study estimates orientation costs $4,720.93 per employee (Bethel, 1990). The newly graduated nurse utilizes significantly more resources than the experienced nurse. Now more than ever, educators are challenged to produce skilled, competent staff at minimal orientation cost.

This chapter provides a brief overview of orientation concepts. For a more comprehensive discussion of emergency nursing orientation, refer to Orientation to emergency nursing: Concepts, Competencies, and Critical Thinking (ENA, 2000).

PROGRAM OVERVIEW

Effective orientation must occur at three specific levels—hospital, department, and unit. Each level builds on content from the previous level to provide the new employee with essential information. A well-run orientation program conveys to orientees they are valued by the organization (Kelly, 1992). Program presentation, required orientee participation, and staff involvement provide the employee with a sense of continuity and organizational support.

HOSPITAL ORIENTATION

Hospital orientation provides information germane to all new employees, regardless of position or assigned department. Upon completion of hospital orientation, the employee goes to the assigned department to continue the orientation process. Topics covered during hospital orientation programs vary; however, most include the following:

- Institution mission statement and philosophy.

- Organizational structure.

- Personnel policies.

- Employee benefits.

- Patient populations.

- Patient services.

- Parking and security.

- Customer service.

- Hospital tours.

DEPARTMENT ORIENTATION

Department orientation introduces the new employee to departmental functions, covering specific policies and performance expectations. During this period, the employee also receives information about cultural norms, values, and communication methods. Performance expectations are provided as concrete, measurable criteria; cultural norms and values are conveyed—consciously and unconsciously—as abstract concepts.

Department orientation targets specific groups, e.g., nurses, technicians, clerks. During department orientation, the new nurse receives information pertinent to all nursing staff, regardless of unit assignment. Content may vary from hospital to hospital, but usually includes:

- Department organization and structure.

- Cardiopulmonary resuscitation.

- Fire safety.

- Infection control.

- Intravenous therapy.

- Nursing Department policy review.

- Quality assurance program.

- Pharmacology review/dosage calculation.

- Medical records, legal aspects, and documentation.

- Age specific competencies.

- Point of care (or Wave) laboratory testing.

UNIT ORIENTATION

Unit orientation provides information on performance expectations, policies, and procedures unique to the unit. Communication of unit-based culture, values, and philosophy is inherent to unit orientation. Subsequent discussion in this chapter covers various aspects of unit orientation.

UNIT ORIENTATION

The new educator may find an orientation program already in place. The educator should evaluate the program to determine its strengths and weaknesses, i.e., "Does it meet unit needs?" There is no need to reinvent the wheel; however, if the current program does not meet unit needs, it should be revised. If an orientation program does not exist, the educator should develop a program to meet these needs. There are several orientation programs available for emergency nurses. ENA's *Orientation to Emergency Nursing: Concepts, Competencies, and Critical Thinking* (ENA, 2000) provides a comprehensive, competency-based orientation. The educator should seize the opportunity to foster learning for all orientees, tap their energies, identify hidden potential, and encourage knowledge sharing among staff.

A variety of approaches has been utilized for unit orientation. Historically, the head nurse or nurse manager provided unit orientation. Numerous other responsibilities often made it difficult for this person to give orientation a significant amount of attention. Consequently, orientation received minimal attention and produced variable outcomes.

In a growing number of institutions, the emergency nurse educator is responsible for unit orientation. Educator responsibility for unit orientation varies between hospitals. The educator may administer the orientation program by coordinating classroom components only, or assume overall responsibility. The benefits of each approach should be considered in light of institutional mandates, resources, and staffing needs.

As health care becomes more complex and the educator role becomes more demanding, clinical orientation of the new nurse may not be the best use of the educator's time. EDs often utilize clinical staff to provide clinical orientation for new personnel. In this process, an experienced staff nurse with the ability and willingness to teach serves as a buddy, mentor, and a preceptor. In addition to providing orientation to the new employee, the precepting nurse becomes the orientee's direct clinical resource person. Utilization of staff nurses to provide clinical orientation conveys to the staff that you recognize their clinical expertise and trust their ability to mentor and teach.

Relieved of some responsibility for clinical orientation, the educator is able to facilitate the process, functioning in a consulting and leadership role. This may lead to better utilization of organizational resources and enable the educator to focus energies on other responsibilities.

LEARNING STRATEGIES

Clinical learning need not be limited to the ED. The educator should consider other arenas for learning experiences. A high-volume ED may provide consistent opportunity for learning, whereas a smaller ED may provide only sporadic learning opportunities. Regardless of ED volume, the educator should use resources creatively and effectively. Clinical rotation to other departments with a close affiliation to the ED—EMS, critical care, labor and delivery—provides exposure to a variety of clinical situations.

FORMAL COURSES

Courses such as basic dysrhythmia review, emergency nursing core review, or a critical care course should also be considered. These classroom experiences provide exposure to more complex concepts and can be interspersed with clinical experience on the unit. When courses are presented by the staff development department, the educator should provide a preliminary assessment of the orientee's learning needs. Ideally, the educator contributes to course development or actually teaches portions of the course.

Effective didactic learning experiences are the result of classroom presentation and subsequent application of concepts and principles in the clinical arena. The clinical component should make the classroom material come alive. For example, the orientee attending a basic dysrhythmia course should be encouraged to care for cardiac patients and review dysrhythmia strips during the clinical experience.

LEARNING CONTRACTS

Learning contracts clearly define expectations or competencies to be achieved during the orientation period. Goals are identified and progress toward goal attainment is monitored.

- The orientee signs the learning contract to indicate he or she understands his or her role in this process and is aware of available resources. (Appendix A provides an example of a learning contract.)

SELF-STUDY MODULES

Self-study modules are based on the assumption that adults can manage their own learning. Mandatory education subjects such as safety and universal precautions lend themselves to this type of learning (Haggard, 1992). Self-study modules may not be appropriate for all topics. The educator must carefully consider various aspects of a topic before development of self-study modules, i.e., topic complexity, skill requirements, and level of difficulty. Self-study modules:

- Focus on a single topic.
- Begin with specific learning objectives—what the orientee must know.
- Are developed after the objectives are identified.
- Are brief, concise, and interesting.
- Use pictures, cartoons, slides, or video to add appeal.
- Evaluate learning with case reviews or other testing.
  - Case review allows the educator to evaluate the orientees' understanding of the module content and evaluate their ability to apply it to clinical practice.
  - When testing is utilized the educator should use multiple choice, matching, and true-false questions to ease the grading process.

PROGRAM DEVELOPMENT

Recognition of existing organizational constraints is essential for the development and implementation of an effective unit orientation program. Selected methods and strategies must be appropriate for the setting. Organization, department, and unit issues must also be considered. Considerations should be given to:

- Available resources.
- Departmental goals.
- Managerial priorities.
- Staffing patterns.

There is no "standard" length of ED orientation for new nurses. Some programs provide the orientee with hospital and department orientation supplemented with two or more weeks of clinical orientation. Managers faced with staff limitations may view orientation length as a luxury they can ill afford. When staffing is short, management may expect the new nurse to assume additional responsibilities, regardless of prior experience or preparation. Unfortunately, patient care may be affected as the orientee is forced to learn by trial and error. It is not always possible to predict staffing shortages; however, the educator should plan for the worst case scenario when developing his or her orientation program. A streamlined, flexible orientation timetable is one strategy to minimize potential disruptions related to staffing shortages.

ORIENTATION STRATEGIES

In addition to content, time frames, and learning strategies, the educator must select a strategy to actually provide the orientation. Methods include internships for graduate nurses, informal buddy systems, and formal preceptor programs.

INTERNSHIPS

Despite significant strain on organizational resources, internships have been very effective in recruiting new, inexperienced nurses. Internships are highly structured transition programs designed primarily for new graduates. Internships combine classroom and clinical instruction to allow gradual adjustment to the work setting, usually over three to 12 months. Clinical rotation through various units (including EMS) is often provided during an internship. In return for education and training, the intern commits employment time to the institution.

Ideally, an internship will assist in a smooth transition from student to practitioner by addressing problems frequently encountered by the new nurse in clinical practice (Kotecki, 1992). Graduation from nursing school and assimilation into the hospital setting often cause conflict for the new nurse. Bureaucratic principles encountered in the hospital setting do not always complement professional ideals stressed in nursing school. The internship needs to provide a review of the "realities" of politics in the institution so as to soften the ambivalent feelings sure to be encountered in clinical practice. The internship should also incorporate interactional strategies so that differences in values can be openly discussed.

BUDDY SYSTEM

Traditional orientation to the clinical unit utilizes a buddy system. A seasoned nurse willing to accept responsibility for orienting new staff is assigned as a buddy. The buddy usually has no formal preceptor training. Buddy selection is generally based on:

- Clinical proficiency.
- Professional role model.
- Willingness to teach.
- Knowledge of hospital policy and procedures.

The buddy system meets learning needs for the newly employed nurse with considerable clinical experience. The orientee and the buddy report satisfaction with the process (Asselin & Barber, 1991). The buddy system may be less effective for the graduate nurse or the nurse with minimal experience. Consistency is important with the buddy system. When a different buddy is assigned each day, fragmentation, inconsistency, and role confusion occur. The buddy may not identify an orientee's subtle learning needs because of a lack of formal training in preceptor techniques and adult learning principles.

PRECEPTOR PROGRAMS

Preceptor programs are widely accepted as an effective method for orienting new staff members. Morrow (1984) defines a preceptor as a person, generally a staff nurse, who teaches, counsels, inspires, role models, and supports the growth and development of an individual for a fixed and limited amount of time with the specific purpose of socialization into the new role. Actual studies are limited; however, preceptor programs may be more effective than the less formal buddy system, resulting in increased satisfaction with the orientation program.

Preceptor programs are particularly beneficial for nurses with limited education and experience (Bellinger & McCloskey, 1992) but work well with the experienced emergency nurse as well. Preceptor programs facilitate role transition for the new graduate (McGrath & Princeton, 1987). Nurse managers found precepted orientees more ready than buddied orientees to assume responsibility when orientation was finished (Giles & Moran, 1989).

Preceptor Selection

Preceptors are selected for their clinical and interpersonal skills as well as willingness to share their knowledge with others. Hartline (1993) identified qualifications to assist in the selection of preceptors. Identified preceptor qualities include:

- Demonstrates needed teaching skills.

- Provides both positive and negative feedback to the novice.

- Demonstrates professional attributes.

- Exhibits leadership skills.

Benner (1984) identified five developmental levels of clinical proficiency—novice, advanced beginner, competent, proficient, and expert clinician. The most suitable preceptor for the novice or advanced beginner may be a nurse at the competent level rather than a nurse at the proficient or expert level. A nurse at the competent level is more likely to remember what it was like as a beginner and be more sensitive to the beginner's needs, whereas the expert nurse may have difficulty identifying and understanding these needs (Benner, 1984). Preceptors with more than five years' experience seem to have more difficulty relating to the novice (Hafer & Sutton, 1990).

Preceptor Training

A comprehensive educational program for preceptor training needs to include:

- Principles of adult learning with a strong emphasis on teaching participants to assess learning needs and evaluate novice performance (Westra & Graziano, 1992).

- Learning styles.

- Assessment of orientee learning needs.

- Teaching techniques.

- Documentation required of the preceptor during orientation.

- Dealing with the challenging orientee.

Successful programs may last four hours (Sheehy, Shaffer, & Ward, 1990) to one week (McGrath & Princeton, 1987).

Increasing cultural diversity in emergency nursing has underlined the need for inclusion of cultural issues in preceptor training programs. Conflict may erupt between a preceptor and orientee as a result of ignorance and misunderstanding of cultural expressions. Confronted with unfamiliar beliefs and behaviors, the preceptor and the orientee may be unable to effectively function in their respective roles. Discussion of pertinent cultural issues during preceptor programs provides the preceptor with essential tools to identify potential cultural conflicts and methods to facilitate cultural adjustment between preceptor and orientee. An added benefit from this exposure is increased preceptor sensitivity to the patient populations and the surrounding workforce (Williams & Rogers, 1993).

The preceptor role is a demanding one. A preceptor can burn out if used too often and if no recognition is in place. Ongoing support, constant reinforcement, continuing education, and formal recognition and/or compensation minimize associated stress and may reduce preceptor burnout. Reward methods may include:

- Formal recognition by title, e.g., staff nurse preceptor.

- Recognition in nursing newsletter or with a recognition program.

- Pay differential.

- Incorporation of the preceptor role in the institution's clinical advancement program (O'Grady & O'Brien, 1992).

- Preceptor recognition lunch, dinner, or breakfast.

COMPETENCY-BASED ORIENTATION

Orientation requires a significant investment of time and money. As health care costs increase and resources decrease, the educator must constantly explore methods to streamline the process without affecting program quality. Competency-based orientation (CBO) is one approach. CBO streamlines the orientation process by focusing on outcomes. This focus shifts orientation emphasis from instruction to learning.

CBO utilizes objective, measurable performance expectations to clearly identify behavioral outcomes. Outcomes may be defined by the educator, the manager, the job description, or peers. When performance outcomes are clearly defined, expectations are explicit. The orientation focuses on what the orientee needs to know rather than what it would be nice to know. A wide range of teaching and learning activities are used to achieve performance outcomes. Traditional methods, such as formal lectures, may be used to facilitate the successful demonstration of competency; however, time spent in formal classroom learning is significantly decreased. Role-playing, case studies, games, poster displays, and many other strategies are utilized to facilitate learning.

Combining CBO with a preceptor program provides an orientation that is flexible, individualized, and built on previous knowledge and skill. For example, the experienced nurse can sign off on certain elements by demonstrating competence. The less experienced nurse is allowed to develop these skills at a slower pace. Length of orientation is determined by orientee competency and clinical performance. Flexible, realistic time frames should be established for achievement of performance outcomes.

Benner (1982) reminds us that the leap to competency is not always automatic. When a basic skill is performed in an actual clinical situation, the characteristics of the situation have as much influence on the individual's performance as does knowledge of steps required for the skill (Benner, 1982). The capacity to perform competently is not the same as performing competently. Actual competency can only be determined by observing actual performance (Alspach, 1992).

ADVANTAGES OF CBO

- Incorporates self-instruction and adult education methodologies.

- Decreases time spent in orientation for the experienced nurse.

- Identifies the need for remediation when a specific competency is not achieved.

- Accrediting agencies view CBO favorably.

- Competency forms and checklists provide documentation that can be included in the individual files.

- Produces consistent and predictable practice from orientees (Grey, Gurvis, & Smith, 1992; Abruzzese, 1992).

ENA developed a CBO program that can be individualized to different institutions (ENA, 2000). The manual provides a framework for development and implementation of an orientation program geared towards the unique needs of the emergency nurse. Related resources available from ENA include *Emergency Nursing Core Curriculum* (ENA, 1999) and *Standards of Emergency Nursing Practice* (ENA, 1995). The emergency nurse educator is encouraged to consider these and other emergency nursing resources to augment the orientation process.

ORIENTATION COMPONENTS

Orientation is a complex, multifaceted process. Essential components include the orientation packet, role clarification, communication, needs assessment, feedback, and evaluation.

ORIENTATION PACKET

A unit-specific guide for orientation identifies essential information, documents clinical experiences, and assures consistency. The orientee should receive an orientation packet at the beginning of the orientation. Content should be comprehensive and logically organized. Essential information includes:

- Program purpose and description.
- Orientation goals and objectives.
- Role responsibilities of the orientee, the preceptor, and the educator.
- Self-study modules.
- Competency-based assessment tools.
- Sample case presentations.
- Unit-specific tools and checklists.
- Forms to document progress.
- Evaluation forms.

ROLE CLARIFICATION

The orientee must have a clear understanding of the orientee role and its inherent responsibilities. Role ambiguity minimizes learning. Role responsibilities should be clearly articulated to the orientee by the nurse manager and the educator. Reviewing the job description with the orientee early in the orientation process is one technique for role clarification. Understanding job responsibilities allows the orientee to focus energies on learning essential information rather than wondering what the job requires.

COMMUNICATION

Communication of essential information is the cornerstone of the orientation process. It is essential that vital information be provided in a manner conducive to understanding and retention. It takes time for the educator and the preceptor to effectively communicate essential information and for the orientee to assimilate the information. When too much information is provided, or it is communicated in a manner difficult to understand, the orientee may feel overwhelmed.

The educator must resist the urge to provide the orientee with an overabundance of information. Utilize the following questions to determine what information should be communicated.

- Is the information relevant?

- Will the information improve performance?

- Does the orientee have the capacity to assimilate and utilize the information?

- Will the information help motivate the orientee by providing a sense of purpose?

- Is the information presented in such a way that it can be easily grasped and used?

Formal and informal communication with the orientee is essential to determine learning needs. Informal discussion over a cup of coffee may reveal a lack of knowledge related to equipment or problems with the preceptor. The educator must provide a climate in which the orientee feels safe to openly and honestly express concerns and needs. The orientee must feel the educator is listening without being judgmental.

NEEDS ASSESSMENT

Learning needs represent the difference between an orientee's skills and abilities and the goals and objectives for the orientation program. Each orientee differs in knowledge, skill, and attitude. Identification of individual skills and abilities for the new employee is the basis for any orientation effort. Without this initial assessment, the orientee may not receive essential information or may receive unnecessary instruction. Refer to Chapter 6 for a comprehensive discussion of needs assessment. These techniques include, but are not limited to:

- Informal conversations.

- Formal interviews.

- Surveys.

- Direct observation.

Learning needs should be assessed for each new nurse, regardless of experience. The graduate nurse and experienced nurse both require orientation. Consideration of experience during the needs assessment clarifies individual needs and individualizes the orientation for each orientee, but never assume that the experienced emergency nurse will require only a short orientation. Individual strengths should be recognized and supported. The knowledge base of the experienced orientee should be viewed as an asset that will ultimately increase the range of talents available to the department. It is important to remember that even the most experienced nurse needs support, direction, coaching, and assistance.

The use of a self-assessment tool is an excellent method to determine the orientee's level of functioning in the clinical setting. Self assessment tools can be used to measure cognitive and psychomotor skills (see Appendix B- Sample Baseline Knowledge Self-Evaluation Tool and Appendix C–Sample Clinical Skills Checklist). Once the educator has reviewed the self-assessments he or she can then tailor the orientation to meet the specific needs of the orientee.

ORIENTEE OBJECTIVES

The use of orientation objectives is very helpful in establishing expectations for the orientee and providing guidelines for preceptors. They can also be used as a basis for orientee evaluation. Appendix D provides a sample set of orientee objectives.

FEEDBACK

The educator and preceptor must monitor and evaluate orientee progress throughout the orientation. Effective and timely feedback is essential for orientee growth. Orientees should have a clear picture of their performance. Lack of feedback may cause orientees to become preoccupied with the question of how well they are doing. This preoccupation limits the capacity to learn.

Feedback should be provided in specific behavioral terms, clearly indicating effect on others and the unit. The purpose of feedback is to change specific behaviors, not alter personalities. Feedback should:

- Reinforce positive performance.

- Indicate how and where performance needs to change and improve.

- Motivate to improve performance (Tracy, 1990).

Frequent informal meetings between the orientee, the preceptor, and the educator facilitate the orientation process through clarification of orientee progress, discussion of specific problems, and identification of pertinent learning experiences.

The orientee should never be surprised at the end of the orientation period with assertions of poor performance. Performance issues should be addressed during the orientation. The educator, preceptor, and orientee must work together to decide how serious a specific situation is and what steps should be taken to correct it.

The educator must guard against the tendency to provide feedback only when problems arise. The average performer needs feedback to elevate performance level and expand motivation. The exceptional performer needs feedback to prevent loss of motivation and return to average performance. The exceptional performer should be supported and encouraged to set higher goals.

PROGRAM EVALUATION

Evaluation of the orientation program assures relevancy of content as well as selected teaching strategies. Poor orientee performance in the clinical area may be related to the orientation program rather than the orientee. Program effectiveness should be regularly evaluated to identify problems and potential revisions. Both formal and informal methods may be used to determine program effectiveness. Regardless of evaluation method, staff must be involved in the process. The educator may have an idea of staff needs; however, needs must be confirmed by the staff.

Methods for Program Evaluation

- Questionnaire.
  - Solicit information from recently oriented staff nurses, preceptors, and nursing management.
  - Suggested questions may relate to:
    - Orientee perception of orientation process.
    - How preceptor assessed competence.
    - Staffing adjustments during orientation (O'Grady & O'Brien, 1992).
  - Interviews with the orientee, the preceptor, and the nurse manager.
  - Direct observation.
  - Review paperwork for attainment of orientation goals and objectives.

SUMMARY

Today's health care environment necessitates high quality at low cost. The challenge is to find innovative, creative ways to accomplish this. Orientees require a well-planned orientation to assure competence and retention. Development, implementation, and evaluation of a successful ED orientation program assures the foundation for a lifetime of learning.

REFERENCES

Abruzzese, R.S. (1992). <u>Nursing staff development: Strategies for success</u>. St. Louis: Mosby.

Alspach, G. (1992). Concern and confusion over competence. <u>Critical Care Nurse</u>, 12(4). 150-153.

Asselin, M., & Barber E. (1991). Unit orientation for the experienced nurse: Process and evaluation. <u>Journal of Nursing Staff Development</u>, 7(3), 126-129.

Bellinger, S., & McCloskey, J. (1992). Are preceptors for orientation of new nurses effective? <u>Journal of Professional Nursing</u>, 8(6), 321-327.

Benner, P. (1982). Issues in competency-based testing. <u>Nursing Outlook</u>, 30(29), 303-309.

Benner, P. (1984). <u>From novice to expert: Excellence and power in clinical nursing practice</u>. Menlo Park, CA: Addison-Wesley.

Bethel, P. (1990). In-service education: Calculating the cost. <u>Journal of Continuing Education in Nursing</u>, 21(3), 105-108.

Emergency Nurses Association. (1998). <u>Standards of emergency nursing practice</u> (5th ed.). Des Plaines, IL: Author.

Emergency Nurses Association. (2000). <u>Orientation to emergency nursing: Concepts, Competencies, and Critical Thinking</u>. Des Plaines, IL: Author.

Grey, M. Gurvis, J., & Smith, F. (1992). Competency-based orientation: A solution. <u>Nursing management: Critical care management edition</u>, <u>23</u>(9), 128A-128H.

Hafer, T., & Sutton, S. (1990). Student internship in emergency nursing: One answer to the nursing shortage. <u>Journal of Emergency Nursing</u>, <u>16</u>(5), 326-330.

Haggard, A. (1992). Using self studies to meet JCAHO requirements. <u>Journal of Nursing Staff Development</u>, <u>8</u>(4), 170-174.

Hartline, C. (1993). Preceptor selection and evaluation: A tool for educators and managers. <u>Journal of Nursing Staff Development</u>, <u>9</u>(4), 188-192.

Jordan, K. (Ed.). (2000). <u>Emergency nursing core curriculum</u> (4th ed.). Philadelphia: Saunders.

Kelly, K. (1992). <u>Nursing staff development: Current competence, future focus</u>. Philadelphia: Lippincott.

Kotecki, C. (1992). Nursing internships: Taking a second look. <u>Journal of Continuing Education in Nursing, 23</u>(5), 201-205.

McGrath, B., & Princeton, J. (1987). Evaluation of a clinical preceptor program for new graduates–Eight years later. <u>Journal of Continuing Education in Nursing, 18</u>(4), 133-136.

O'Grady, T., & O'Brien, A. (1991). A guide to competency-based orientation: Develop your own program. <u>Journal of Nursing Staff Development, 8</u>(3), 128-133.

Sheehy, S., Shaffer, A., & Ward, C. (1990). Designing an orientation preceptorship: Development, delivery and evaluation. <u>Journal of Emergency Nursing, 16</u>(6), 408-412.

Tarcinale, M. (1988). The role of evaluation in instruction. <u>Journal of Nursing Staff Development, 4</u>(3), 97-103.

Tracy, D. (1990). <u>Ten steps to empowerment: A common sense guide to manage people</u>. New York: William Morrow.

Westra, R., & Graziano, M. (1992). Preceptors: A comparison of their perceived needs before and after the preceptor experience. <u>Journal of Continuing Education in Nursing, 23</u>(5), 212-215.

Williams, J., & Rogers, S. (1993). The multicultural workplace: Preparing preceptors. <u>Journal of Continuing Education in Nursing, 24</u>(3), 101-104.

RECOMMENDED READINGS

Biancuzzo, M. (1994). Staff nurse preceptors: A program they "own." <u>Clinical Nurse Specialist, 8</u>(2), 97-102.

Carroll, P. (1992). Using personality styles to enhance preceptor programs. <u>Dimensions of Critical Care Nursing, 11</u>(2), 114-119.

Cox, D.G. (1988). A teaching triad: Preceptor, learner, manager. <u>Journal of Nursing Staff Development, 3</u>(2), 22-26.

Hartshorn, J. (1992). Evaluation of a critical care nursing internship program. <u>Journal of Continuing Education in Nursing, 23</u>(1), 42-48.

Hodges, J., & Hansen, L. (1999). Restructuring a competency-based orientation for registered nurses. <u>Journal of Nurses Staff Development, 15</u>(4), 152-158.

Inman, L.F., & Haugen, C. (1991). Six criteria to evaluate skill competency documentation. <u>Dimensions of Critical Care Nursing, 10</u>(4), 238-245.

Kelly, M.M., & Matlin, C.S. (1993). Use of a conceptual framework in planning and implementing an orientation program. <u>Journal of Nursing Staff Development, 9</u>(4), 174-178.

Kidd, P., & Sturt P. (1995). Developing and evaluating an emergency nursing pathway. <u>Journal of Emergency Nursing, 21</u>(6), 521-530.

Kokiko, J. (1993). Desiging a competency based orientation for the emergency department.<u>Journal of Emergency Nursing, 19</u>(6), 538-540.

Laskowski-Jones, L., & Bartley, M.K. (1995). Trauma resource nurse orientation program. <u>Journal of Emergency Nursing, 21</u>(1), 78-79.

McBee, M. J. (1996). Pocket guide to ED orientation. <u>Journal of Emergency Nursing, 22</u>(5), 446-450.

Mikos-Schild, S. (1999). Competency-based orientation (CBO). <u>Today's Surgical Nurse, 21</u>(3), 14-19.

Panno, J. (1992). A systematic approach for assessing learning needs. <u>Journal of Nursing Staff Development, 8</u>(3), 269-273.

APPENDIX A
ORIENTATION LEARNING AGREEMENTS

⅃ **NewYork-Presbyterian**
⅂ The University Hospital of Columbia and Cornell

NEW YORK WEILL CORNELL MEDICAL CENTER
OFFICE OF ORGANIZATIONAL LEARNING
Department of Nursing Education

ORIENTATION LEARNING AGREEMENT

NAME: _____

UNIT: _____   DATE OF HIRE: _____

I _____, understand that orientation is a mutual process for which I am partly accountable. I will be facilitated in this process by the Nursing Education Department and my assigned preceptor(s).

I agree to be responsible for completing the following:

1. _____   by _____
2. _____   by _____
3. _____   by _____
4. _____   by _____
5. _____   by _____
6. _____   by _____

If I miss any orientation classes, I will make arrangements for acquiring that content. Should I be unable to fulfill my responsibility in this agreement, I will make suitable alternate arrangements with my preceptor, instructor and nurse manager.

_____   _____
Instructor   Orientee

_____   _____
Date   Date

G:\Forms\AGREE-97.DOC: 2/92; Rev. 3/93; 12/94; Rev. ME 2/97, 6/97; 12/98; 4/99; 9/99

APPENDIX B
BASELINE KNOWLEDGE SELF-EVALUATION TOOL

NEWYORK-PRESBYTERIAN HOSPITAL
New York Weill Cornell Medical Center
Department of Nursing Education

EMERGENCY NURSING ORIENTATION
Baseline Knowledge Self-Evaluation Tool

SECTION I: TRIAGE/COBRA/ADMISSIONS/PATIENT DISCHARGE

COMPETENCY STATEMENT: At the conclusion of orientation the registered nurse will be able to verbally and clinically demonstrate an understanding of the triage process, inpatient admissions, inter/intrafacility patient transfers, and patient discharge.

Patient Problem/Complaint	TE	T	NoTE
1) General considerations for the triage of patients in the ED			
2) Admission of walk-in patients to the treatment areas			
3) Admission of EMS patients to the treatment areas			
4) Admission of patients to the inpatient hospital units			
a) Med/Surg admits			
b) Critical Care/Trauma/Telemetry admits			
c) Transfer to the OR			
5) Considerations for the intrafacility transfer of patients for special procedures (i.e. CT, XR, arteriogram...)			
6) Considerations for the transfer of patients out of the ED to other facilities			
7) Considerations of COBRA-EMTALA regulations			
8) Considerations for the discharge of patients home from the ED			

TE=   Theory & Experience in this area
T=   Theory & No Experience in this area
NoTE= No Theory or Experience in this area

COMMENTS:

EMERGENCY NURSING ORIENTATION
Baseline Knowledge Self-Evaluation Tool

SECTION 2: RESPIRATORY EMERGENCIES

COMPETENCY STATEMENT: At the conclusion of orientation the registered nurse will be able to verbally and clinically demonstrate an understanding of the care for patients presenting with complaints of the respiratory system

Patient Problem/Complaint	TE	T	NoTE
1) General considerations for patients presenting with respiratory complaints			
2) Respiratory distress syndrome			
3) Asthma/COPD			
4) Epiglottitis			
5) Croup			
6) Hyperventilation syndrome			
7) Acute bronchitis			
8) Pneumonia			
9) Pulmonary embolus			
10) Tuberculosis			
11) Pneumothorax (spontaneous & traumatic)			
12) Hemothorax			
13) Tension pneumothorax			
14) Pulmonary edema			
15) Use of neuromuscular blocking agents/Rapid sequence intubation			

TE= Theory & Experience in this area
T= Theory & No Experience in this area
NoTE= No
Theory or Experience in this area

COMMENTS:

EMERGENCY NURSING ORIENTATION
Baseline Knowledge Self-Evaluation Tool

SECTION 3: CARDIOVASCULAR EMERGENCIES

COMPETENCY STATEMENT: At the conclusion of orientation the registered nurse will be able to verbally and clinically demonstrate an understanding of the care for patients presenting with CV complaints

Patient Problem/Complaint	TE	T	NoTE
1) General considerations for patients presenting to the ED with suspected CV disease			
2) Acute coronary syndrome/Angina/AMI			
3) Congestive heart failure			
4) Cardiogenic shock			
5) Hypovolemic shock			
6) Obstructive shock			
7) Hypertension			
8) Deep venous thrombosis			
9) Sickle cell crisis			
10) Aortic aneurysm			

TE=   Theory & Experience in this area
T=   Theory & No Experience in this area
NoTE= No Theory or Experience in this area

COMMENTS:

APPENDIX C
EMERGENCY NURSING ORIENTATION CLINICAL SKILLS/PROCEDURES CHECKLIST

⌐ NewYork-Presbyterian
¬ The University Hospitals of Columbia and Cornell

NEW YORK WEILL CORNELL MEDICAL CENTER
DEPARTMENT OF NURSING EDUCATION

EMERGENCY NURSING ORIENTATION
CLINICAL SKILLS/PROCEDURES CHECKLIST

Orientee: _____

Instructor: _____

Hire Date: _____

Preceptor(s): _____

Dept./Unit: _____

_____

In order to assist in the individualization of your orientation, please assess your level of expertise in the following nursing skills by completing the "Orientation Self-Assessment." This checklist will also be utilized by your preceptor(s) and instructor(s) in evaluating your orientation experience in the applicable skills. The preceptor or instructor will place his/her initials and date in the column "Skill Performed Satisfactorily" or in the column "Simulated Experience" when the skill has been demonstrated by you.

EMERGENCY DEPARTMENT	Orientee Self-Assessment			Preceptor-Instructor Assessment		
LIST	I HAVE NO EXPERIENCE	I WANT SUPERVISION	I CAN PERFORM INDEPENDENTLY	SILL PERFORMED SATISFACTORILY	SIMULATED EXPERIENCE	**COMMENTS**
SAFETY:						
Room set up						
Side rails						
Conscious Sedation Procedure						
Standard Precautions						
Location of MSDS sheets						
Hazardous Material Decontamination						
Psych seclusion room						
Use of Physical and Chemical Restraints in the ED						
EQUIPMENT (Generic):						
Use of stretchers/pediatric cribs						

· **1**

EMERGENCY DEPARTMENT	Orientee Self-Assessment			Preceptor-Instructor Assessment		
LIST	I HAVE NO EXPERIENCE	I WANT SUPERVISION	I CAN PERFORM INDEPENDENTLY	SILL PERFORMED SATISFACTORILY	SIMULATED EXPERIENCE	COMMENTS
Use of Scales						
Tympanic / Electronic Thermometer						
Ultrasound Doppler (OB & Vascular)						
-a) Doppler peripheral pulse assessment						
- b) Doppler fetal heart rate assessment						
PYXIS location and use						
Dirty utility hopper						
Morgan Lens eye irrigation						
Radiant warmers (Resus 1 & 2)						
Bair Hugger						
SPECIMEN COLLECTION:						
Pneumatic tube system						
Clean catch urine collection						
Urine dip testing						
Urine pregnancy testing (UPT)						
Blood glucose monitoring						
Occult testing of blood in stool and gastric contents						
Venipuncture						
Venous access device cannulation (i.e. PICC line, Infuse-aid, etc…)						
IV MANAGEMENT:						
Peripheral IV access						
Tubing/Bag Change						
IV Site Care / Assessment						
Saline Lock						
Secondary IV infusion						
Baxter Pump						
Blood Products Transfusion						
Manage Central Line (single / multilumen)						
Level I Rapid Infuser/Fluid Warmer						

EMERGENCY DEPARTMENT	Orientee Self-Assessment			Preceptor-Instructor Assessment		
LIST	I HAVE NO EXPERIENCE	I WANT SUPERVISION	I CAN PERFORM INDEPENDENTLY	SILL PERFORMED SATISFACTORILY	SIMULATED EXPERIENCE	COMMENTS
Insite Safety System						
TRIAGE						
- Triage Classifications						
- Pediatric Triage						
- Psychiatric Triage						
- Urgent Care Center Triage						
- Triage Documentation						
RESPIRATORY SYSTEM:						
Respiratory Assessment						
Oxygen Delivery Devices						
Portable Oxygen Tank						
Flow Meter						
Mechanical Ventilator Set-up						
Oral/ETT / Trach Suctioning						
Pulse Oximetry						
Rapid Sequence Protocol						
Assist with Intubation						
CARDIOVASCULAR:						
CV Assessment						
Blood Pressure						
Pulse Assessment						
Bedside Cardiac Monitoring						
Set-up of Cardiac Monitor (including SaO_2, Non-invasive BP)						
Obtaining 12 Lead EKG						
Set-up Transport Monitor						
Titrate Vasopressors / Antiarrhythmics						
Defibrillation / Cardioversion						
Transvenous & Transcutaneous Pacemaker						
Arterial Line Monitoring:						
a) Line setup						

EMERGENCY DEPARTMENT	Orientee Self-Assessment			Preceptor-Instructor Assessment		
LIST	I HAVE NO EXPERIENCE	I WANT SUPERVISION	I CAN PERFORM INDEPENDENTLY	SILL PERFORMED SATISFACTORILY	SIMULATED EXPERIENCE	COMMENTS
- b) Arterial line blood sampling						
Pleuravac / Autotransfusion Set-up						
GASTROINTESTINAL:						
GI Assessment						
Gastric Lavage/Nasogastric tube insertion						
Diagnostic Peritoneal Lavage (DPL)						
Gastric						
NEUROLOGICAL SYSTEM:						
Neuro Assessment/GCS						
ICP Monitoring/Ventriculostomy						
Spinal Immobilization						
INTEGUMENTARY SYSTEM (Also see section on Burn Care)						
Integumentary Assessment						
Dressings						
Assessment and staging of pressure ulcers						
OB-GYN/GU						
Foley catheter insertion						
Urine dip-stick/daily controls						
Urine pregnancy test/controls						
Assist with pelvic examination						
Sexual assault evidence collection						
BURN CARE:						
Burn Wound Assessment						
Fluid Resuscitation (Burn Fluid Formula)						
Appropriate dressing of burns						
PEDIATRIC:						
Pediatric triage						
Pediatric mediation administration						
Transport of pediatric patients						
Holding Pediatric Patients for Procedures						

EMERGENCY DEPARTMENT	Orientee Self-Assessment			Preceptor-Instructor Assessment		
LIST	I HAVE NO EXPERIENCE	I WANT SUPERVISION	I CAN PERFORM INDEPENDENTLY	SILL PERFORMED SATISFACTORILY	SIMULATED EXPERIENCE	COMMENTS
Pediatric Conscious Sedation						
Pediatric Vital Signs						
Pediatric Catheterization (male & female)						
Pediatric U-bag						
EMERGENCY EQUIPMENT:						
Crash Cart (Adult and Pediatric)						
Safe Response Mask						
Bag Valve Mask (Ambu-bag)						
Resuscitation Rooms Set-up (Adult & Peds)						
Transport monitor and drug bag						
NURSING DOCUMENTATION / COMMUNICATION:						
Triage Documentation						
Nursing Documentation						
Admission documentation						
Transfer documentation						
Discharge documentation						
Patient / Family Teaching--DC Instructions						
Patient Care Assignments						
Shift Report						
Faxing Orders/Requisitions						
E-Track System						
Computerized Laboratory System						
Investigational drug use in the ED						

Comments:

Preceptor Initials/Signature

Emergency Department Instructor
Initials/Signature

G:\CKL-OBJ\AER-1.DOC: BG/gv 5/91 Rev. 6/94; NC 1/95;1/96; TZ 12/96; SW 1/98; 12/98; 9/00

APPENDIX D
EMERGENCY NURSING
ORIENTATION OBJECTIVES

⌐ NewYork-Presbyterian
⌐ The University Hospitals of Columbia and Cornell

NEW YORK WEILL CORNELL MEDICAL CENTER
DEPARTMENT OF NURSING EDUCATION

EMERGENCY NURSING
CLINICAL ORIENTATION OBJECTIVES

The clinical assignment given to an orientee should coincide with the content being taught in class. Therefore, specific clinical objectives are written for each clinical experience. Each day's assignment are built on the previous days experience. For example, week three patient selection should be inclusive of any task or procedure from week two in addition to the objectives for week three.

Emergency Nursing Specialty Orientation:
All orientees will receive a specific emergency nursing didactic orientation. The content of this specialty orientation is based on the Core Curriculum for Emergency Nursing (ENA 1999), age specific orientation content related to the pediatric, adult, and geriatric patient populations, and a skills/procedures day. The didactic component will include live lecture, self-learning modules, computer based education, or a combination of all three.

PRE-HIRE TESTING:
Pharmacology Examination
Challenge Examinations
- Basic Dysrhythmia Exemption Examination
- Emergency Nursing Exemption Examination _or_
- Critical Care Exemption Examination

WEEK ONE:
Didactic Orientation
Human Resources Orientation (Monday of orientation week one)
Nursing General Orientation (Tuesday – Thursday of week one)
Emergency Nursing Specialty Day 1 (Friday of week one)

WEEK TWO:
Didactic Orientation
Nursing General Orientation
Basic Dysrhythmia Course (if indicated)
Emergency Nursing Specialty Days 2 & 3

1

Meet with the Emergency Department Director _or_ Designee regarding scheduling, vacation requests and holiday time.

Clinical Orientation
Work up of one (1) acute or two (2) non-acute patients.
Patient selection should include:
> - initial physical and psychosocial assessment
> - discharge
> - patient/family education
> - standard precautions
> - lab computer/pneumatic tube system
> - telephone and paging system
> - blood glucose monitoring, QC check, and fingerstick (contact superuser)
> - administration of medications
> - cardiac monitoring set up

Documentation should reviewed daily for:
> - all assessment data entered on the ED Nursing Progress Note
> - treatments/interventions/procedures
> - patient education
> - reassessment of interventions for effectiveness
> - discharge/admit documentation

WEEK THREE:
Didactic Orientation
Basic Critical Care Course (if indicated)
Emergency Nursing Specialty Orientation Days 4 & 5 (as indicated)

Clinical Orientaiton
Initial work-up of two (2) to three (3) patients and simultaneous care of at least two (2) other patients. The orientee may work with a preceptor in caring for one (1) critically ill patient.

Clinical activities should include (if already completed the preceptor will monitor for competence):
> - patients on isolation
> - non-acute peds patients (during rotation in the Pediatric ED)
> - Performs IV therapy per HOSPITAL policy
> - patients receiving blood or blood component transfusion
> - checks emergency cart and defibrillator
> - preop patients
> - 12 lead EKG
> - assists preceptor in assuring all assigned areas are stocked
> - oxygen delivery systems
> - Assist preceptor in the transport of a critical patient to radiology and to critical care inpatient unit

2

WEEKS FOUR THROUGH SIX:
Clinical Orientation
Initial work-up of all patients (by week 6) and simultaneous care of at least five (5) non-acute patients by week Five. At the end of week Six, the orientee should be able to provide simultaneous care for six (6) non-acute patients in a patient care area.

Patient care should include (if already completed the preceptor will monitor for competence):
- volumetric infusion pumps
- chest drainage systems
- suctioning
- use of chemical and physical restraint(s)
- mechanical ventilation with supervision
- assessment of a critical trauma victim
- spinal immobilization
- care of a patient with respiratory problems (asthma)
- basic burn care
- insertion of a morgan lens
- musculoskeletal trauma
- chest pain (management of a stable MI)
- sickle cell crisis
- altered mental status
- alcohol/substance abuse
- NG tube insertion
- selected psych patients
- violent patients
- abused patients
- sexual assault
- abdominal pain
- gyn problems
- triage observation

WEEK SEVEN:
The orientee should have responsibility for an entire patient care area with the preceptor assistance. Simultaneously care for two (2) critically ill patients in the south ED who are stable. Care for one (1) unstable critically ill patient.

Patient selection should include (if already completed the preceptor will monitor for competence):
- care of the critically patient with multi-system problems
- interpretation of all dysrhythmias
- stable pediatric patients for orientees who rotate to the Pediatric ED.
- participate in a cardiac arrest (if applicable) or trauma
- Arterial line set up, calibration, monitoring, blood sampling, and troubleshooting

Documentation should be reviewed daily for adequacy & completeness

3

WEEKS EIGHT, NINE, TEN, AND ELEVEN (as indicated):

Orientees will have rotated through the Psychiatric & Pediatric ED and will receive 24 hours of basic Triage orientation. The start time for rotation will depend upon an orientee's progress and the number of orientees in total needing to be circulated through the rotations. Each rotation will be six, 12 hour shifts. The Triage experience may be for 1/2 of each shift, allowing for experience in the patient care areas in the afternoon. Rotation to the Pediatric ED will involve caring for two (2) to three (3) patients and will work up towards assuming responsibility for the entire patient care area with the preceptor.

Patient selection as outlined above. Rotation to Pediatric Emergency Department should include:
- care of the stable pediatric patient
- care of a pediatric patient undergoing conscious sedation
- pediatric septic work-ups
- participation in pediatric emergencies with supervision
- pediatric triage observation (4-6 hours)

Documentation should be reviewed daily for adequacy & completeness

WEEK TWELVE (as indicated):

The orientee should be able to assume responsibility for a patient care area with minimal supervision. The preceptor will serve as a resource to the orientee.

Patient selection should include (if already completed the preceptor will monitor for competence):
- thoracic trauma
- massive transfusion protocol
- shock
- countershock
- pacemakers
- head and spinal cord trauma
- obstructed airway
- abdominal trauma
- hypo/hyperthermia
- spontaneous delivery
- disasters/hazardous materials
- use of the Level I rapid transfuser/warmer
- autotransfusion
- diagnostic peritoneal lavage
- Lead nurse in transport of a critical patient to radiology and to critical care inpatient unit

G:\CKL-OBJ\AER.DOC: NC/90; Rev. 5/93; 10/93; 1/94; 7/95; 1/96; Rev. TZ 1/97; SW 11/99, 12/2000

4

CHAPTER 6

Keys to Planning
Successful Educational Activities

OBJECTIVES

Upon completion of this chapter, the emergency nurse educator will be able to:

1. Conduct a learning needs assessment.

2. Design an educational event based on identified needs.

3. Identify three options for in-service education.

4. Recall the process of annual and long-range educational planning.

5. Identify the purpose of continuing education for professional nurses.

6. Describe the process for obtaining contact hour approval for a continuing education activity.

INTRODUCTION

Nursing as a profession is rich with teaching opportunities. Mandatory education, orientation, in-services, community outreach, and continuing nursing education programs are just a few of the available educational opportunities. Without question, patient teaching is a cornerstone of nursing practice. Regrettably, this type of teaching does not prepare the nurse for the role of educator.

Educational planning and program development can be a challenge for even the most experienced educator—the novice educator may feel overwhelmed. An educational plan or curriculum makes the task more manageable. The plan enables the educator to coordinate multiple educational experiences for diverse target audiences and meet the educational needs of staff with varying educational backgrounds and experience levels. It is important for the educator to remember that education competes with other health care related activities for limited resources; therefore, education programs must be designed for efficiency and effectiveness.

INTENT

Education within nursing may be classified by intent of the educational opportunity:

- **Continuing education** – "planned learning experiences beyond a basic nursing educational program. These experiences are designed to promote the development of knowledge, skills, and attitudes for the enhancement of nursing practice, thus improving health care to the public" (ANA, 1984, p. 15).

- **In-service education** – "learning experiences provided in the work setting for the purpose of assisting staff in performing their assigned functions in that particular agency" (ANA, 1992, p. 5).

- **Staff development** – "process consisting of orientation, in-service education, and continuing education for the purpose of promoting the development of personnel within any employee setting, consistent with the goals and responsibilities of the employer" (ANA, 1992, p. 3).

EDUCATIONAL OPPORTUNITIES

The American Nurses Credentialing Center (1991) identified three types of educational opportunities that may be developed by the educator in the emergency setting:

- **Offering** – "single educational activity that may be presented once or repeated" (p. 49).

- **Program** (conference/course) – "series of offerings or educational sessions that have a common theme and common overall goals. Examples of a program might be a course, e.g., critical care, or a conference with multiple educational sessions" (p. 53).

- **Independent study** – "self-paced learning activity developed by an organization for use by an individual learner" (p. 59).

COURSE DESIGN

Educational opportunities within a staff development program should be structured to promote professional growth and enhance acquisition of competency in specialized areas. A systematic approach to educational planning and program development clarifies intent and improves outcomes. Essential steps in developing an educational experience are:

- Assessment of learning needs.

- Identification of target audience.

- Generation of outcomes or objectives from identified needs.

- Selection of teaching strategies to achieve objectives.

- Determination of content outline.

- Identification of instructors.

- Determination of evaluation strategies.

ASSESSMENT OF LEARNING NEEDS

A needs assessment identifies learning needs for a defined population of individuals. Strategies utilized to conduct a needs assessment should be consistent with the principles of adult learning. The goal of the needs assessment is to obtain accurate information from the target population so that identified learning needs can be prioritized and addressed. Utilizing a systematic approach to assessment of learning needs increases validity of the findings and reflects group needs rather than perceived needs of the educator.

The process of conducting a needs assessment may be formal or informal. More than one assessment strategy may be utilized. Information may be gathered from the target population as well as those familiar with the needs of the target population, such as nurse managers, clinical specialists, charge nurses, and preceptors.

ASSESSMENT STRATEGIES

Carefully designed assessment strategies gather information directly from the target population to identify continuing education needs. A poorly conducted assessment wastes time and undermines validity of further educational planning.

Recognition of education programming developed to meet learning needs—real or perceived—constitutes the most elemental needs assessment. New emergency nurse educators should identify existing education programs prior to development of new programming. This initial assessment of existing programs reveals programs that effectively meet staff learning needs as well as programs that only appear to meet these needs. Established programs should be continued while the educator evaluates their effectiveness in meeting current learning needs.

Interviews

Interviews are useful as a formal or informal means of gathering information. Interviews allow exchange of ideas and clarification of responses through dialogue. Informal interviews occur when time permits and are often the result of casual conversations or observations in the immediate environment. Formal interviews required planning and preparation.

Formal interview process:

- Formulate a list of questions prior to the interview.
- Schedule time with the individual providing the information.
- Focus discussion to make efficient use of scheduled time.
- Record and validate responses.

Advantages:

- Allows exchange of ideas.
- Ability to clarify responses.
- Familiar technique.

Disadvantages:

- Time-consuming to collect data from a large group.
- Recording results during an interview may interfere with spontaneity.
- Recording results after an interview may decrease accuracy of findings and bias prioritization of needs.

Tips for successful interviews:

- Be prompt for scheduled interview.
- Explain reason for interview.
- Utilize open-ended questions to elicit learning needs.
- Redirect responses as needed to focus interview.
- Summarize results of interview for clarification.

Focused Group Discussions

These discussions provide collective exchange of ideas and the opportunity to validate and record group data in a relatively short period of time. Multiple groups with no more than six to eight individuals are usually more productive than a single large group.

Focused group discussion process:

- Pose prepared questions to groups of no more than six to eight people.
- Allow the group time to discuss their responses.
- Ask spokesperson to report responses.
- Display responses.
- Encourage the group to prioritize responses by developing a list of needs.
- Summarize discussion and validate findings.

Advantages:

- Assess larger groups in relatively short period of time.
- Participants work together to identify learning needs.
- Validate data by summarization.

Disadvantages:

- Some participants may be reluctant to participate.
- Participants have to adjust work schedules.

Tips for successful focused group discussions:

- Determine time frame for introduction, discussion, prioritization, and summarization during the planning session.
- Advertise time and purpose.
- Prepare questions prior to group meeting (see Table 2).
- Focus questions on the purpose.
- Develop questions that provoke discussion.
- Pose only one or two questions to the group.
- Write discussion results on flip chart.
- Tape flip chart sheets to wall.
- Record prioritization results on flip chart.
- Adhere to time frame.

TABLE 2. SAMPLE DISCUSSION QUESTIONS

1. What information do you feel would help you increase competency and proficiency in your position?

2. Considering changes that have occurred in the health care setting, what information do you feel would be helpful to you as a professional?

Nominal Group Technique

This technique provides a group structure that "allows individual judgments to be effectively pooled and used in situations in which uncertainty or disagreement exists about the nature of the problem and possible solutions."

Nominal group technique process:

- Generate ideas.
  - Group of six to eight people write responses to a stimulus question.
- Record ideas.
  - After a designated time, each participant contributes a single response in round-robin fashion until all responses are recorded and displayed. No comment is made on individual responses.
- Discuss ideas.
  - The group discusses each item for clarity of meaning.
- Prioritize.
  - After discussion, each individual prioritizes the items by rank-ordering. To rank order, an index card is provided for each item. Group members stack cards in order of need, from highest to lowest need. Participants then number cards beginning with one for the lowest need, progressing numerically to the most pressing needs. Results are then tallied and displayed. Items with the highest score reflect the highest needs (Puetz, 1992).

Nominal group technique process with large groups:

- Provide large group with stimulus question.
- Subdivide large group into smaller groups of six to eight people.
- Provide time for the process.
- Record small group discussion findings rather than individual written items.
- Reconvene small groups to identify top priorities.
- Record and display small group priorities as a consolidated list.
- Allow time for serial discussion of consolidated list before final rank-ordering by the large group.
- Consolidate prioritizations from each group to represent the work of the entire group when necessary.
- Tally and display results.

Advantages:

- Allows expression of individual judgments in a group.
- Assesses needs of large group.
- Identifies learning needs of individuals and groups.

Disadvantages:

- Coordinating staff schedules may be difficult.
- Requires additional time to assure all members are heard.

Tips for successful nominal group technique:

- Determine time frames during the planning session.

- Advertise time and purpose.

- Prepare questions prior to group meeting (see Table 2).

- Pose only one or two questions to the group.

- Write discussion results on flip chart.

- Tape flip chart sheets to wall.

- Record prioritization results on flip chart.

- Adhere to time frame (Puetz, 1992).

Checklists

Checklists are a list of skills or information used to determine individual learning needs through the process of self-appraisal. Collective patterns of learning needs for a target population also are determined. Checklists may be used to ascertain knowledge, values, or skill proficiency subsequent to orientation or as part of the clinical promotion process.

Checklist process:

- Develop list of skills or concepts familiar to the target population.

- Determine frequency of skill utilization in practice setting.

   I Learning needs related to frequently performed skills take precedence over those skills that are seldom performed.

- Have participants rank each item using a numerical scale or by placing a check in a column for specific ranking categories.

- A significant number of responses in an area that indicates a need for additional resources warrants further investigation to determine if the identified need is related to knowledge deficit, i.e., real education need.

Advantages:

- Assesses population's perceived knowledge and ability against an identified standard or expectation.

- Determines collective patterns of learning needs for the target population.

Disadvantages:

- Unless checklist identifies every potential learning need, data may be limited.

- Little opportunity to validate results.

- Prioritization is determined by the educator rather than the target audience.

Tips for successful checklists:

- Develop the checklist in conjunction with individuals familiar with practice expectations in the clinical setting.

- Identify response categories to provide nonthreatening evaluation, e.g., needs to seek additional resources, able to perform independently, serves as a resource.

- Determine validity of the tool by comparison of checklist items to actual practice.

- Clarify checklist return date.

- Provide easy system for checklist return such as envelope posted in a prominent location.

Questionnaires

These are surveys that may be used to collect data from large groups.

Questionnaire process:

- Develop questionnaire (see Table 3).
- Pilot questionnaire on small group.
- Modify questionnaire based on pilot results.
- Distribute questionnaire.
- Tally results.

Advantages:

- One of most cost-effective strategies available.
- Able to survey large numbers in a short period of time.
- Does not disrupt work schedules.

Disadvantages:

- Developing reliable, valid questions may be difficult.
- Return frequently less than 50%.
- Open-ended question or sentence completion is cumbersome and analysis is susceptible to bias.
- Closed-ended questions restrict amount of information obtained.

Tips for a successful questionnaire:

- Develop questionnaire in collaboration with a consultant experienced in this area.
  - I The marketing department is a good place to find an expert in this area.
- Ask consultant to review questions for validity.
- Define due date of completed questionnaires.
- Design systematic reminders to encourage questionnaire return.
- Provide for easy questionnaire return such as envelope posted in a prominent location.

TABLE 3. Sample Questionnaire Questions

Open-Ended Question: Please indicate information you need to improve or enhance your nursing practice.

Sentence Completion: In order to improve my practice, I need to learn more about:

Closed-Ended Question: Do you need to learn more about 12-lead ECG interpretation?

Delphi Technique

The Delphi Technique uses a series of questionnaires to identify learning needs, achieve consensus, and prioritize identified needs (Chaney, 1987). The first survey is generated from initial assessment of the target audience. Initial assessment techniques include but are not limited to:

- Interviews.
- Observations.
- Exit interviews.
- Questionnaires.

Delphi Technique process:

- First round of questionnaires.
  - Previously identified items are listed.
  - Respondents rank items in order of importance.
  - Other pertinent items may also be added.
- Second round of questionnaires.
  - Developed from first round responses.
  - Participants rank each item.
- Third round of questionnaires.
  - The average (calculated mean) and the most frequently selected response (mode) are identified for each item.
  - Includes comments from the second survey.
  - Participants rank each item for consensus.
- Analysis.
  - Third round of questionnaires collected.
  - Mean and mode are calculated again.
  - Comments summarized.
  - If consensus is not obtained by round three, further attempts to achieve it will probably be futile (Puetz, 1992).

Advantages:

- Data collection, even for large groups, is fast, inexpensive, and convenient.

Disadvantages:

- Each round of questionnaires increases the risk of diminished return.

Tips for successful Delphi Technique:

- Advertise process and purpose.
- Rank items with scale of one to four, according to importance or degree of need.
- Clearly define due dates for questionnaire return.
- Design systematic reminders to encourage return.
- Provide for easy questionnaire return such as envelope posted in a prominent location.

Assessment Results

The needs assessment is a critical first step in educational planning and program development. On completion of a needs assessment, the educator must analyze results to determine the types of needs that have been identified. Identification of need type allows the educator to develop an appropriate plan to address specific needs identified by the assessment.

- **Real needs** reflect objective deficiencies that actually exist.
  - This type of need may or may not be recognized by the one who has the need.
- **Real education** needs refer to specific understanding, skills, or attitudes that are lacking.
  - The specific deficiency can be improved with a focused learning experience.
  - The individual with the learning need may not be concerned with satisfying the educational need until the need is recognized.
- **Felt needs** are regarded as necessary by the involved individual.
  - This type of need is limited by individual self-awareness, i.e., the individual may want an educational experience without really needing it.
- **Normative needs** reflect the gap between a desired standard and the existing standard (Atwood & Ellis, 1971; Monette, 1977).

Not all needs identified through a needs assessment require educational resolution. Real needs may reflect a system or environmental problem. For example, poor documentation may be the result of a cumbersome documentation tool rather than a knowledge deficit related to documentation. In this instance, chart modification would be more effective than an education session on the importance of documentation. Real education needs and normative needs receive highest priority in educational planning because of their direct link to improved patient outcomes. Felt needs have little direct impact on patient outcomes; however, these needs may motivate an individual to participate in professional development programs.

TARGET AUDIENCE

Any group who will benefit from a specified educational opportunity may be defined as a target audience or target population. In the health care setting, target audiences include such diverse groups as registered nurses, licensed practical nurses, nursing assistants, secretaries and clerks, technical support staff, community groups, and others. "The profile of the target population is particularly significant in planning learning behavior outcomes, for the level of achievement designated must be compatible with the background of the population" (Reilly & Oermann, 1990, p. 116).

Target populations may be defined by age, educational level, and life experiences. Further delineation may be determined by need or defined by role. For example, the need for orientation identifies new employees as a target population. Examples of target populations defined by role are:

- Direct patient care roles – RNs, LPNs, nursing assistants, patient care technicians.
- Management and leadership roles – nurse managers, administrators, clinical specialists, clinical coordinators, educators.
- Support roles – secretaries, clerks, unit secretaries, nonlicensed care assistants.

Target populations also extend beyond the health care environment. Community outreach programs, adult education settings, or geriatric centers pose special considerations for targeting education to a defined population.

OUTCOMES OR OBJECTIVES

Objectives define expected outcomes for an educational experience. Properly written objectives clarify expected achievement level, focus learning behaviors, and provide evaluation guidelines. In essence, they are the foundation of educational design. Goals or objectives are developed to promote learning and measure this learning through changed behavior. Changed behavior occurs when the learner:

- Understands the process and rationale for the change.

- Values the learned behavior over previous behaviors.

- Possesses the ability or skill to execute the desired change.

LEARNING DOMAINS

The dynamic relationship between understanding, valuing, and acting represents the three domains of learning (Bloom, 1956).

- **Cognitive** – intellectual ability.

- **Affective** – the states of feeling and valuing.

- **Psychomotor** – manipulative and motor skills.

Learning occurs within each domain from simple to complex, building on previous levels. Taxonomies are classification systems that define levels of learning (Bloom, 1956; Krathwohl, Bloom, & Masia, 1964; Schweer, 1981). Bloom's taxonomy (see Appendix A) serves as a reference for developing objectives that reflect levels of learning. Objectives written for each domain differentiate various aspects of problem-solving, attitudes, acting, thinking, and feeling (Reilly & Oermann, 1990).

When the **cognitive domain** is addressed, the educator must consider participant education level to determine prior exposure to proposed content. More program time is required for the participant with no prior knowledge of proposed content.

Objectives in the **psychomotor domain** describe skill performance desired at the conclusion of the learning experience. Activity reinforces learning; therefore, practice time should be incorporated in learning experience. Skill evaluation should occur after the participant has had time to practice.

Knowledge within the cognitive and psychomotor domains is gauged by evaluation of measurable behaviors. Learning in the **affective domain** may be demonstrated indirectly through actions; however, evaluation tools lack sophistication to differentiate the extent of goal attainment. For this reason, objectives written in the affective domain are not defined in measurable terms. With the strong emphasis on defining objectives in measurable terms, many educators avoid the affective domain entirely.

Knowledge in the affective domain relates to empathetic, holistic aspects of care. For example, affective knowledge is expressed in the clinical setting when the nurse learns to appreciate the impact of cardiac arrest on patients and their families. How well the nurse understands and applies this knowledge is reflected in attentiveness to stressors of the patient and family who have experienced a cardiac arrest situation.

WRITING OBJECTIVES

Effective learning objectives should contain the following essential elements:

- Time frame when the learning should occur.

- Selected teaching strategy or educational experience.

- Target audience.

- Expected behavior after learning has occurred.

Multiple objectives are frequently used to define educational goals; therefore, objectives should provide linkage between the objectives as well as clarity of content. In general, time frame, teaching strategy, and target audience combine to form the stem, a statement common to each objective. The stem is followed by a list of expected behaviors. Table 3 illustrates objectives that represent each domain of learning.

TABLE 4. Sample Objectives

At the conclusion of the code management seminar, the nurse will be able to:

1. Evaluate the appropriateness of selected treatment interventions in a code management scenario.

2. Demonstrate safe, appropriate defibrillation.

3. Appreciate the impact of cardiac arrest on patients and their families.

The objectives presented in Table 4 illustrate how specific information is communicated through objectives.

- **Time frame** – expected behaviors should be attained by the conclusion of the seminar.

- **Educational experience** – defined by this objective as a seminar.

- **Target audience** – defined as nurses, excluding other health care professionals.

- Expected behaviors after learning has occurred:

  I The first objective is written at a high level in the cognitive domain.

    ♦ Evaluation of treatments implies the learner will be able to assess the need for intervention, identify the cause of the clinical presentation, know available treatment options, and understand the rationale for selecting one option over another.

  I The second objective is written in the psychomotor domain and requires that the learner understands indication, technique, and safety issues of defibrillation.

    ♦ Evaluation of learning focuses on the learner's ability to integrate cognitive knowledge with the motor skill of defibrillation.

    ♦ Teaching strategies that include opportunities in the cognitive and psychomotor domain allow integration of content and skill.

  I The third objective is written in the affective domain.

    ♦ This objective is not measurable; however, it does address a fundamental aspect of nursing practice—empathetic, holistic care.

    ♦ To address this objective, course content should provide beginning awareness of stressors related to cardiac arrest.

    ♦ Evaluation of learning in the clinical setting occurs through observation of the nurse's interactions with patients and families who have experienced a cardiac arrest situation.

TEACHING STRATEGIES

Creativity in teaching is virtually limitless; however, creativity without focus quickly leads to chaos. Teaching strategies consistent with program objectives and learning domains set the stage for learning. Consideration should be given to availability of resources and characteristics of the target population. Table 5 provides a brief summary of teaching strategies that facilitate learning in each domain. See Chapter 3 for additional discussion of teaching strategies.

TABLE 5. LEARNING DOMAINS AND TEACHING STRATEGIES

LEARNING DOMAIN	APPROPRIATE TEACHING STRATEGIES
Cognitive domain	**Gain knowledge** Lecture Panel discussion Reading Self-study packets Instructional video Computer-assisted instruction **Increase understanding** Lecture Group discussion Case presentation Debate Dramatization—role-play, video Problem solving Computer-assisted instruction
Psychomotor domain	**Develop or refine skills** Demonstration Coaching Return demonstration Practice sessions Simulations Clinical observation/practice
Affective domain	**Change/reinforce attitudes/values** Dramatization—video, film, role-play Sharing experiences Debate Panel discussions Gaming

CONTENT OUTLINE

The content outline may be developed before selection of teaching strategies, concurrently, or after strategies have been finalized. Development of the content outline has two essential components:

- Determine topics to be presented.
- Identify time allotment for designated topics.

Educators may develop content outlines individually or in collaboration with others, such as an experienced staff member or clinical nurse specialist. This is particularly important when the individual has agreed to teach the content. Regardless of who creates the content outline, it is essential that the outline be consistent with:

- Course description and purpose.
- Target audience.
- Learning objectives.
- Current literature.
- Institutional practice standards.

INSTRUCTORS

The educator may frequently serve as the only instructor for an educational program; however, certain programs may require the expertise of other individuals. Depending on program content, instructors may include:

- Experienced staff nurses.
- Clinical nurse specialists or nurse practitioners.
- Other health care professionals.
- Experts not employed by the sponsoring institution.

Prior to contacting potential speakers outside the sponsoring institution, the educator must identify applicable institutional reimbursement policies. Speaker reimbursement must be considered when determining the budget for an educational event. An outside speaker may be required to complete a disclosure statement and provide a current curriculum vitae to obtain contact hours. A sample disclosure statement is provided in Appendix B.

EVALUATION STRATEGIES

As competition for resources increases, it is imperative that a return on investment is demonstrated. Evaluation is one method to demonstrate tangible benefits from various education programs. Evaluation is an ongoing process that compares goals, accomplishments, and cost-effectiveness of staff development/continuing education efforts. Abruzzese (1992) describes a four-tier, hierarchical evaluation system "with simple to complex levels of evaluation, frequencies of implementation, and cost factors" (p. 238).

- **Process evaluation** addresses participant satisfaction with course structure, coordination of course, facilities, and relevancy of content and objectives to personal goals.
- **Content evaluation** evaluates cognitive, psychomotor, and affective learning.

- **Outcomes evaluation** measures change in behavior that has occurred and persisted after the learning experience.

- **Impact evaluation** explores the operational result of educational programming, e.g., increased quality of care, reduction in cost.

Process and content evaluation are used most frequently in staff development and continuing education. Outcome and impact evaluations are considered more advanced evaluation strategies. New educators should seek assistance when designing evaluation strategies at these levels.

PROCESS EVALUATION

The American Nurses Association Commission on Accreditation identifies the following key elements for process evaluation:

- Learner achievement of each objective.

- Effectiveness of each instructor.

- Relevance of content to stated objectives.

- Effectiveness of teaching strategies.

- Conduciveness of environment to learning.

- Learner achievement of personal objectives (New Jersey State Nurses Association, 1992).

Data from process evaluations should be utilized for program revision and future educational planning. Identified concerns should be addressed and resolved when possible. A sample program evaluation form is provided in Appendix C.

Questionnaires are the most frequently utilized tool for process evaluation. Questionnaires are designed with a ranked Likert Scale response for each question. A scale with an even number of possible responses allows for differentiation between negative and positive responses because of omission of a neutral response. If a neutral response is desired, a scale with an odd number of responses should be used.

CONTENT EVALUATION

Content evaluation measures cognitive, psychomotor, and affective learning (Abruzzese, 1992). Written tests are an effective technique for evaluation of learning in the cognitive domain, whereas observation is the best way to evaluate learning in the psychomotor domain.

WRITTEN TESTING

This begins with a test plan. In the most elementary form, a test plan is based on the number of lectures within an educational experience and the time allotted for each presentation. The number of test questions for each objective should correlate with the time allotted for each topic. Time allotment for test completion should allow one minute for each multiple choice, true/false, and matching question. Construction of a quality examination remains one of the greatest challenges an educator faces. Educators are encouraged to review pertinent literature and attend seminars in test construction.

Computer software packages for test construction, also called test banks, store test questions by designated categories. To construct a test, the instructor selects desired categories and the required number of questions from each category. The program then selects the questions and constructs the test. Educators should trial test bank programs before purchase to determine ease of utilization and verify adherence to basic principles of test construction.

Options available for written testing are summarized below (Gronlund, 1988; Cox & Ewan, 1988; Schoolcraft, 1989).

Multiple Choice Exams

These exams remain the most commonly used tool in staff development and continuing education despite the fact that most instructor-produced multiple choice exams are neither valid nor reliable (Abruzzese, 1992). A multiple choice question consists of a stem followed by a series of possible answers.

- Stem of the question.
  - Presented as a single, clearly stated problem.
  - Able to elicit an answer before options are read.
  - Worded so there is no repetition of stem in the possible answers.
  - Stated in a positive form when possible.
  - Negative words such as **not** or **except** should be highlighted in the stem.
- Possible responses to the stem.
  - Similar in structure.
  - Grammatically consistent with the stem.
  - Free of verbal clues that may bias a potential response.
  - Structured with the correct response in varied positions to exclude patterned responses.
  - Ranked in a logical fashion according to length and numerical progression.
    - Rank length from shortest to longest.
    - Numerical progression should be from the lowest to highest number.
  - Designed to eliminate overlap of content.
  - Avoid use of all of the above or none of the above.
    - When you do use these choices, they must also be used as an incorrect response.
- The correct response must be:
  - Correct.
  - Clearly the best choice.
- Distractors or incorrect responses should:
  - Appear feasible to those unfamiliar with the content.
  - Be approximately the same length as the correct response.

True or False

These questions consist of a stem that is either true or false. Students may be asked to simply select the answer or may also be required to explain the rationale for their response.

- The stem must be:
  - Presented as a single statement.
  - Stated in simple, concise language.
  - Able to elicit an answer.
  - Entirely true or entirely false.

Matching

Matching questions consist of a list of items and a list of corresponding definitions, terms, or concepts.

- Items are listed in left column, preceded by a blank line.

- Responses are listed in the right column, preceded by a letter or number.

- Including one additional response avoids answering through the process of elimination.

- Check and recheck to assure only one correlation can be made between items and responses.

- Utilize similar format to list items.

- Responses should have the same structure and be approximately the same length.

Written testing provides an opportunity for additional learning through the evaluation process. To enhance learning at this point, every effort should be made to decrease anxiety associated with testing. Inability to pass a written test does not necessarily mean an employee is unable to meet the expectations of a specific position. Poor test scores may be caused by poor teaching, poor test construction, poor test-taking skills, or a combination of the three. Strategies to diminish test anxiety include:

- Define expectations of the test.

- Define test format.

- Eliminate punitive consequences for poor test performance.

- Provide opportunities for remedial tutoring.

PSYCHOMOTOR TESTING

Psychomotor testing is used to evaluate learning in the psychomotor domain. Some individuals may be able to explain a task in great detail without being able to execute required psychomotor skills. Conversely, an individual may not be able to explain a process, but demonstrates the skill without difficulty. Successful psychomotor testing includes the following:

- Identify critical criteria for skill performance. What steps must be done to assure safety?

- Develop a checklist for evaluation of demonstrated psychomotor skills.

- Highlight critical components on the checklist.

- Provide students with the checklist prior to evaluation.

- Allow practice time before testing begins. Students should feel comfortable with the skill before the performance evaluation.

OUTCOMES EVALUATION

Outcomes evaluation measures change in behavior that has occurred and persisted after the learning experience. Outcomes evaluation usually occurs three to six months after an extensive learning experience (Abruzzese, 1992). Strategies to measure long-term changes in behavior include:

- Questionnaires completed by the staff and/or supervisors.

- Self-assessment reporting scales.

- Observation of clinical practice.

- Audits.

IMPACT EVALUATION

Impact evaluation explores the operational result of educational programming, e.g., increased quality of care, reduction in cost. Impact evaluation studies are complex, utilize research designs, and require strong technical support. These studies are best left to the seasoned educator.

COURSE IMPLEMENTATION

The time required to prepare and organize an educational event depends on the type, complexity, and length of the event. Guidelines for organization and implementation of an educational program are provided in Appendixes D, E, and F. During implementation, the educator should evaluate effectiveness of preparation for the event. Careful observations may identify methods to improve the existing program or enhance future planning and design.

ANNUAL EDUCATION REQUIREMENTS

Three universal components of the educator role are mandated by external controls. These are mandatory education, record keeping, and competency evaluation.

MANDATORY ANNUAL EDUCATION

Mandatory education in the hospital setting is defined by state and federal laws, regulatory agencies, and hospital policy. Mandatory education is often provided as in-service education. The JCAHO and OSHA are two regulatory agencies that require specific annual in-services. Requisite topics include:

- Fire.

- Safety including body mechanics.

- Infection control including HIV/AIDS.

- Cardiopulmonary resuscitation (CPR).

- Tuberculosis with respirator fittings.

- Hazardous material exposure.

Hospitals may also require additional in-services for the emergency nurse. Content may be a specific topic identified through quality improvement initiatives, selected high-risk skills, or new policy/procedure. Verification of selected credentials may also be required, e.g., advanced cardiac life support (ACLS), trauma nurse specialist (TNS), Trauma Nurse Core Course (TNCC), and mobile intensive care nurse (MICN).

Mandatory in-services are closely linked to merit raises. In most institutions, staff must attend mandatory in-services to assure a merit raise. Staff are always paid for attendance at mandatory in-services. These requirements challenge the educator to provide mandatory in-services to all staff in a manner that is cost-effective and easily accessible. Concurrent with this demand is the need to provide the information in a manner conducive to adult learning.

IN-SERVICE PRESENTATION

When selecting the best strategy for in-service delivery, the first consideration is cost. The educator should estimate which method is the most cost-effective in terms of material, man-hours, and availability. A variety of options are utilized to present mandatory in-services.

- Monthly in-services.
    - One required in-service is presented each month.
    - In-service may be presented every day for an entire week at various times to accommodate all shifts and staff.
- Marathon in-service day.
    - All required in-services are presented in one day.
    - Each nurse is expected to attend one in-service day each year.
- Self-study/Self-learning module.
    - Critical information on required topics such as fire, safety, and infection control is printed and placed in a manual. Nurses sign the manual out to study on their own.
    - When the manual is returned, a short test with two or three questions per subject is given.
    - Knowledge is verified by a predetermined score.

IN-SERVICE FORMAT

Once a presentation method is selected for in-services, the format for delivery must be determined. Delivery options are limited only by the imagination of the educator.

- Games.
    - Develop a board game for the various topics.
        - ◆ Examples include Safety First board game (Schoessler, Yount, Marshall, & Gilson, 1991).
    - Fortune cookie contest.
        - ◆ Place questions in fortune cookies. Award prizes (Petersen, 1994).
- Posters.
    - Work most efficiently for monthly education days.
    - Develop a poster for the in-service of the month.
    - Use different formats for different months.
- Case studies - Using case studies to provide mandatory information may generate fresh interest. Most nurses perceive case studies as information that is useful rather than simply mandatory (Yoder, 1990).
- Ten minute learning break - Develop flyers on requisite in-service information which can be read in 10 minutes, i.e., during a break.
    - Post new flyers on a weekly or monthly schedule.
    - Placing the flier in the bathroom, by the time clock, or on the refrigerator door makes the flier accessible to the majority of the staff.
    - Size of the print on the flier should be easily read from the seating area.

- Staff presentations – staff volunteer topic. The educator works with staff to select a method for poster presentation of the selected topic.

- Videos.

  - Simple videos.

  - Interactive videos.

- Lectures.

- Computer-assisted instruction programs.

- CPR marathon/blitz – CPR may be included in regular in-service days or held as a separate class. In addition to standard CPR classes, a CPR marathon/blitz may be used. This format has demonstrated efficient use of time and resources.

  - Fifteen-minute appointments are created.

  - Nurses sign up for a specific 15-minute appointment. A CPR booklet is provided at sign up.

  - Staff must arrive at their scheduled time fully prepared to demonstrate requisite skills and complete the required written test.

    - The instructor tests rather than teaches.

    - If the student is not prepared, he or she must return on another marathon day.

RECORD KEEPING

Record keeping is an extremely important aspect of education in the health care setting. It provides verification that mandatory in-services were held. The educator must know information required by various state, federal, regulatory, and licensing agencies.

If in-services are held on a monthly basis, records can be maintained in a three-ring binder with a tab for each month. The record for the monthly in-service should include a sample of the in-service—poster or flier, handouts, sign-up sheets, roster of original signatures, and the marketing piece distributed to announce the in-service. Marketing pieces should include dates, times, objectives, format, topic, and location. Evaluation summary and faculty information may be required by some states or institutions.

Individual records should also be maintained for each staff member. An index card, a simple sheet of paper, or a computer file can be used. Staff name and the time frame of the record should be included, e.g., Jane Doe, January 1999-January 2000. Cards may be kept in a card box, sheets in a three-ring binder. The record should be available to the nurse at all times. Responsibility for maintenance of individual records belongs to the employee. Providing record sheets at in-services is an effective reminder and encourages the nurses to record the in-service when they sign the roster. Preprinted record sheets or index cards with required in-services allows the educator to quickly ascertain status on mandatory in-services.

COMPETENCY EVALUATION

Competency is the ability to perform required skills in a safe and proficient manner. Evaluation of competency is an ongoing concern. The JCAHO requires that all staff be competent in their respective roles. Competency includes the ability to perform routine care activities and the ability to provide safe care in situations not encountered on a regular basis (JCAHO, 2000).

Nurse managers are responsible for day-to-day unit operations and for the delivery of safe care to patients and families. In the process of conducting annual performance appraisals, the nurse manager verifies that each staff member is a safe, competent practitioner. In this context, competency evaluation is a management function.

The educator participates as a member of the management team for competency evaluation with specific involvement in developing strategies for ongoing evaluation and documentation of staff competency. Educators also assess staff competency throughout the orientation process. The educator's determination that an orientee is ready to leave orientation may be the primary impetus for termination of the orientation process. *Orientation to Emergency Nursing: Concepts, Competencies, and Critical Thinking* (ENA, 2000) focuses on competency-based orientation for the emergency nurse.

Education strategies for ongoing competency evaluation of staff include, but are not limited to:

- Skills fairs.
  - Staff are monitored by experienced nurses at various stations in the performance of selected, essential skills.
- Essential skills checklists.
  - Identify essential skills.
  - Skill performance is evaluated by designated experienced nurses throughout the year.
  - Compliance with utilization of skills checklists is enhanced when a completed checklist is required prior to annual performance appraisal.
- Continuing education.
  - Required in some states as part of maintaining competency.
  - Institutions often require a specified number of contact hours, even in states where continuing education is not mandated for professional licensure.
- Sharing expertise.
  - Strategy where the educator serves as a mentor for individual staff nurses who research and develop expertise in one or more areas of specialized nursing practice.
  - These experts provide in-services in their respective area of expertise and serve as a resource to other staff.

These educational strategies are somewhat limited since each strategy utilizes a time-limited demonstration of competency. Ongoing competency includes critical thinking, interpersonal relationship skills, and clinical expertise. Educational strategies for competency evaluation should be linked with ongoing processes that reflect competency, such as quality management and outcome management.

ANNUAL EDUCATION PLANNING

Curriculum development is the process to structure and organize educational experiences for development of a target population. A curriculum is defined as a program of learning activities designed to achieve specific educational goals (Bevis, 1989). It allows for systematic development of expertise through logical progression of learning activities and gives consideration to the changing environment and learner needs (Leroux, 1992). Curriculum development provides for thoughtful educational planning in a proactive manner as well as organized implementation of educational programming. A sequence of core educational opportunities enables the educator to build on previous knowledge and experiences when providing education.

All educational experiences in an acute health care setting cannot be mapped through curriculum development. When unexpected changes in practice or technology occur, educational programming must be developed and promptly implemented to meet urgent educational needs. Evaluation of educational outcomes as a component of curriculum development allows adaptation and response to changing needs of the learner and the environment.

CURRICULUM PLANNING

In most settings, the new educator finds many existing courses designed to meet staff learning needs. Examples of such programs include:

- Orientation.
- Specialty courses.
- Mandatory education programs.
- Continuing professional education seminars.

Despite the presence of existing educational programming, the new educator should develop an annual education plan. The education plan provides structure and focus to all educational endeavors. Development of an annual education plan includes the following steps:

- Identify current educational programming.
- Evaluate the effectiveness of existing educational programming in meeting current learning needs.
- Determine the need for additional programming.
- Identify educational opportunities to develop staff on the continuum from novice to expert (Benner, 1984).
- Map core educational programs.
- Identify continuing education programs.
- Market annual education plan.

CURRENT PROGRAMMING

The first step in annual planning is identification of existing programs. Current offerings should be systematically evaluated for effectiveness. Appropriate revision within the existing educational structure should be considered. The novice educator should maintain previously scheduled programs unless there is strong evidence to support change or deletion of an educational event. Evaluation of programs as they occur allows the educator to:

- Become familiar with the system and staff expectations.
- Determine if expected competencies are identified.
- Evaluate consistency of content and teaching strategies with expected outcomes.
- Decide if courses are logically sequenced to promote professional development.
- Critique strategies utilized to evaluate outcome.

ADDITIONAL PROGRAMMING

The second step of annual planning is to determine the need for additional programming. Given the educator's responsibility for required educational program, it is imperative that the educator define expectations for various positions (see Assessment of Learning Needs in this chapter). The following documents are valuable resources that can be used to define expectations of staff positions:

- Institutional mission statement.
- Departmental philosophy and conceptual framework.
- Institutional and departmental standards, policies, and procedures.
- Professional standards.
- JCAHO guidelines.
- OSHA standards.
- Center for Disease Control and Prevention standards.
- State regulations related to nursing care, particularly in specialty areas.
- Job descriptions and performance appraisal tools.

STAFF DEVELOPMENT

During the final phase of annual education planning, the educator should review and clarify professional expectations with those individuals who are accountable for maintaining standards of practice, i.e., directors of nursing, nurse managers, clinical specialists, risk managers, and quality management coordinators. Competency identification should progress through levels of professional development from novice to expert practitioner. "Nursing staff development educators are responsible for facilitating a successful transfer from acquiring context-free knowledge as a student to performing effectively in the new role of a professional nurse" (Avillion & Abruzzese, 1992, p. 35).

Orientation programs are designed to facilitate transfer of knowledge to clinical practice and to define expectations for beginning practice level competencies. Continuing education, in-services, and mandatory education build on beginning competencies and provide the framework for progression of courses in a curriculum design.

CORE PROGRAMMING

Thorough planning and mapping of the core educational program allows the educator to manage time and resources wisely. The core educational program consists of sequenced educational experiences for professional development of a target population. For the emergency nurse, minimal content of a core educational program is orientation and mandatory education defined by the institution and pertinent regulatory guidelines. Other educational experiences that may be included in the core educational program relate to use of increasingly complex technology, ongoing competency concerns, and continuing education. Additional educational requirements in the core program may consist of a prescribed number of continuing education hours related to practice area or participation in specialty courses designed by professional organizations, e.g., the Trauma Nursing Core Curriculum (ENA) or Advanced Cardiac Life Support (American Heart Association).

Mapping Tips

- Large wall-size calendars facilitate mapping because they provide immediate visualization of educational activities for the year.

- Educational events should be evenly distributed throughout the year.

Continuing Education Programs

In addition to the core education program, the educator must address changing learning needs of a diverse staff.

- Continuing education programs should be planned on an annual basis and included on a calendar of scheduled educational events.

- In-service education is provided in response to rapidly changing needs in the environment and allows for minimal long-range planning.

Marketing the Annual Plan

The annual education program should be approved through institutional protocol, then disseminated to all appropriate individuals and units. Education notebooks or annual calendars are two formats used to share information related to the core program and continuing education offerings. Course titles, dates, objectives, target audiences, teaching strategies, times, locations, and specific registration instructions should be posted. The calendar of education programs should be updated promptly as changes occur.

Long-Range Planning

Long-range planning uses goal setting to define future education programming in the health care setting. Long-range planning requires cooperation and collaboration of all members of the management team to effectively and efficiently meet educational needs of staff while supporting the institution's mission and long-range goals. Such plans should be guided by educational evaluations and projected trends in education and the health care industry. As a member of the management team, the educator must build relationships and initiate behaviors to create an environment that encourages and supports the integration of learned behaviors in the clinical setting.

CONTINUING EDUCATION CREDIT IN NURSING

The American Nurses Association (ANA) is the national professional association for registered nurses and is responsible for developing standards for professional development. Professional development can be described as the lifelong process of active participation in learning activities to enhance professional practice. While orientation and staff development refer to those learning activities designed to facilitate job-related performance, continuing education (CE) refers to professional learning activities designed to enrich the nurse's contribution to health care, therefore improving quality (ANA, 1994). These activities are not facility specific and include information that can be utilized across settings. CE activities meet specific criteria. It is important to remember that contact hours can only be awarded for learning activities that are continuing education in nature. Information related to in-service, basic nursing education, or mandatory education does not qualify for continuing education credit.

Approximately 20 states and three territories have continuing education requirements for both renewal of registration and reentry into active practice, or reactivation of a license for RNs, licensed practical/vocational nurses, and advanced practice nurses. In addition, nurses certified in professional specialty practice require contact hours to meet recertification requirements, e.g., the Certified Emergency Nurse (CEN®). Although professional nurses are responsible for their own professional development, employing organizations can support this by providing credit for educational programs.

The measure of participation in CE in nursing is the contact hour. Nursing no longer recognizes the Continuing Education Unit (CEU). One contact hour is equal to 50 minutes of an organized learning activity, either didactic or clinical. Time for breaks, lunch, etc., is not eligible for contact hour award.

Individual courses, seminars, conferences, and independent study activities can be approved for contact hour credit. There are **approvers** and **approved providers** of CE that can approve education activities for contact hour credit. Organizations, such as state nurses' associations or specialty organizations, undergo a formal review process to become nationally accredited as approvers of CE. ENA is an approver and provider of CE. An accredited approver can then approve courses for those that meet their application criteria. Qualified organizations can apply to be approved as providers of CE, by the state nurses' associations or specialty organizations. Your hospital/institution may be a provider.

APPLICATION PROCESS

There are two types of education activities that can be submitted for contact hour approval:

1. *Educational Design I (EDI)* – educational activity involving participant attendance. The pace of the activity is determined by the sponsor who plans and schedules the activity.

2. *Educational Design II (EDII)* – educational activity designed for completion by learners, independently, at the learner's own pace and at a time of the learner's choice.

Application to an approver: Approvers of continuing education have written guidelines for CE approval. There is usually a fee. ENA guidelines for CE submission can be obtained by calling the national office. The completed application is submitted and is approved if all criteria are met. The application needs to be submitted to the approver at least eight weeks prior to the date of the education activity.

Application to an approved provider: Approved providers of continuing education have a nurse planner who is required to be involved in planning, developing, implementing, and evaluating the education activity. This makes the process easier for those unfamiliar with CE approval.

It is important to be aware that retroactive approval is not permitted. Approval for contact hour credit cannot occur after the education activity has been presented, as approval must be granted prior to the first presentation of the activity.

Regardless of the approving body, CE approval requires:

1. Purpose

2. Objectives (content, time frame, teaching strategies, faculty)

3. Biographical data—documented qualifications, expertise of faculty

4. Evaluation method

A planning committee of experts should be assembled to plan the program according to the guidelines of the approver or provider, including date, time, place, financial resources, objectives, and content that will be presented. The activity is developed in response to the educational needs of potential participants. The appropriate speakers should be identified and reserved for the date of the program, and then included in any planning.

As the nursing knowledge base increases at a rapid rate, continuing education, although not mandatory in most states, is essential for nurses to maintain and increase competence in nursing practice. Many nurses are certified in specialties and must either meet continuing education requirements or be retested to maintain certification. Continuing education is necessary for nursing professional development, to enhance professional practice, and to maintain and improve quality health care.

Please refer to Appendix G for a sample application.

BEHAVIORAL OBJECTIVES

Program development begins with identification of the target audience. The next step is determination of what the participant should learn from the program, e.g., behavioral objectives. A brief description of behavioral objectives is provided below. For a comprehensive discussion of behavioral objectives, refer to Chapter 3.

Behavioral objectives are written by completing the following statement: "Upon completion of this program (course, lecture), the participant will be able to…"

GUIDELINES FOR BEHAVIORAL OBJECTIVES

- Objectives should be obtainable.
- The number of objectives should be appropriate for the program. Two to five objectives for a single program is reasonable.
- Learning is evaluated by measuring attainment of stated behavioral objectives.
  - Objective. Upon completion of this program, the participant will be able to name the four chambers of the heart.
  - Learning evaluation question. Name the four chambers of the heart.
- Combining objectives or asking too much in one objective makes it difficult to ascertain attainment of the objective.
  - Identify the vessels that carry deoxygenated blood and the vessels that carry oxygenated blood" is actually two objectives written as one. A learner may be able to identify only a portion of the objective, making evaluation difficult.
- A seminar with more than one lecture should have overall objectives for the seminar and specific objectives for each lecture.

BEHAVIORAL CATEGORIES

Behavioral objectives measure learning in various levels of cognition. Bloom's taxonomy is one system used to systematically categorize behaviors from the simplest to the most challenging. Specific categories are:

- Knowledge.
- Comprehension.
- Application.
- Analysis.
- Synthesis.
- Evaluation.

Within each category of Bloom's taxonomy, specific verbs are identified to measure accomplishment at that particular level. Written objectives should always begin with a measurable verb.

- Utilizing the previous example regarding the four chambers of the heart, the objective "Name the four chambers of the heart" measures knowledge. The verb "name" verifies knowledge.

- The objective "Contrast the four chambers of the heart" verifies analysis. A copy of Bloom's Taxonomy is provided at the end of the chapter in Appendix A and in *CECH Guidelines* (ENA, 1995).

OUTLINE

Once objectives have been established, an outline is created. The contact hour application must show the approving body the relationship between the objectives and the outline. This is the reviewer's only mechanism to determine that course content supports the objectives. An orderly, logical outline is essential.

SUGGESTIONS FOR OUTLINE WRITING

- Roman numeral I should relate to objective number 1; Roman numeral II should relate to objective number 2, etc.

- Under each Roman numeral use sequential capital letters to identify information pertinent to that particular Roman numeral.

- Table 6 presents an example of an outline that demonstrates the relationship between objectives and content.

The outline should include time allotment for each Roman numeral. Fifty minutes of content equals one contact hour. Total time on the outline should be the same as course time in the marketing brochure.

The final issue related to the time allotment and the outline is teaching method. The reviewer compares outline content and teaching method to determine appropriateness. Commonly used teaching methods include slides, lecture, handouts, and demonstration.

TABLE 6. OBJECTIVE DRIVEN OUTLINE

OBJECTIVES

Upon completion of this chapter, the participant will be able to:

1. Write two behavioral objectives.

2. Develop an outline that supports stated objectives.

OUTLINE

I. Behavioral Objectives

    A. Definition

    B. Purpose

    C. Measurement
       -Bloom's taxonomy

    D. Examples

II. Outline

    A. Content Identification

    B. Format
       -Relationship to objectives

    C. Examples
       -Relationship to objectives

                                               Basics and Beyond

BIOGRAPHICAL DATA FORMS

Biographical data forms are completed for each speaker, each member of the planning committee, and the activity coordinator. The form should include name, education, and experience related to the program topic. This documents speaker qualification and planning committee expertise.

EVALUATION

Participant feedback is vital for the continued success of education efforts. An evaluation should be completed for each speaker and lecture. An overall course evaluation should be completed when more than one lecture is offered.

EVALUATION CONTENT

The educator should identify specific evaluation requirements from the approving body. Most approving bodies require evaluations that answer the following questions:

- Was the speaker knowledgeable?
- Were the objectives obtained?
- Were audiovisuals beneficial?
- Was the environment conducive to learning?

Please refer to Appendix C for a sample participant evaluation form.

EVALUATION MONITORING

Some approving bodies require submission of summary evaluations. Others do not require summary evaluations; however, random audits are conducted throughout the year on records maintained by the activity coordinator. Most approving bodies require that evaluation records be kept for a minimum of four years.

PARTICIPANT ROSTER

Rosters provide the planning committee with names for completion of attendance certificates. Submission of participant rosters may or may not be required by the approving body. The approving body may randomly audit participant rosters or review them annually.

CERTIFICATES

Approving bodies may require use of a specific certificate or simply ask for specific information on a generic certificate. Typically, the information required on a certificate of attendance includes program name, date, location, activity coordinator, and number of contact hours obtained.

COST

Applying for contact hours is not extremely expensive. In addition to a possible charge for obtaining contact hour guidelines, there is a charge for the contact hours. This charge usually covers the cost to obtain the credits. Most approving bodies have a cost scale based on the number of contact hours. For example, a program with less than 10 contact hours may cost $30.00, a program with 10 to 20 contact hours may cost $50.00. This fee is usually paid regardless of program approval. Fortunately, most approving bodies work diligently with the program coordinator to assure program approval.

INDEPENDENT STUDY

A recent concept receiving approval for continuing education is independent study. Independent study may be a video, computer program, or monograph. Contact hour approval for independent study requires more information than traditional programs.

- Documentation of pilot studies. Time for program completion is determined from pilot studies.

- Evaluation tool to validate learning.

- Guidelines used to determine minimum score for contact hour award.

- Mechanisms for participant feedback.

REFERENCES

Abruzzese, R.S. (1992). Evaluation in nursing staff development. In R.S. Abruzzese (Ed.), <u>Nursing staff development: Strategies for success</u> (pp. 235-248). Philadelphia: Mosby.

American Nurses Association Council on Continuing Education. (1992). <u>Roles and responsibilities for nursing continuing education and staff development across all settings</u>.

Washington, DC: American Nurses Association.

American Nurses Association. (1994). <u>Standards for nursing professional development: Continuing education and staff development.</u> Washington, DC: American Nurses Publishing.

American Nurses Credentialing Center. (1996a). <u>American Nurses Credentialing Center's Commission on Accreditation manual for accreditation as a provider of continuing education in nursing</u>. Washington, DC: Author, 103-106.

American Nurses Credentialing Center. (1991). <u>Manual for accreditation as a provider of continuing education in nursing</u>. Washington, DC: American Nurses Association.

Atwood, H., & Ellis, J. (1971). The concept of need: An analysis for adult education. <u>Adult Leadership, 19</u>, 210-212, 244.

Avillion, A., & Abruzzese, R.S. (1992). Conceptual foundations of nursing staff development. In R.S. Abruzzese (Ed.), <u>Nursing staff development: Strategies for success</u> (pp. 29-44). Philadelphia: Mosby.

Benner, P. (1984). <u>From novice to expert: Excellence and power in clinical practice</u>. Menlo Park, CA: Addison-Wesley.

Bevis, E. (1989). <u>Curriculum building in nursing</u> (3rd ed.). New York: National League for Nursing.

Bloom, B. (Ed.). (1956). <u>Taxonomy of educational objectives, Handbook I: Cognitive domain</u>. New York: Longman.

Chaney, H. (1987). Needs assessment: A Delphi approach. <u>Journal of Nursing Staff Development, 3</u>(2), 48-53.

Cox, K., & Ewan, C. (1988). <u>The medical teacher</u>. New York: Churchill Livingstone.

DeSilets, L. (1998). Accreditation of continuing education: The critical elements. <u>The Journal of Continuing Education in Nursing 29</u>(5), 204-210.

Emergency Nurses Association. (2000). <u>CECH guidelines</u>. Des Plaines, IL: Author.

Emergency Nurses Association. (2000). <u>Orientation to emergency nursing: Concepts, Competencies, and Critical Thinking</u>. Des Plaines, IL: Author.

Gronlund, N. (1988). <u>How to construct achievement tests</u>. Englewood Cliffs, NJ: Prentice-Hall.

Joint Commission on Accreditation of Healthcare Organizations. (1999). <u>2000 Comprehensive manual for hospitals</u>. Chicago: Author.

Krathwohl, D., Bloom, B., & Masia, B. (1964). <u>Taxonomy of educational objectives, Handbook II: Affective domain</u>. New York: Longman.

Leroux, D. (1992). Curriculum planning and development. In R.S. Abruzzese (Ed.), <u>Nursing staff development: Strategies for success</u> (pp. 203-214). Philadelphia: Mosby.

Monette, M. (1977). Need assessment: A critique of philosophical assumptions. <u>Adult Education, 29</u>(2), 83-94.

Morton, P.G. (1991). The 10-minute learning break. <u>Journal of Continuing Education in Nursing, 22</u>(1), 39.

New Jersey State Nurses Association. (1992). <u>Continuing education approval program manual</u>. Newark, NJ: Author.

New York State Nurses Association. (1997). Bridging the Gap: Continuing education in nursing. New York: NYSNA.

Petersen, J. (1994). Increasing standards awareness through a fortune cookie contest. Journal of Continuing Education in Nursing, 25(1), 48.

Puetz, B. (1992). Needs assessment: The essence of the staff development program. In K. Kelly (Ed.), Nursing staff development: Current competence, future focus. Philadelphia: Lippincott.

Reilly, D., & Oermann, M. (1990). Behavioral objectives – Evaluation in nursing (3rd ed.). New York: National League for Nursing (Pub. No. 15-2367).

Schoessler, M., Yount, S., Marshall, D., & Gilson, M. (1991). Brief: Safety first – A board game for safety education. Journal of Continuing Education in Nursing, 22(6), 263.

Schoolcraft, V. (1989). A nuts-and-bolts approach to teaching nursing. New York: Springer.

Schweer, J. (1981). Defining behavioral objectives for continuing education offerings in nursing: A four level taxonomy. Thorofare, NJ: Charles B. Slack.

Yoder, R.E. (1990). Teaching tips. Journal of Continuing Education in Nursing, 21(6), 276.

Yoder-Wise, P.S. (1999). State and association/certifying boards CE requirements. The Journal of Continuing Education in Nursing 30(1), 5-12.

RECOMMENDED READINGS

Coffey, M., & Billiard, J.R. (1990). A comprehensive needs analysis equals training department credibility. Hospital Topics, 68(2), 27-28.

Discenza, D.J. (1993). A systematic approach to selecting and evaluating instructional materials. Journal of Nursing Staff Development, 9(4), 196-198.

Duchin, S., & Sherwood, G. (1990). Posters as an educational strategy. Journal of Continuing Education in Nursing, 21(5), 205.

Packard, S.A., Polifroni, C., & Shah, H.S. (1994). Rules and regulations governing nursing education. Journal of Professional Nursing, 10(2), 97-104.

Resko, D., & Chorba, M. (1992). Enhancing learning through use of games. Dimensions of Critical Care Nursing, 11(3), 173-177.

Speers, A.T. (1993). Crossword puzzles: A teaching strategy for critical care nursing. Dimensions of Critical Care Nursing, 12(6), 52-55.

Speers, A.T. (1993). Games in nursing staff development. Journal of Nursing Staff Development, 9(6), 274-277.

Stein, A. (1998). History of continuing nursing education in the United States. The Journal of Continuing Education in Nursing 29(6), 245-252.

Thompson, C., & Crutchlow, E. (1993). Learning style research: A critical review of literature and implications for nursing education. Journal of Professional Nursing, 9(1), 34-40.

Waddell, D.L. (1993). A reliable and valid evaluation instrument for continuing nursing education. Journal of Nursing Staff Development, 9(4), 184-187.

Wright, D. (1993). The princess and the chemo spill – A policy magically turned into a fairy tale. Journal of Continuing Education in Nursing, 24(1), 37.

APPENDIX A
BLOOM'S TAXONOMY

This is an excellent reference if one is unsure of writing behavioral objectives. Simply determine what it is that you would like your participant to accomplish, find an appropriate verb in the listings below, use that verb to begin your statement, and you have a behavioral objective. Different verbs can verify different products. If you want to verify knowledge, use a verb from the knowledge list, comprehension from that particular group, etc. Also included are a few samples of general objectives.

CATEGORY	VERB	EXAMPLE
Knowledge: knowledge involves the rather elementary skill of recalling or remembering specific information or experiences.	to: select, describe, recall, define, state, identify, recognize, name, and list	-Describe the stages of the so-called scientific "method." -Define the term "light." -State the relationship between temperature and pressure.
Comprehension: comprehension involves understanding or perceiving. It includes taking in, grasping, insight, and as such is highly stressed in school learning. Three subcategories of comprehension are recognized: translation, interpretation, and extrapolation.	Transform, predict, interpolate, extrapolate, interpret, translate, illustrate, draw, rearrange, reorder, explain, and associate	-Interpret the following situation. -Illustrate what is meant by a warranted and unwarranted conclusion. -Give two examples of the above rule.
Application: application involves using something in a specific manner. As such it includes relevancy, as well as the capacity for close attention to detail. The skill of application underlies a great part of school learning, and is intimately concerned with some of the primary objectives of education.	Plan, record, employ, use, revise, formulate, apply, show, demonstrate, investigate, perform, relate, develop, transfer, construct, and infer.	-Apply the principle of resistance to a novel situation in aerodynamics. -Transfer the concept of a field of force from physics to human behavior. -Infer the appropriate principle behind each of the following reactions.
Analysis: analysis involves the breaking down or separation of a whole into its component parts. In its simplest form, analysis includes a simple listing of elements.	Analyze, separate, break down, discriminate, distinguish, detect, categorize, compare, contrast, and diagram	-Analyze this topic into its component parts. -Distinguish the literary and stylistic techniques used in the following poem. -Categorize the relationship between the phenomena list above.
Synthesis: synthesis is the opposite of analysis. It involves combining together a number of elements in order to form a coherent whole.	Combine, restate, summarize, relate, generalize, conclude, derive, organize, design, deduce, classify, formulate, propose, and compose	-Summarize the normal cycle of erosion for streams and rivers. -Design a module describing the concept of the sonnet. -Propose three ways in which a hypothesis might be tested.
Evaluation: evaluation is concerned with making judgments about value.	Evaluate, judge, contrast, criticize, defend, support, attack, avoid, seek out, reorder, weigh, modify, verify, and decide	-Evaluate a curriculum in terms of its announced aims and agreed objectives. -Contrast two major theories accounting for the formation of volcanoes. -Decide the several advantages for using a taxonomy of educational objectives.

APPENDIX B
DISCLOSURE STATEMENT

DISCLOSURE STATEMENT

Please read the following statements carefully and place a check in the space opposite the statement which applies to you. A symbol beside your name in the final program will indicate your disclosure of some type of financial interest or affiliation with an organization.

Please note: (Your organization's name) does not view the existence of such interests or commitments as necessarily implying bias or decreasing the value of your participation.

_____ I, the undersigned, declare that neither I nor any member of my immediate family knowingly have a financial arrangement and/or direct affiliation with any corporate organization that may have direct interest in the subject matter of my presentation/publication.

_____ I, the undersigned (or an immediate family member), have a financial interest/arrangement or direct affiliation with a corporate organization that has a direct interest in the subject matter of my presentation/publication.

_____

Signature

_____

Print Name

_____

Date

Failure to disclose or false disclosure will require (your organization's name) to identify a replacement for your participation.

APPENDIX C
PROGRAM EVALUATION FORM

NAME OF PROGRAM _____

UNIT OR AREA OF EMPLOYMENT _____

Information provided on evaluation forms is used by individual speakers and course planners to improve future courses/presentations. Please circle the number or write in requested information that most closely matches your feelings in each area of evaluation. Thank you for your effort in honestly completing this form.

1	2	3	4
STRONGLY DISAGREE	DISAGREE	AGREE	STRONGLY AGREE

The objectives of this course were met.	1	2	3	4
The speakers were knowledgeable and well prepared.	1	2	3	4
The facilities provided an environment conducive to learning.	1	2	3	4
It appeared that this course was well organized.	1	2	3	4
The content of the course flowed in a logical fashion.	1	2	3	4
I will be able to apply the content of this course to my clinical practice.	1	2	3	4
I would recommend this course to a professional colleague.	1	2	3	4

Strengths of this course are: _____

_____

_____

_____

Suggestions for course improvement: _____

_____

_____

_____

Topics I would like to see presented in the future: _____

_____

_____

_____

Additional comments: _____

_____

_____

APPENDIX D
GUIDE TO PROGRAM PREPARATION

- Submit proposed program budget for approval.

- Determine the date and time of the program.

- Develop the beginning sections of the syllabus.

  ▮ Title, date, time, description, purpose, target audience, format, learning objectives, content outline (may be developed with faculty).

- Develop evaluation tool.

- Reserve room or facility.

  ▮ Inspect room or facility prior to reservation.

  ▮ Specify room design for seating, equipment, special needs.

  ▮ Reserve instructional equipment.

  ▮ Order food—snacks and meals. Verify cost and time limit required to confirm number of registrants.

- Contract with speakers.

  ▮ Make any necessary arrangements—transportation, parking, meals, hotel.

  ▮ Obtain disclosure statement and curriculum vitae resume if indicated.

- Support materials.

  ▮ Review and order texts or pertinent materials.

  ▮ Develop and print course packet (usually includes completed syllabus).

- Update syllabus.

  ▮ Location, speaker list, content outline, bibliography.

  ▮ Syllabus to print shop.

- Distribute confirmation letter and syllabus to each speaker.

- Apply for continuing education credit.

- Market the course.

  ▮ Mailings:

    ◆ Design brochure or flyer.

    ◆ Send to print shop.

    ◆ Obtain mailing labels.

    ◆ Mail or send to mailing distribution company.

- Advertisements:
  - ◆ Determine extent of advertising, e.g., national journals, local media.
  - ◆ Develop wording for advertisement.
  - ◆ Meet deadlines to utilize free advertising.
  - ◆ Design, print, and distribute flyers to in-house staff.
- Registration.
  - Develop roster of registrants.
  - Type and sign contact hour certificates.
  - Track money submitted for registration and materials.
  - Distribute "confirmation of registration" letter to registrants.
  - Produce name tags.
  - Arrange for assistance with conference registration.
  - Arrange for assistance with packing up at end of program.
  - Design and print directional signs if necessary.
- Peace of mind.
  - Review this list and reconfirm essential arrangements.
  - Package course materials to facilitate transport: attendance roster, name tags, course packets, printed materials, texts, evaluation tools, typed contact hour certificates, additional contact hour certificates, pens, pencils, tape, phone and beeper, list of all faculty.
  - Arrange for assistance in transporting supplies and materials.

APPENDIX E
GUIDE TO PROGRAM IMPLEMENTATION

- Before program starts:
  - Arrive early.
  - Post directional signs.
  - Verify room design.
  - Verify food arrangements.
  - Check operation of all equipment.
  - Set up registration table or instruct assistants.
  - Assist with registration.
- As the program begins:
  - Welcome participants.
  - Provide vital information.
    - ◆ Location of bathrooms, telephones, schedule of activities.
    - ◆ Pertinent information related to meals, continuing education credit information, evaluation process, upcoming events.
  - Welcome each speaker.
  - Introduce each speaker.
  - Verify contact hour certificates against attendance roster.
- Throughout the day:
  - Smile, appear relaxed, confer with speakers and registrants.
- As the program ends:
  - Thank participants and speakers.
  - Collect evaluations.
  - Distribute contact hour certificates.
  - Pack up materials and leave.

APPENDIX F
GUIDE TO PROGRAM COMPLETION

- Notify payroll of nonattendance if participants paid for attendance.

- Tally and review evaluations.

- Distribute thank-you letters and speaker evaluation results to faculty.

- Deposit checks and pay invoices.

- Submit required course paperwork for inclusion in education file.

- Note time to begin outcomes and impact evaluations if required.

APPENDIX G
APPLICATION FOR NURSING CONTINUING EDUCATION

NEW YORK-PRESBYTERIAN HOSPITAL
NEW YORK WEILL CORNELL CENTER
SCHOOL OF CONTINUING EDUCATION FOR NURSES

Approved as Provider of Nursing Continuing Education by the New York State Nurses Association's Council on Continuing Education.

Application for Approval
Nursing Continuing Education

Educational Design I (ED I)

Educational Design I (ED I) is an educational presentation which involves participant attendance. The approval period is two years.

SUBMIT FOUR (4) COPIES OF THE PACKET AND ALL ATTACHMENTS.
MAINTAIN THE MASTER COPY OF ALL SUBMISSIONS FOR YOUR RECORDS.

1. _____
   Education Design I Title

2. _____
   Date of First Scheduled Presentation

3. _____
   Name of Primary Sponsoring Agency

4. _____
   Address for Correspondence

5. _____
   Name and Title of Individual to Contact for Further Information

6. _____
   Number of Contact Hours Requested-Divide total time (in minutes) by 50

EDUCATION DESIGN I

> *An Education Design I (ED I) activity involves participant attendance. It is distinguishable by the fact that the pace of the activity is determined by a sponsor who plans, schedules, and presents the activity. Contact hour credit awarded is based on the time allocated for the activity. Examples of ED I activities include but are not limited to, conventions, courses, seminars, workshops, lecture video series, and distance learning activities such as telephone and audio conferences. Knowledge and use of adult learning principles should be reflected in all aspects of the education design (e.g., objectives, content, teaching methods, physical facilitates).*

I.   PLANNING

A.   Resources

1.   Name the administrator responsible for the activity.

_____

2.   Name two registered nurses involved as planners in the activity. (NOTE: At least one nurse must have earned a baccalaureate or higher degree in nursing).

_____

_____

3.   Identify faculty participation in the planning of their presentations.

☐ Development of objectives   ☐ Selection of handouts
☐ Development of content   ☐ Selection of teaching methods
☐ Other (please describe) _____

Complete the attachment entitled Biographical Data Form for the administrator, the nurse planners, and each faculty presenter. (Do not attach CV or any additional information to this form).

B.   Physical Facilities

Describe the facilities to be used in relation to how they will accommodate teaching strategies, environmental comfort and audience accessibility.

_____

_____

C.   Target Audience and Needs Assessment

1.   Indicate the target audience for this activity.

☐ Registered Nurses   ☐ Specific Registered Nurses

☐ Other (please describe) _____

2

2. Indicate the approximate number of learners per session _____

(In activities with a clinical component, group work or return demonstration, a learner/teacher ratio of more than 10 to 1 is suggested).

3. Identify how need was identified and how learner input was considered in such areas as content, location, and scheduling. (Check all appropriate boxes).

☐ Periodic Needs Survey   ☐ Informal Needs Assessment

☐ Analysis of Past Attendance   ☐ Past Program Evaluation

☐ Regulatory requirements   ☐ Institutional Policy

☐ Identified Need for Content Areas (i.e., findings from quality assurance, new issues and trends, technology, etc.)

☐ Other (please describe)_____

II.   DESCRIPTION OF THE ACTIVITY

A.   Purpose/Goals

The purpose must be consistent with ANCC's definition of continuing education, which is as follows: Continuing education in nursing consists of those planned activities intended to build upon the educational and experiential bases of the professional nurse for the enhancement of practice, education, administration, research, or theory development to the end of improving heath care to the public.

Describe the purpose of this activity, i.e. **who** is this activity for, **why** is this activity being held and **what** do you expect the learners to gain from attending.

_____
_____
_____

B.   Overview

Submit a brochure, flyer, or outline which lists each content/topic area and its time frame.

C.   Documentation of Representative Lesson Plan: Objectives, Content Outline, Time, Frame Teaching Strategies & Faculty.

*Note: If the activity is **150 minutes (3.0 contact hours)** or less, submit the ED I Documentation Format for the entire activity.*

*If the activity is longer than **150 minutes (3.0 contact hours)**, submit the ED I format for 150 minutes of the program that are representative of the overall activity. (It is expected that objectives, content, time allotments, teaching strategies, and faculty for the entire program be documented in your own records).*

3

III. VERIFICATION OF ATTENDANCE AND SUCCESSFUL COMPLETION

A. Identify how attendance will be determined (check all appropriate boxes).

☐ Sign In ☐ Roll Call ☐ Completion of Registration Forms

☐ Room Monitors ☐ Other (describe) _____

B. Identify criteria for successful completion.

☐ Attendance for Specified Time (describe) _____

☐ Post Test/Exam ☐ Skill Demonstration/Completion

☐ Submission of Evaluation Forms ☐ Other (describe) _____

If credit for attendance at any part of the activity is allowed (less than the entire activity), clarify how that is determined.

C. Documentation of Attendance

NYSNA criteria specify that the sponsor of an approved activity must provide each participant with a document containing the following information:

1. Successful completion of the educational activity.
2. Number of contact hours awarded.
3. Name and address of the sponsor of the educational activity.
4. Official statement of approval:
   "This activity has been approved by the New York States Nurses Association's Council on Continuing Education, which is accredited by the American Nurses Credentialing Center's Commission of Accreditation, and is assigned approval code _____."
5. Title, date, city and state (location) of the educational activity.

NOTE: *Clarify how different contact hours will be awarded for partial attendance, if allowed.*

With this application, please provide a sample of the certificate that will be awarded to learners.

IV. EVALUATION

The evaluation process must address the following areas:

A. Relationship of objectives to overall purpose.
B. Learner's achievement of objectives and content.
C. Appropriateness of teaching strategies.
D. Expertise of each individual presenter.
E. Appropriateness of the physical facilities.

4

Attainment of the activity's objectives can be evaluated in a number of ways: (1) actual measurement of objectives through such as exams, attitude measurement scales or performance checklists; (2) participants' evaluations of how well they believe they met the objectives through questionnaires with a rating scale.

Submit a copy of the evaluation instrument.

V. COSPONSORSHIP

(The process of planning, developing, and implementing an educational activity by two or more sponsors).

A. Is this activity cosponsored? ☐ YES ☐ NO

If **YES**, a copy of the cosponsorship agreement must be submitted.

B. If the activity is cosponsored, a written agreement must be developed between your agency and the cosponsors which states that **your organization is responsible** for:

1. Administration of the budget for the activity.
2. Determination of objectives and content.
3. Selecting faculty/presenters.
4. Awarding contact hours.
5. Recordkeeping for this activity.
6. Evaluation.
7. Copy of marketing material, e.g. brochures, announcements, flyers.

VI. RECORDKEEPING SYSTEM

A. A recordkeeping system must be established for this activity. You are required to maintain the following essential material for a period of five years:

1. A complete copy of the Education Design I application and all supporting documentation.
2. A copy of the certificate awarded to participants.
3. A summary of participants' evaluations.
4. Names and addresses of all participants and number of contact hours awarded to each.
5. The approval letter from provider indicating the code number and the contact hours awarded.
6. A cosponsorhip agreement (if applicable).

B. Briefly describe how records are stored and retrieved and how confidentiality is maintained: _____

_____

_____

_____

5

EDUCATIONAL DESIGN I DOCUMENTATION FORMAT

Objectives	Content (topics)	Time Frame	Faculty	Teaching Methods
List objectives in measurable behavioral terms, objectives must be consistent with the purpose. The learner will be able to:	List each topic area to be covered and provide a description or outline of the content to be presented.	List minutes for each topic post testing and evaluation	List the faculty person or presenter for each topic.	Describe the teaching method(s) used for each. (lecture, discussion, group work, Q & A, etc.)

CHAPTER 7

Concepts of Marketing and Promotion of Educational Activities

OBJECTIVES

Upon completion of this chapter, the emergency nurse educator will be able to:

1. Define marketing.

2. List three methods to solicit vendor support.

3. Define cost analysis.

INTRODUCTION

How does marketing relate to design and dissemination of nursing continuing education programs? Continuing education is a service that nurses purchase. Every continuing education program needs participants or customers to succeed and survive. Marketing must be based on understanding customers and their needs. Marketing is essential to attain participants for current and future programs.

The emergency nurse educator may not feel comfortable thinking of continuing education programs in terms of profits and losses. The educator may think money will interfere with the quality of the program. Just as financial resources have dried up for the participant, so is the case for the educator. It is unrealistic and foolhardy to ignore the importance of finances. Programs that do not at least break even or make a profit are short-lived. Many educators have also found it hard to gain administrative support for future projects if these events fail to self-propagate themselves financially. Getting the word out and making your program stand out from others is what it will take for continued success.

MARKETING TERMINOLOGY

Many terms used in marketing literature may not be familiar to the emergency nurse educator. This section provides an overview of key marketing terms.

- **Market.**
  - Refers to the population you are targeting. This is "who the customers or participants are" (Shragge, 1989, p. 18).
  - Is not synonymous with marketing. It defines the specific group that you want to attend the program.
- **Marketing.**
  - Refers to a process. This is the process that educators utilize to make the target population aware of the product (or program).

- ∎ "All the things a business does to get goods and services from the producer to the consumer in such a way that the consumer is satisfied and the producer has met the objectives of his or her organization" (Schragge, 1989, p. 25).

- ∎ "A social and managerial process by which individuals and groups obtain what they need and want through creating and exchanging products and values with others" (Kotler, 1988, p. 3).

- **Marketing research.**

  - ∎ Refers to a "systematic process of designing the study of a specific marketing problem, collecting and analyzing the data, and reporting findings" (Alward & Camunas, 1991, p. 69).

- **Marketing orientation.**

  - ∎ Also called customer orientation.

  - ∎ Implies the energy from the individual or the organization that is focused on identifying the needs and wants of its customers and delivering services that satisfy these needs or desires.

- **Market plan.**

  - ∎ Detailed business plan tailored to the organization's product, services, and customers.

  - ∎ Well-prepared market plan involves extensive market research.

  - ∎ Elements of a market plan include the four Ps of marketing: product, price, place, and promotion.

  - ∎ A sample market plan is presented below.

MARKET PLAN

This sample market plan addresses continuing education programs for emergency nurses inside or outside the institution. The plan is modeled on the plan in *Marketing for a Small Business* (Alberta Economic Development and Trade Department, 1989). It is intended as a practical exercise. Not all marketing plans involve a series of direct questions; however, answering these questions provides structure to the process of market plan development. By answering these questions, you have given your business a great deal of thought and have a greater chance of success. Answering these questions often requires detailed market research for an actual market plan. The responses provided in this exercise are intended as examples.

GENERAL INFORMATION

What business are you really in?

- Define the business from the customers' point of view.

- Describe personal improvement, networking opportunities, social opportunities, and investment in the future.

What are the main products or services you offer?

- Activities, such as workshops, evening seminars, conferences, and short courses are both product and service.

What do you do best?

- Provides a basis for setting marketing objectives. Examples may include:

  - ∎ Offer current, timely topics relevant to emergency nurses.

- Use innovative, creative teaching methods, e.g., small group dynamics, case studies, increase participant participation.

- Adhere to principles of adult learning.

- Maintain awareness of adult stages of development.

- Demonstrate sensitivity to multiple life demands of nurses (try to offer program at times and in sufficient quantity to meet the needs of your target audience).

- Demonstrate awareness of current issues regarding formal degrees, mandatory continuing education, and specialty certification.

What business do your customers think you are in? What are they buying? What does your product or service really do for people?

- Define your business position in the community (let your nurses, administrators, other EDs in the area, and other health care providers know who you are).

- Conduct market research to answer these questions.

  - Qualitative methods include interviews with emergency nurses and other local educators.

    - Interviews can be formal and scheduled or informal and impromptu during the course of a workday or social outing.

  - Quantitative methods include a short, concise questionnaire distributed at workshops and conferences.

    - These methods are similar to techniques used for needs assessment. Refer to Chapter 6 for additional discussion of needs assessment.

How many customers do you have?

- Identify size of existing markets (number of EDs in market area).

- Review attendance records over several years to identify demographic trends related to the number and origin of participants.

How large is your potential market?

- Estimate the potential market and the total market for all businesses of this type.

- Determine the number of emergency nurses in your area. Membership lists can be purchased from various nursing organizations such as:

  - Emergency Nurses Association.

  - Air and Surface Transport Nurses Association.

  - American Association of Critical Care Nurses.

  - State licensing body for nursing.

    (Professional organization member lists will only list a fraction of the actual number of target nurses in a given geographic area.)

  - Identify other nursing groups who may be interested in emergency nursing continuing education programs (e.g., ambulatory care, school nurses, etc).

What is your approximate share of the market?

- Compare the total number of potential customers with the number of actual customers.

- How many other educators are also marketing their programs in your area?

How many competitors do you have? In town? In the state? Outside the state?

- Potential sources of information on competitors include:
  - Business directories (including telephone directory) may indicate educators or consultants who may impact your market share.
  - Brochures on similar programs mailed to individuals and hospitals.
  - Notices of upcoming education programs listed in nursing journals, e.g., *Journal of Emergency Nursing*, or local/regional nursing periodicals, e.g., *Nursing Spectrum or Newletters*.
  - Word of mouth on upcoming programs.

What strengths do your competitors have that you don't?

- Examine available sources of information on the competition.
- Formulate a chart or table comparing your programs with the competition.

What are your business resources?

- Identify all resources available to you.
- Realistic marketing objectives are based on available resources, i.e., personnel, services, space, and administrative support.
- The marketing budget is derived from available resources.

How does your share of the market compare with your resources?

- Should you compete with competitors head-to-head or reposition the business to minimize competition and attract different customers?
- Study the competition to estimate their sales and customers.
  - Attend a competitor's program to investigate the competition.
  - Become a member of competitor mailing lists.
    - ◆ This provides constant information on competitor activities.
  - Telephone the competition and obtain information by posing as a potential customer.
    - ◆ This yields information on the competitor's service image.
  - Speak with nurses who attended competitors' programs to obtain details not available by other methods.

TARGET MARKETS

- Define your target population.
  - Develop a profile of customers based on:
    - ◆ Demographic information, such as age, sex, marital status, and number and age of children.
    - ◆ Years of nursing experience.
    - ◆ Years of emergency nursing experience.
    - ◆ Educational background.
    - ◆ Current job description.
    - ◆ Geographic location of residence and employment.

- ◆ Salary.

- ◆ Pursuit of education for formal degree.

  ▮ A written survey conducted at the end of education sessions, professional meetings, and by mail to selected zip codes facilitates development of a customer profile.

When do customers attend programs? Are certain times of year more popular than others?

- • Include a survey question on the number of continuing education sessions attended per year and when the sessions were held.

How will your target markets change next year? In five years?

- • Awareness of changing trends in emergency care, hospital staffing, and economic predictions is essential for long-term marketing and planning.

- • A survey question related to customers' plans for formal education courses may forecast decreased enrollment in continuing education programs.

PRODUCT/SERVICE

- • Determine which products or services to emphasize in the marketing plan.

- • Identify the products or services that appeal to the target markets.

What are the main products or services sold by the business? How do they appeal to specific target customer groups? What are the benefits to customers? Should any products/services be phased out? Should any products/services be added?

- • List education programs offered by your organization during the last five years.

- • Review evaluations to determine which programs received the highest marks.

- • Structure survey questions to identify reasons for the high rating.

- • Look at attendance figures for repeat sessions.

  ▮ Was attendance better or worse than the first offering?

- • Word of mouth is a powerful source of advertisement.

- • Review suggestions for future programs.

  ▮ If any of the suggested programs were offered, were they well attended?

- • Brainstorm to identify potential topics and speakers.

- • Keep a list of the most popular instruction techniques and educational formats.

- • Consider a theme for programs one day or more in length.

  ▮ Select topics and speakers to support the theme.

- • Track consumer trends in continuing education and in lifestyle.

  ▮ Read emergency care and continuing education publications.

  ▮ Watch the top 10 television shows and movies to identify influences on consumer behaviors and purchasing decisions.

  ▮ Speak with at least 100 customers per year regarding continuing education programs they attend and why they selected specific programs.

PRICE

- The best pricing strategy for a given product and service depends on multiple factors, e.g., speaker fees, travel expenses, and local education market.

- Awareness of these factors is essential for competitive pricing strategies.

Do present prices cover all costs? Does the pricing method account for speaker fees, promotional costs, supplies for the programs? Are meals/refreshments included with the program price?

- Look at budgets from past courses to determine profit status.

  - Did the course make a profit, lose money, or break even?

  - Determine the philosophy of your organization.

    - Is making a profit one of the goals?

    - Does the organization wish to provide a service at a break-even price rather than at a profit?

  - Most organizations strive to break even or make a profit.

  - There may be times when a program is offered to a few enthusiastic learners if the loss can be offset by other profitable programs.

Tips for effective pricing:

- People want value for their education dollars.

- Make your prospective participants think they are getting a good value.

  - Offer programs for $99.00 instead of $100.00.

- Offer a discount for early registration.

  - Conferences may identify several prices based on target registration dates.

- Offer group rates.

  - Discount registration when three people register together or three people register from the same institution at the same time.

- Start a Frequent Attendee club.

  - Offer a 50% discount for the fourth program the participant attends.

- Offer member discounts when the program is offered through a professional association.

- When program length is two days or more, offer a purchasing option for participants to attend only one or two days.

  - To attract participants for the entire program, the price for the entire program is usually less than combined daily fees.

- Identify items covered by the course fee, such as program, syllabus, refreshments, lunch, continuing education credits, etc.

  - All items covered should be clearly identified in the program brochure.

- Establish firm deadlines for registration and refunds.

  - The refund policy should be clearly stated in the program brochure.

  - If registration will be accepted at the door for the same or a higher fee, state this in the brochure.

- Use previous evaluations to determine if a meal is included in the price.

I If participants will be responsible for their own lunch, the location should provide accessible restaurants.

• Handouts enhance the image and effectiveness of any offering.

I The price of the program should include handouts.

• Consider vendor sponsorship for the event.

I Vendor contributions lower the price. See the section titled "Vendors" later in this chapter for a more detailed discussion.

PLACE

• The location should be suitable to the type of program and convenient for the participants.

What locations are currently utilized for continuing education programs?

• Programs can be held in a variety of locations.

I Hospital conference rooms, hospital auditoriums, hotels, convention centers, universities/colleges, and schools of nursing are just a few possible locations.

I Advantages and disadvantages are discussed in Appendix A.

• The site must complement the objectives and format of the meeting while satisfying physical and logistical requirements.

• Site selection requires six basic steps:

I Identify objectives for the educational event.

I Develop the format of the event.

I Determine physical requirements (see Appendix B).

I Define participant interests and expectations.

I Select the general area and type of facility.

I Evaluate potential sites.

• Some programs include on-site child care for participants with small children.

I This should be considered if the target market has a significant number of participants unable to attend without on-site child care.

PROMOTION

• Evaluate existing promotional methods and determine a promotional mix to reach target markets. Budget issues related to promotion are discussed later in this chapter.

How do you best reach and inform your existing customers?

• Look at promotional methods used for past programs.

• Include a question on the program registration or evaluation form related to how the participant learned of the program.

I Answers identify effective promotional methods.

I Word of mouth is still a powerful form of advertising.

How will you best reach participants?

- Use color, diagrams, and photographs for program posters and brochures whenever possible.

  ▮ Desktop publishing software produces attractive brochures at a minimal cost.

  ▮ Clip art is a good source of copyright-free pictures and diagrams.

- Have posters and brochures available at least three months before the program.

- Take advantage of free advertising in the *Journal of Emergency Nursing* and other journals read by your target market.

  ▮ Check with magazine staff for deadlines.

  ▮ Three to six months advance notice is standard.

- Post a program listing on the Internet.

- Utilize your sponsoring institution's website to post a program listing.

- If the educator has a website then that will also be utilized.

- Some hospitals permit local advertising with employee paychecks.

- Employee newsletters are another way to publicize educational events free of charge.

- Utilize designated bulletin boards for in-house promotion.

  ▮ This method reaches a broad spectrum of customers.

- If the program theme or topic has public appeal, issue a press release.

  ▮ Invite the media.

  ▮ This helps with advance publicity and coverage on the day of the event.

  ▮ Public exposure is good advertising for future events.

- Distribute promotional material for future sessions at a current session.

  ▮ Conclude the program with announcements of upcoming events.

- Include positive testimonials from past participants in brochures.

  ▮ Obtain appropriate consent.

- Use action words to describe program objectives, content, and speakers.

  ▮ Information in the brochure should help participants determine if the program will meet their needs.

  ▮ There will be dissatisfied customers if the content is more basic or advanced than indicated by the brochure.

- Include a map of the surrounding area with the program location highlighted.

- Secure parking, when possible.

  ▮ Advertise this in the brochure.

- Include considerations for hotel/motel listing as needed.

- Identify the type and number of continuing education credit hours applied for or approved.

- If your event targets participants outside your institution, develop a comprehensive mailing list.

  ▮ Obtain the names of key individuals in outside agencies for future mailings.

  ▮ Use follow-up telephone calls to determine receipt of brochures.

▌ Mailing lists can be purchased from nursing organizations, e.g., ENA, universities, colleges, and licensing boards.

ADVERTISE YOUR PROGRAM IN PRINT

Reaching your market is not as difficult as you might think. There are several methods the educator can use to "get the word out" about a program.

Post Signs in the Targeted Clinical Areas

Placing colorful signs in areas that are frequently visited by staff will assist in getting the attention of your staff. Avoid wordy signs and placing more than two or three signs in an area at any given time (you will overload your staff and they won't read any of them). Place signs in areas where the staff will go to relax, such as the lounge, break room, locker room, and even the bathroom.

Advertise in Your Local Nursing Newspaper

Many metropolitan areas have nursing news publications marketed to nurses and health professionals in a specific city or geographic region. These news publications are an excellent way to market your program. For approximately $50-$100 your program can be seen by hundreds or thousands of nurses.

Journal of Emergency Nursing

The *Journal of Emergency Nursing (JEN)* provides complimentary continuing education listings for educators. This is a great way to get your program noted internationally. For additional information contact the Journal at ENA's website.

Website Advertisement

If you have a website or access to a website you can promote your program to the world and add graphics and animation. Consult your institution's web administrator for details. Many local and state ENA chapters have web sites that list upcoming education events. Contact your local or state president for information.

FLYERS AS A SOURCE OF PROGRAM PROMOTION

Flyers are the most commonly used method to promote educational activities. Distribution may be limited to key areas within an institution or extend to local, regional, or national arenas. Flyers effectively advertise a single education program or a series of educational offerings. The cost of flyer development and mailing is a marketing and budgetary consideration.

Advantages:

- Serves as marketing tool for the institution.
- Advertises educational events to numerous individuals.

Disadvantages:

- Return on the dollar is directly related to participant response. A poor response is a poor return on the dollar because of costs for labor and mailing.

Tips for designing a flyer:

- Consult someone familiar with graphic design or an informational text on layout and design. Some health care agencies have a graphics, art, or advertising department to assist with the production of advertising material.

- Include essential information for registration and attendance.
  - ▌ Program name.
  - ▌ Date, time, and location.
  - ▌ Registration instructions and fees.
  - ▌ Name and telephone number of contact person.

- Minimize the number of inquiring phone calls by including:
  - ▌ Purpose and description of the course.
  - ▌ Target audience.
  - ▌ Faculty and their qualifications.
  - ▌ Content outline.
  - ▌ Continuing education credit.
  - ▌ Evaluation strategies.

- Provide the following for attendees not familiar with the institution or location:
  - ▌ Travel routes.
  - ▌ Mass transit.
  - ▌ Parking availability and fees.
  - ▌ Specific room location.
  - ▌ Meal arrangements.

- Design flyer with following considerations in mind:
  - ▌ Standard format and cover design provides visual recognition.
  - ▌ Sequence information logically.
  - ▌ Use no more than two type/font styles per flyer.
  - ▌ Avoid use of all capital letters. Text entirely in capital letters is difficult to read.
  - ▌ Use **bold** for emphasis.
  - ▌ Use short, concise sentences.
  - ▌ Avoid jargon.
  - ▌ Judicious use of color increases cost but does enhance design.

- Flyer should be proofread carefully by at least two individuals before distribution. Ideally, one person should be experienced in design and distribution of flyers.
  - ▌ If the format is new or represents a change from a previous design, circulate the flyer to a pilot group before distributing it.

VENDORS/EXHIBITORS

A vendor exhibition held in conjunction with an educational event benefits participants and vendors alike. Exhibits are often the largest nontuition, revenue-producing activity for the sponsoring organization. Revenue is produced when the sponsor sells exhibit space to vendors. If a hotel or convention center is used, the sponsor initially leases the exhibit space from the hotel or convention center, then sells to the vendor at a profit. Vendor revenue provides a significant amount of the money required for an event, allowing the sponsor to offer programs at a reasonable rate.

Exhibits or vendor displays should complement the education program. Equipment and products should interest the participants. For example, a program on cardiac care should target exhibitors of monitoring equipment, defibrillators, and cardiac pharmaceuticals.

Advantages of Vendor Exhibits

- Generates revenue for the educational event.

- Provides hands-on education with new products.

- Allows comparison shopping for products.

- Enables vendors who do business with the program sponsor to show their appreciation as well as educate staff about products.

- Enhances clinical practice through educational products, such as pocket guides, calipers, etc.

- Adds variety to an event.

- Provides activity during refreshment and meal breaks.

- Permits vendors to view competitive lines and new products presented by other exhibitors.

- Encourages participants to discuss ideas for new products with vendors.

Considerations When Using Vendors

- Federal Drug Administration (FDA) Guidelines.

  - There are certain ethical concerns related to vendor involvement.

  - The FDA has published the guidelines titled, **Final Guidance on Industry-Supported Scientifc and Educational Activities Notice.** A copy of this document can be viewed at the FDA web-site at at www.fda.gov.

- Complying with Continuing Education Unit requirements.

  - In response to the FDA guidelines, many organizations have developed their own guidelines related to vendor support and sponsorship.

  - When vendors are included in an educational event, ensure compliance with applicable guidelines.

  - Appendix C provides an example of guidelines for commercial vendor support of continuing medical education.

- Recognition.

  - Vendors may not provide an exhibit, but may wish to contribute financially to the event.

  - Ways to recognize these contributions include:

    - List contributors in the syllabus or handout.

    - Display a large poster of all contributors at the registration table or in the refreshment area.

- ♦ Acknowledge contributors during opening or closing remarks.
- ♦ When a vendor sponsors a meal or coffee break, post signs in the area to recognize the sponsors.
  - Budget enough time to allow participants to visit with vendor
  - Combine breaks with vendor exhibitions to maximize vendor time

DEVELOPING THE VENDOR PACKAGE

Information sent to prospective vendors should describe what is expected as a result of participation and the costs of such participation. The following information has been adapted from *Professional Meeting Management, Third Edition* (Polivka, 1998).

EVENT IDENTIFICATION

- Name of sponsoring organization.
- Title of educational event.
- Place and dates of the exhibition.
- Event format.
- Name, address, and telephone number of the contact person for the exhibition.

MARKET IDENTIFICATION

- Brief profile of the organization.
- Profile of expected participants.
  - ▎ Who they are and what they do.
- Anticipated number of participants.
- Previous exhibition locations and attendance by profession or field of interest.
- Types of products and services of interest to participants.

EXHIBIT DESCRIPTION

- Specific location.
- Dates and hours for move-in and deadline for completion of the setup.
- Dates and hours the exhibition is open to participants.
- Dates and hours for move-out and time when dismantling must be finished.
- Method of booth assignment, e.g., first-come, first-served, lottery, etc.
- Size of available space.
- Number of tables, chairs, and tablecloths that will be provided.
- When the event is longer than one day, indicate availability of overnight security in the exhibit area.

VENDOR COSTS AND BENEFITS

- Cost of booth space.
- Cost of other options for event contributions, e.g., coffee breaks, sponsoring a guest speaker, sponsoring a meal, general monetary contributions, sponsoring the printing of the event syllabus.
- Methods for recognizing vendor contributions.
- Number of vendors permitted per exhibit.
  - Many exhibits limit vendor participation to two vendors, including lunch and refreshment breaks for the vendor.
  - If the company exceeds the specified number of vendors, the company must pay for the meal and refreshment breaks for extra vendors.
- Opportunity for vendors to attend the educational program if space permits.
- Availability of a vendor lounge.

VENDOR REGISTRATION

- A registration form is necessary if large numbers of vendors are anticipated.
  - Provide a space for vendors to indicate electrical requirements.
  - Ask vendors to indicate pieces of equipment larger than original space allotment, e.g., stretchers and beds.
- Deadline for registration and receipt of fees.
- Provide information on local hotels and restaurants if there will be vendors from out of town.
- If event is at a hotel and a block of rooms has been reserved for participants, pass this information on to vendors.

DEVELOPING A PROGRAM BUDGET

Many emergency nurse educators have limited experience formulating and adhering to a budget. With growing limits on education resources, proficiency at budgeting is essential for nurse educators. This section is not intended to replace formal training in budget design. Many nursing administration courses include an entire module on working with a budget. Basic definitions, rationale for skilled budget preparation, and references are provided.

BUDGET TERMINOLOGY

Budget

- "An operational financial plan, stated in terms of income and expense, which covers all phases of activity for future division of time. It is a document that expresses a plan of operation in action" (Swansburg, 1993, p. 105).

Revenue

- "Income from sale of products and services" (Swansburg, 1993, p. 106).
- In education departments, revenue comes from tuition, grants, donations, and vendors.

Expenses

- "The costs of providing services . . . they are frequently called overhead and include wages and salaries, fringe benefits, supplies, food service, utilities and office supplies" (Swansburg, 1993, p. 106).

Budget Specifics for Educational Programs

The nurse educator may be required to justify dollars dedicated to personnel development. Cost-benefit analysis "compares the dollars spent on the staff development program with the dollar benefits expected of the program" (Kelly, 1992, p. 147). Cost analysis and cost-benefit analysis of educational programming are growing areas of research; it is essential that education programs demonstrate productivity and effectiveness. Without program effectiveness and efficiency, education budgets will be among the first cut when resources are slim.

COST ANALYSIS

Kelly (1985) outlined specific items related to cost analysis. These items can be used as categories for your budget.

- Planning costs, including salary and benefits of the planning committee and the education specialist.
- Cost of curriculum development, usually includes the education specialist's salary.
  - May also include resources, such as books and library search costs.
- Faculty fees, including travel and lodging. May include development of materials and audiovisuals.
- In-house instructor salary and benefits.
- Coordinator salary and benefits.
- Secretary and clerical support, including salary and benefits.
- Program expenses, such as folders, work materials, and name tags.
- Software and hardware, such as films, videos, and equipment.
  - Prorate cost over life of the materials.
- Marketing costs, including brochure development, printing, postage, and mailing.
- Telephone expenses.
- Program administration costs.
- Overhead, such as rental space.
- Miscellaneous supplies.
- Learner salaries.
- Replacement costs for learners if overtime is necessary to replace learners in the clinical area

Reporting a cost analysis without delineation of the associated benefits is an incomplete study. Educational outcomes quantify the benefits of education efforts. A cost-benefit analysis should be included in an overall financial analysis to demonstrate program effectiveness.

BENEFITS OF EDUCATION PROGRAMS

- Improved patient care.
- Decreased length of stay.

- More efficient care delivery.

- Decreased errors.

- Reduced turnover.

- Decreased absenteeism.

- Less medical supply use.

- Fewer worker's compensation claims.

- Decreased litigation costs.

- Fewer grievances.

- Increased productivity.

- Higher employee job satisfaction (Kelly, 1992, p. 148).

FORMULATING A BUDGET

- Model the budget for a specific event or department on other budgets within the institution.

  ▌ Administrators use a model for the institution budget, specific guidelines, and essential terminology.

  ▌ Utilize the institution's experts in the field of financial planning for assistance with the budget process.

- Refer to Appendix D for a sample budget of a two-day educational conference.

  ▌ The sample budget incorporates hospital space used at no charge, outside catering, hospital catering, local speakers, and outside speakers.

REFERENCES

Alberta Economic Development and Trade Department. (1989). <u>Marketing for a small business</u>. Edmonton, Alberta: Author.

Alward, R., & Camunas, C. (Eds.). (1991). <u>The nurse's guide to marketing</u>. Washington, DC: Delmar.

Federal Register (1997). <u>Final Guidance on Industry-Supported Scientific and Educational Activities Notice 62</u>(232), 64, 073-64, 100.

Herkimer, A. Jr. (1978). <u>Understanding hospital financial management</u>. Rockville, MD: Aspen.

Kelly, K. (1985). Cost-benefit and cost-effectiveness analysis: Tools for the staff development manager. <u>Journal of Nursing Staff Development, 1</u>, 9-15.

Kelly, K. (1992). <u>Nursing staff development</u>. Philadelphia: Lippincott.

Kotler, P. (1988). <u>Marketing management: Analysis, planning, and control</u> (6th ed.). Englewood Cliffs, NJ: Prentice-Hall.

Polivka, E.G. (1998). <u>Professional meeting management</u> (3rd ed.). Birmingham, AL: Professional Convention Management Association.

Shragge, P. (1989). <u>Starting your own consulting business</u>. Edmonton, Alberta: Northern Alberta Institute of Technology.

Swansburg, R. (1993). <u>Introductory management and leadership for clinical nurses</u>. Boston: Jones and Bartlett.

RECOMMENDED READINGS

Aghababian, R. V., & Volturo, G. A. (1997). Marketing and outreach. In Salluzzo, R. F., Mayer, T.A., Strauss R. W., et al (Eds.). Emergency department managment: Principles and applications. pp. 817-821. St. Louis: Mosby.

Kotler, P., & Clarke, R. (1987). <u>Marketing for health care organizations</u>. Englewood Cliffs, NJ: Prentice-Hall

Nelson, L.J., Staebell, S.L., & Cooper, J.W. (1987). Marketing and public relations for the ED. In J.H. van de Leuv (Ed.). <u>Management of emergency services</u>, pp. 133-137. Rockville, MD: Aspen.

Tilbury, M., & Fisk, T. (1989). <u>Marketing and nursing: A contemporary view</u>. Owing Mills, MD: National Health Publishing.

van de Leuv, J.H. (1987). Public relations in the ED. In J.H. van de Leuv (Ed.). <u>Management of emergency services</u>, pp. 139-145. Rockville, MD: Aspen.

Wilson, S. (1992). Market research techniques-A synopsis for CE providers. <u>Journal of Continuing Education in Nursing, 23</u>(4), 182-183.

APPENDIX A
CHOOSING THE LOCATION FOR
AN EDUCATIONAL EVENT

ADVANTAGES	DISADVANTAGES

Hospitals

• Often free.	• May not provide sufficient space. Space is difficult to obtain in a hospital.
• Good PR.	
• Catering may be less expensive.	• In-house participants may want a change.
• Can use own instructional equipment.	• Hospital catering may not provide adequate selection.
• Can use hospital staff as on-site workers and avoid expensive hotel staff.	

Hotel/Convention Center

• More space available.	• Must reserve early.
• Good choice of catering.	• Catering is expensive.
• May have free parking.	• Rush hour traffic may be problem in urban setting.
• Often pleasant surroundings.	• Pay for instructional media, equipment, and staff.
• Convenient for out-of-town speakers and participants.	
• Staff trained to assist with conferences. Able to troubleshoot.	

Universities/Colleges

• Often free of charge.	• Space limited during school.
• May use outside catering.	• Catering is expensive.
• Often no charge for instructional equipment.	• Large campuses confusing. Need many signs to direct participants to the event.
• Parking available.	

APPENDIX B
DETERMINING PHYSICAL
REQUIREMENTS FOR YOUR EDUCATIONAL EVENT

Utilize the following questions to determine space requirements for any educational event:

- What has been the attendance at previous events of this type?

- What is anticipated attendance for this event?

- How many rooms will be required?

    ▮ Large rooms for keynote speakers and/or smaller break-out session rooms.

- How many rooms will be used simultaneously?

- What is the estimated attendance for each individual session of this event if there will be more than one?

- Are the participants to be seated theater-style or classroom-style?

    ▮ Theater style mimics an auditorium.

    ▮ Classroom style is set up with tables.

- Is space needed in or near the room for refreshment breaks?

- Are rooms with high ceilings and no columns needed because the event will include film or slide projection?

- Does the audiovisual equipment supplier need a headquarters or storage room?

- Will a room be needed where speakers may review their slides and prepare for their presentations?

- Are there exhibits in conjunction with the meeting?

- Is a room needed for guest/exhibitor hospitality?

- How large a registration area is required?

- Is a storage space for registration materials needed?

- How many food and beverage functions will be held?

    ▮ When will these functions be held?

- What restroom facilities are required?

- What parking facilities are required?

Basics and Beyond

APPENDIX C
GUIDELINES FOR COMMERCIAL VENDOR
SUPPORT FOR CONTINUING EDUCATION

COMMERCIAL SUPPORT OF EDUCATIONAL OFFERINGS

Educational offerings are provided by the Emergency Nurses Association (ENA) with the intent of enhancing the knowledge base of emergency nurses. ENA often receives financial and other means of support from commercial organizations to assist in providing educational offerings of high quality.

ENA supports the policy statement established by the Food and Drug Administration regarding Industry-Supported Scientific and Educational Activities. In an effort to adhere to this statement, the following guidelines have been developed and enforced by ENA.

CONTENT

1. ENA, as the provider, will be responsible for the design and implementation of educational offerings.

2. All offerings will be educational and nonpromotional in nature.

3. Any products discussed in an educational offering will be objective, balanced, and have scientific merit. When a product of the sponsoring company is an important element of an educational offering, the presenter will ensure that the data regarding the company product and competitive products will be objectively presented with a fair representation of both favorable and unfavorable information.

4. If unapproved uses of a product are discussed, the presenter will disclose that the product usage is unapproved.

PRESENTER

1. ENA is ultimately responsible for the planning of program content including the selection of presenters and moderators. Sponsors agree to play no role in the selection of presenters other than responding to ENA requests for recommendations or sources of possible presenters. ENA also will consider opinions from other sources and make an independent judgment to determine the most appropriate presenter for the topic.

2. All presenters and moderators will be required to complete an ENA Disclosure Statement.

3. ENA will disclose to program participants those presenters or moderators that have a specific relationship with the sponsoring company.

SPONSORS

1. ENA will disclose to program participants the sponsors of offerings.

2. No promotional products or advertisement will be distributed in the program room before, during, or after an educational offering.

3. Exhibit placement has no relationship to the consideration of an educational offering.

4. Educational events will take precedence over commercially sponsored social events.

APPENDIX D
SAMPLE BUDGET
TWO-DAY EDUCATIONAL CONFERENCE

EXPENSES

Two round trip airline tickets for two outside speakers (2@ $375) $750.00

   • Must purchase 14 days in advance and stay Saturday night.

One return airline ticket 850.00

   • Speaker cannot stay Saturday night.

Hotel rooms for two outside speakers (4 nights x 150/night x 2 speakers) 1200.00

   • Four nights each

Hotel room for one speaker 100.00

   • One night

Speakers' meals not already provided (4 days x 50/day x 2 speakers) 400.00

Honorarium for outside speakers 1,000.00

Gifts for local speakers 600.00

Catering expenses 5,000.00

   • $50.00 per person for two days

   • Based on 100 people

Handouts, registration packs, name tags 600.00

Brochure 100.00

Slide Show 100.00

Postage 250.00

TOTAL $10,950.00

REVENUE

Vendor Sponsorship $3,600.00

- $300.00 base price for each booth

- Anticipate 12 booths

Anticipate additional vendor sponsorship 3,500.00

Tuition Fees 8,500.00

- $85.00 for two days

- 100 paying customers

TOTAL $15,600.00

REVENUE–EXPENSES = $4,650.00

- May be considered profit.

- Allows flexibility if expenses are more than anticipated or less than 100 paying customers attend.

CHAPTER 8

Effective Creation and Use of Visual Aids

OBJECTIVES

Upon completion of this chapter, the emergency nurse educator will be able to:

1. List various types of visual aids and their role in the education process.

2. Select appropriate visual aids to enhance educational activities.

3. Create quality, cost effective visual aids.

WHY USE VISUAL AIDS?

A picture is worth a thousand words, or so it is said. Unfortunately a picture can't speak, making it sometimes difficult to get your point across. Words alone can't always get your point across either. Together, they are more effective in communicating your message. We learn through our five senses. The more senses involved in the learning process, the greater the retention of knowledge. We remember 20% of what we hear, 30% of what we see, 50% of what we see and hear, and 70% of what we see, hear, and discuss. Of all the senses, we rely heavily on sight. Seventy-five to eighty-five percent of what we learn comes to us through visual impressions.

A University of Minnesota and 3M Company research study discovered that an audience is 43% more likely to be influenced by a speaker who uses visual aids. Using visual aids can communicate your message to your audience in an interesting and dramatic way (or at least they should). The inappropriate selection, creation, and use of visual aids can make a presenter look unprofessional and turn an audience off.

When created and used correctly, visual aids will:

- Facilitate the communication process.
- Enhance your presentation.
- Gain and maintain learner attention.
- Emphasize important points.
- Clarify confusing/complex points.
- Assist in generating discussion.
- Improve audience retention.

Visual aids should be designed to supplement your presentation, not be a substitute for it. A common mistake is when presenters put the majority of their presentation on visuals. If your presentation revolves around your visual aids, why do the learners need you? When planning your presentation and designing visual aids, ask yourself this important question, "If I had to, could I deliver this presentation without the use of visual aids?"

If the answer is no, go back to the drawing board. You can never predict power or equipment failure, misplaced transparencies, or slides spilling all over the floor prior to a presentation. Therefore, you need to be prepared to present without the use of visual aids should disaster strike!

Remember: Visual aids should complement your presentation, never overshadow it.

This chapter will provide helpful tips on how to create and use visual aids that will enhance your presentation, not detract from it.

TYPES OF VISUAL AIDS

As a presenter, you have more visual aid choices than ever before, from the traditional to the increasingly popular computer generated. There are several types of visual aids:

- Overhead projectors and transparencies.
- 35mm projectors and slides.
- Flipcharts.
- Posters.
- Handouts.
- Videotape.
- LCD/Multimedia presentations.

Which visual aid you select depends on several factors, including the type and size of your audience; the content, time frame, and length of your presentation; the location, set-up, and size of the presentation room; available resources; and your comfort level using the visual aid. It is crucial as a presenter to master the basic skills involved in the design and use of visual aids. Know the advantages, disadvantages, and differences of each of the visual aids before making a selection. Take the time to familiarize yourself with all types of visual aids. Varying their use can make your presentations more interesting and dynamic!

OVERHEAD PROJECTION

Overhead projection remains one of the most popular visual aids in the presentation world, mostly because of its versatility, flexibility, and low cost. Overhead projectors have been streamlined over the years, making them more reliable, lightweight, portable, and easier to use. These newer models project brighter, crisper images thanks to stronger lights and higher resolution. Depending on the technology, overhead projectors range in price from the low hundreds to several thousands of dollars.

Constructed of clear or colored acetate, precut to 8½ x 11, overhead transparency film is relatively inexpensive, approximately 20 cents per clear, 30 cents per color, or 90 cents per laser printer sheet. Transparencies can be simply created by hand printing before or during a presentation using color felt-tipped markers or wax pencils. Water-based markers can be erased off the acetate so it can be reused. Permanent markers give a better appearance, but the writing cannot be erased off the acetate. Transfer letters or stencils can be used to create the visual on paper and then photocopied onto the transparency film. For more sophisticated, professional looking transparencies, use a computer graphics program coupled with a color inkjet or laser printer.

Advantages to Using Overhead Projection:

- Projector is portable.

- Can be used for small to medium sized audiences.

- Projected image can be, to some degree, adjusted based on audience size.

- Transparencies are quickly and inexpensively produced.

- Flexibility – transparency sequence can be easily changed based on audience response.

- Specific points can be emphasized during the lecture by writing, underscoring, or marking on a prepared transparency.

- Lights do not have to be dimmed in the room.

- Editing ease – only those transparencies that need updating can be replaced.

- Can use progressive disclosure to reveal information sequentially. Place an opaque material on top of the transparency and move it downward to disclose information as it coincides with the presentation.

- Sequenced overlays can show progression of complex ideas or concepts.

- Instructor can visualize the transparencies before projection.

Disadvantages to Using Overhead Projection:

- Projector requires electrical power.

- Can only use front projection – the projector is placed in front of the screen.

- Transparencies are large and bulky.

- Transparencies have to be changed by hand. (There are transparency feeders that can be attached to an overhead projector and operated with a wireless hand control, but they are very noisy.)

- Projector distance cannot be more than 10 to 12 feet away from the projection screen or the light dims.

- Projector and instructor may obstruct the audience's view if the screen is in the front center of the room.

- If the projection lamp beam does not meet the screen at a 90° angle, image distortion known as "keystoning" can occur. The distorted image is a trapezoid shape—larger at the top than the bottom. Angling the screen forward corrects this distortion.

PREPARING TRANSPARENCIES

Effectively designed transparencies can add a professional touch to any presentation. The degree of color, the style of typeface, and the amount of information on the transparency can greatly impact the audience's response to the presentation. Therefore, careful planning and preparation are required. Below are some "how-to" tips to consider when designing transparencies.

- Use a horizontal format. It has a larger appearance than a vertical format. Enclose information in a maximum work area of 7½ x 10". This will maintain a one-inch margin all around and ensure visibility of the content.

- Keep it simple. Limit each transparency to one idea.

- Put a heading on each transparency.

- For computer designed, use one font style that is easy to read (a sans serif style, such as Helvetica and Arial is advised) in no more than three sizes (between 24 and 40 pt.). For hand designed, use legible print or large transfer letters, at least $1/3$" in height. If writing while presenting, use legible hand print using water-based markers.

- For easier reading, use upper case letters for titles, and upper and lower case letters for text.

- Think simple and uncluttered. Apply the rule of "7"— seven words per line, seven lines per transparency. Remove all unnecessary words to make each statement as concise as possible.

- Double-space the text.

- Use bullets to cue the beginning of each new line. Capitalize the first letter after each bullet.

- Use dark colors for text on clear or color transparency film. Colored film reduces the glare.

- Bold and drop shadow text to increase readability.

- Use correct grammar, punctuation, and spelling.

- For variety, add graphics, clipart, and color, but do not overdo it! Use a maximum of three colors per transparency. Use the same three throughout the presentation. Other colors can be used to highlight or draw attention to key points.

- DO NOT copy pages out of a book or journal and make into a transparency. The information will be too small and overwhelming for the audience to read. Use a handout instead.

- Divide complex diagrams, detailed illustrations, formulas, charts, or forms into parts and show on separate transparencies.

- To test readability, place the finished transparency on a piece of white paper on the floor in front of your feet. Looking down, attempt to read it. If you can read the transparency, it will be readable when projected onto the screen.

The two most common techniques used for creating preprinted transparencies are a photocopy machine or a laser or inkjet printer.

Photocopied transparencies are produced from an original paper design that is copied onto the transparency using a photocopy machine. Text and graphics may be computer generated, photocopied from another source, or created freehand. Color designs are appropriate if a color copier is available.

Computer-generated transparencies are printed from a computer program via a laser or inkjet printer on transparencies specifically designed for use in these printers. Computer presentation packages allow for easy preparation of text, bullet lists, diagrams, charts, and the addition of graphics.

GUIDELINES FOR USING OVERHEAD PROJECTION

Operating an overhead projector is a skill that comes with practice. Poor delivery techniques will overshadow your transparencies no matter how creative and professional they may look.

Below are guidelines to adhere to when using overhead projection. Some may seem very simplistic, but when not applied, a presentation will look unorganized and unprofessional.

- The projector must be a maximum distance of 10 to 12 feet from the screen. Any farther, the light beam begins to dim.

- Use the 2 x 6 rule to match screen size with the room seating. The distance from the first row of seats to the screen should be equal to two times the width of the screen. The distance from the screen to the last row should be equal to six times the width of the screen.

- Bottom of the screen should be 42 inches from the floor.

- For optimal visibility, place the screen in the corner of the room. If possible, tilt it towards the audience at a 45° angle to prevent keystoning.

- Place the projector into a recessed stand to prevent obstruction of audience visibility.

- Stand to the side of the projector when presenting and face the audience, not the screen.

- Teach off the screen, not the projector, to avoid blocking all or part of the audience's view. Avoid turning your back to the audience as you do so.

- Practice your presentation using the transparencies and projector several times before the actual delivery. Make sure the transparencies can be viewed from all angles of the room.

- Don't prematurely pull the transparency off the projector platform. Allow the audience enough time to read the information.

- Don't leave a transparency projected onto the screen if it has no relevance to the topic being discussed.

- Never leave the projector beam shining onto the screen when not using a transparency. The bright light is very distracting to the audience. Cover the projector platform with a piece of cardboard or other opaque material to obscure the light.

- Never walk in front of the projector when it is turned "on." It looks unprofessional and can temporarily blind you from the very bright light.

- Avoid cutting off parts of the transparency when placing it on the projector. A piece of masking tape placed strategically on each side of the projector platform will assure proper transparency placement every time.

- Change the transparencies smoothly by sliding one off the platform as you immediately slide the next one onto the platform. This will avoid the bright white light from annoying the audience. Or, turn the projector off between each transparency change. This practice, however, increases the risk of blowing the bulb out.

- Put a clear transparency over a premade transparency to adlib or add content. If writing on the transparency, stand to the projector's left if you are right-handed and right if you are left-handed to avoid turning away from the audience.

- Put transparencies in cardboard frames for protection and ease of handling. Arrange in sequence and number. Notes or reminders can be written on the frames for easy reference when presenting.

- Prevent static cling by placing paper between each transparency. If the transparencies slide when placed on the projector platform, wipe the platform with a damp cloth and the sliding will stop.

- Place transparencies in clear sheet protectors and store in a binder.

- Keep a spare bulb with the projector and know how to change it. A pair of hemostat clamps can be used to remove a burned out bulb that will be very hot.

35MM PROJECTION

Thirty-five millimeter projection was once thought of as the replacement for overhead projection. Instead, it has managed to co-exist with the overhead projector and transparency, vying for the visual spotlight among presenters. Slide projector features have been enhanced over the years, including auto-focus, wireless remotes, built-in automatic timers, and a wide variety of zoom lenses that can be used for different size audiences. Designing and creating 35mm slides has become easier over the years thanks to user-friendly computer software and photographic processing laboratories. Information is formatted on the computer and brought to a photographic laboratory where it is imaged and converted into a slide.

ADVANTAGES TO USING 35MM SLIDE PROJECTION

- The projector is portable.
- Can be used with any size audience due to a variety of projection lens sizes.
- Can use front or rear screen projection systems.
- Slides can be easily produced using a computer graphics program and photographic laboratory.
- Slides are small and easy to carry around. Can be stored in a carousel tray.
- Can easily view and sequence slides by placing in a clear slide sheet protector and holding them up to normal room lighting.
- Flexibility – slide sequence can easily be rearranged for each presentation based on need.
- Projected image can be adjusted based on audience size.
- Editing ease – can replace only those slides that need revision.
- Pictures, photographs, or other preprinted material can easily be converted into a slide.
- Can synchronize to music or recorded narration.
- Quality, premade slides are available for purchase from media companies and health care organizations.

DISADVANTAGES TO USING 35MM SLIDE PROJECTION:

- Costly to produce in comparison to transparencies. Worthy investment if the presentation will be given multiple times.
- Projector requires electrical power.
- Room lights must be dimmed unless a rear projection unit is utilized.
- Instructor must maintain awareness of slide progression since the slide cannot be visualized immediately before projection.
- A seated audience member's head or an audience member who walks in front of the projector lens can disrupt the projected image.

PREPARING 35MM SLIDES

Creating quality 35mm slides using computer graphics software has become more economical over the years, making their use more popular with presenters. Designing slides using a computer graphics software program is similar to that of overhead transparencies. Once designed, the slides are saved to a disk and sent to a photographic processing center for production. An easy and inexpensive alternative is to photograph the slides in a darkroom on a high-resolution, color monitor with a 35mm camera on a tripod. However, the resolution of the monitor and the skill of the photographer limit slide quality. Some tips for slide development include:

- Use a horizontal format. It has a larger appearance than a vertical format. Make sure to select the 35mm format on the computer graphics program to assure the correct design proportions. Maintain a one-inch margin all around to ensure visibility of the content.

- Keep it simple. Limit each slide to one idea.

- Put a heading on each slide.

- For computer designed, use one font style that is easy to read (a sans serif style, such as Helvetica and Arial is advised) in no more than three sizes (between 24 and 40 pt.). To test readability, hold the slide at arm's length. If you can read it, your audience will be able to read it once projected.

- For easier reading, use upper case letters for titles, and upper and lower case letters for text.

- Think simple and uncluttered. Apply the rule of "7"— seven words per line, seven lines per slide. Remove all unnecessary words to make each statement as concise as possible.

- Double-space the text.

- Use bullets to cue the beginning of each new line. Capitalize the first letter after the bullet.

- Use correct grammar, punctuation, and spelling.

- For variety, add graphics, clipart, and color, but do not overdo it! Use a maximum of three colors per slide. Use the same three throughout the presentation. Other colors can be used to highlight or draw attention to key points.

- Dark colored backgrounds, such as royal or navy blue, black, or green are easiest for the eyes to adjust to.

- Text should be light colored; white, yellow, and gold work best. Avoid using red text, except as an occasional highlight, especially on a blue, black, or green background.

- Bold and drop shadow text to increase readability.

- DO NOT copy pages out of a book or journal and make into a slide. The information will be too small and overwhelming for the audience to read. Use a handout instead.

- Use progressive disclosure – add more information to the original information for each successive slide until all the information is visible on the final slide for that topic. This prevents the audience from reading ahead of what you are saying if a lot of material is on one slide (Figure 7).

- Divide complex diagrams, detailed illustrations, formulas, charts, or forms into parts and show on separate slides.

- Utilize actual or staged photographic slides to enhance written content. If actual people are being photographed, consent needs to be obtained.

- Pictures, drawings, cartoons, graphics, etc. can be converted into a slide by a photographic processing center. Obtain copyright permission when necessary.

FIGURE 7 EXAMPLE OF THE USE OF PROGRESSIVE DISCLOSURE.

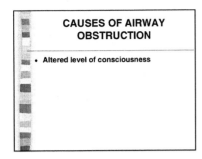

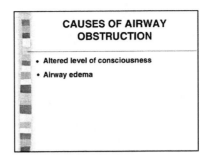

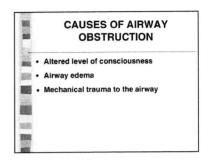

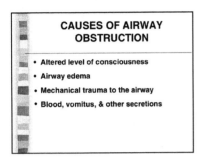

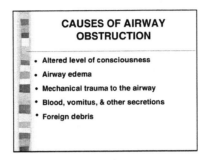

GUIDELINES FOR USING 35MM SLIDE PROJECTION

- Place slides in order in a slide protector sheet or carousel tray before the presentation.

- Number slides in sequence. If slides spill from the carousel, they can quickly be replaced in the appropriate order.

- To assure correct placement of slides in the carousel tray, hold the slide upright so the content can be read, then mark the lower left corner. Turn the slide upside down and place in the carousel tray; the mark should now be in the upper right corner, facing the screen.

- Secure the carousel tray locking ring before picking up or transporting to prevent the slides from spilling out.

- Projector should be 12 to 60 feet away from the screen. Image should be five feet wide or larger.

- Project the slides prior to the presentation to assure that they are in the correct sequence and orientation, i.e., not upside down or backwards.

- If a slide needs to be repeated, make additional copies to avoid flipping back and forth.

- When using older projectors, black slides can be placed in between content slides where pauses are desired to eliminate white light projection. Newer projectors do not project a white light when there is no slide in the carousel tray slot.

- Practice your presentation using the slides and projector several times before the actual delivery. Make sure the slides can be viewed from all angles of the room.

- Stand to the side of the projector when presenting and face the audience, not the screen.

- Don't change the slides too quickly on the screen. Allow the audience enough time to read the information.

- Don't leave a slide projected onto the screen if it has no relevance to the topic being discussed.

- Never walk in front of the projector when it is turned "on." It looks unprofessional and can temporarily blind you from the bright light.

- Use carousel slide trays that accommodate 80 slides instead of 120. The spaces are larger, making the slides less likely to jam.

- Hemostat clamps can be used to remove a jammed slide. Keep one tied to the projector for easy access.

- A wireless remote allows the speaker to move and continue to control the projector.

- Keep a spare bulb with the projector and know how to change it. A pair of hemostat clamps can be used to remove a burned out bulb that will be very hot.

- Use a small light box or flat surfaced light source to sort slides.

- Write a title or subject on each slide to assist with sorting.

- To preserve slide quality, avoid touching the slide surface. Handle by the edges only.

- Store slides in a carousel tray or in slide protector sheets that can be placed in a 3-ring binder.

- Store in a dark, cool, humidity controlled area.

FLIPCHARTS

Flipcharts are still a popular visual aid for presentations. Composed of a pad of paper and easel, they can be found wherever presentations are made. They are favorable due to their flexibility and adaptability when used in an interactive manner. The presenter can control and redirect the flow of the presentation based on the audience's involvement.

ADVANTAGES TO USING FLIPCHARTS:

- Economical.

- Easily accessible.

- User friendly, portable, and versatile.

- Do not require electricity.

- Can prepare pages ahead of time or write on the pages while presenting.

- Used for interactive presentations such as group discussions, teambuilding, or brainstorming. Audience members can physically write on the flipchart page.

- Completed pages can be torn off the pad and posted on the wall for easy reference.

- Can save prepared pages and reuse.

DISADVANTAGES TO USING FLIPCHARTS:

- Should not be used for audiences greater than 25 to 30 people. Difficult to read after approximately 20 feet. This is also based on room size, seating arrangements, and the presenter's handwriting.

- Pages cannot be easily turned into handouts.

- For hand-prepared pages, the presenter needs good penmanship, grammar, and spelling.

PREPARING/USING FLIPCHARTS

Flipcharts can be prepared ahead of time or during the presentation. Although a popular visual aid, many presenters shy away from using flipcharts because of inexperience and lack of comfort with their creation and use during a presentation. A flipchart as a visual aid is a nice change to the traditional overhead transparencies or 35mm slides favored by most presenters. As a presenter becomes more comfortable with using a flipchart, it will be a nice addition to his visual aid repertoire. This comfort level can occur with practice. The following suggestions on preparing and using flipcharts can assist with developing that comfort level.

- Stand in different parts of the room to determine if all audience members will be able to see the flipchart.

- Ensure there are sufficient sheets of paper on the flipchart pad.

- Write clearly and legibly. Test letter size to assure it is readable—a minimum of 2" to 3" in height.

- Keep it simple—use basic language; abbreviate when possible; use bullets; draw simple pictures or illustrations.

- Apply the rule of "7"— seven words per line, seven lines per flipchart.

- Write on the top 2/3 of the flipchart page to ensure that all can see the content.

- Use watercolor markers in dark colors for text. Watercolor markers do not bleed through the paper and wash off your hands easily.

- Emphasize key points or areas by using lighter color markers to underline, circle, etc.

- Stand to the side (opposite of your writing hand) of the flipchart when writing to avoid blocking the audience's view. Always face the audience when writing. Comfort with this skill takes practice.

- Put the marker down when not writing.

- If posting sheets on the wall, have preripped tape or stick-on putty easily accessible.

- Use more than one flipchart for variety

- If preparing ahead of time, print text or use stencils or project text from an overhead transparency onto the flipchart and trace the letters. Fill with color. This technique is good for copying pictures or illustrations, especially if you have difficulty drawing.

- Put blank pages between prepared pages.

- Pencil in points to remember along the edges of the paper as quick reference notes.

- Tab the sides (closest to where you are standing) of each prepared page with a piece of masking tape or stick-on tab to assist with flipping back and forth between pages.

- Flipchart pages can be placed in protector sheets designed specifically for flipcharts that protect them from damage so they can be reused. The presenter can write with erasable markers directly onto the protector sheet if desired. The original sheet is untouched.

- Save and store prepared flipchart pads in a holder or the box the pads come in to protect the sheets from ripping or getting damaged

POSTERS

In recent years, posters have gained popularity as an effective visual aid for providing educational information. An instructional poster has the potential of reaching more individuals than a traditional lecture. After a few weeks of display, posters can be circulated to other areas within the institution with similar educational needs. Posters can be self-produced or professionally created by an art department or graphic artist.

A well-designed, strategically-placed poster can target nurses, ancillary staff, and other members of the health care team. Despite published guidelines, many unattractive and poorly constructed posters are designed which ineffectively communicate the creator's message. Following are some tips to adhere to when creating posters that will attract the reader's attention.

ADVANTAGES TO USING POSTERS:

- Cost effective – relatively inexpensive to self-produce. One can also acquire professionally prepared posters at little or no cost from many organizations, such as the American Heart Association, the American Cancer Society, and pharmaceutical and patient care equipment/product companies contracted with your institution.
- Portable.
- Learning is self-paced and individualized.
- Time-effective – provides 24-hour education.
- Can display for a long period of time, reaching a large number of learners.
- Reusable.
- Can supplement with handouts.
- Can be used individually, in groups, or to enhance a presentation or skills lab.
- Once developed, can respond to educational requests more quickly by using a poster instead of planning a live presentation.

DISADVANTAGES TO USING POSTERS:

- Time-consuming to produce. Can take weeks to months of preparation.
- Expensive – can be costly if professionally produced.
- Little or no opportunity for exchange of learner ideas.
- Provides only essential information. The learner is not furnished with theoretical or background information.
- Requires motivation of learner to read information.
- Without a post-test or other exercise, there is no way to determine if an individual actually read the content.

PREPARING POSTERS

The goal of a poster is to attract attention and convey a message quickly. Therefore, it should be designed with that goal in mind. Some guidelines for preparing posters are discussed in this section.

- Determine the essential information that needs to be communicated. Include only critical facts but enough information to get the reader's attention.

- Design how to communicate the information to the reader using text, graphics, pictures, etc. Be creative! You want the poster to be appealing.

  - Sketch a rough draft of the poster layout. Keep it simple, yet eye-catching.

  - Materials required:

    - Mounting board, such as foam core, which is lightweight and sturdy.

    - Colored paper that complements the color of mounting board. Used for printing text on or for bordering pictures or graphics.

    - Paper cutter or a straight edge and sharp bladed knife for cutting paper to size.

    - Computer generated or written text.

    - Pictures, photographs, graphics, charts, etc.

    - Map pins, thumbtacks, Velcro, glue stick, or adhesive mounting spray to mount text and graphics to board.

  - Title should be as short as possible, not to exceed 10 words.

  - Layout text and graphics in a logical sequence.

  - Text should be as concise as possible and augment the graphics, photographs, charts, etc. that you are using. Sometimes a picture says it all!

  - Title and text must be visible and easy to read from four to six feet away. Title size should be 2" to 3" in height (font size of 216 to 310 pt in Times New Roman). Text size should be a minimum of $1/3$" to $1/2$" in height (font size of 36 to 48 pt in Times New Roman). (Figure 8.)

  - For easier reading, use upper case letters for titles, and upper and lower case letters for text.

  - Use correct grammar, punctuation, and spelling.

  - Double-space the text.

  - Use bullets to assist in guiding the reader. Capitalize the first letter after the bullet.

  - Use no more than three colors – one main, two to accent. The colors should contrast with each other.

  - Use graphics instead of text when possible. Graphics break up the necessary text and can add interest and appeal to the poster.

  - Create a three-dimensional effect by mounting text and graphics on foam board, cut them out and then mount them on the poster board.

  - Before mounting text and graphics, proof copy and check for accuracy. Arrange the layout on the poster board and rearrange for visual appeal and logical progression of ideas.

  - Mount text and graphics onto foam board, index paper, Oaktag, or another sturdy piece of material using either:

    - A photo mount adhesive spray that is found in most art supply or camera stores. It is a permanent adhesive that will not bleed or discolor. Since it generates fumes, use in a well-ventilated area.

    - Some type of glue, such as rubber cement or glue stick. Neither is as permanent as the adhesive spray, but cheaper.
      (The adhesive spray mounts paper smoother and more evenly than glue, which can create a bumpy, uneven mount.)

- Then mount the mounted text and graphics onto the posterboard using one of the materials above or with map pins, thumbtacks, or Velcro.

- Don't overload the poster with text and graphics. Maintain approximately 50% of blank space.

- Maintain an even margin all around.

FIGURE 8. SAMPLE FONT SIZES IN TIMES NEW ROMAN.

36 pt

48 pt

72 pt

GUIDELINES FOR DISPLAYING/USING POSTERS

Once developed, plan how to display the poster to maximize its impact. Some guidelines to consider:

- Determine where to display the poster. Select the most visible area to reach as many readers as possible.

- Determine how to display the poster and the materials needed. It can be displayed on an easel or mounted to a wall or bulletin board. Make sure the mounted area can support the poster for the desired length of time and that the poster will not cause damage to the mounted area.

- Provide clear directions for the readers if a post-test or exercise needs to be completed after reading the poster so they understand what is expected of them and the time frame for completion.

- The type of attendance tracking for those who read the poster.

- Establish time frame length for each display location and make sure to move the poster at the scheduled time.

HANDOUTS

The easiest visual material to create and use is the handout. The purpose of handouts is to support and expand upon a presentation. Handouts are prepared prior to a presentation and can be distributed before, during, or after. Handouts can be created using a computer software program for a professional look or by hand for a more personal, casual look. If not created properly, handouts can be confusing and misleading to the audience. A handout should be used whenever you create a visual aid that prompts you to say "I know you can't read this but. . ."!

Handouts are often used to provide more detailed information not covered in a presentation or for information too complex or too lengthy to be made into an overhead transparency, 35mm slide, or written on a flipchart. Handouts can be the sole visual aid during a presentation. The learner follows along with the presenter, taking notes as the presentation progresses. The handouts can consist of the presentation's purpose, objectives, content outline, bibliography, and any other supplemental information, such as, charts, diagrams, etc. Handouts can also be used in conjunction with other visual aids. Copies of the presenter's overhead transparencies or 35mm slides, usually three to a page, coupled with space for notetaking, can be made into a handout for the learner to use during the presentation and for future reference. Unfortunately this practice is being overdone and becomes tiresome to the learner, who tends to read ahead and not listen to what you are saying. In addition, you are freely giving out your lecture, which you worked hard to develop, for anyone else to use. Avoid this form of handout as much as possible.

Poorly designed and disorganized handouts or those hastily designed will often end up in the trash bin and are not much better than having no handouts at all. That is why it is important to take the time to plan and prepare handouts that your audience will want to keep.

ADVANTAGES TO USING HANDOUTS:

- Easy to create and produce using a computer, laser printer, or photocopy machine.

- Economical to duplicate in large quantities.

- Easily revised.

- Easy to transport and use.

- Can be used anywhere and with any size audience.

- Can be placed in a binder or folder for a professional look.

- Guide the learner through the presentation.

- Can provide the learner with very detailed or complex diagrams, charts, etc. or supplemental information, such as an article, that will not be covered in the presentation but is important to know. Be sure to obtain copyright permission for anything borrowed from copyrighted material!

- Assist the learner with remembering the presentation after it is over.

- Depending on the amount of preprinted information given, can reduce the degree of notetaking.

DISADVANTAGES TO USING HANDOUTS:

- Can become a distraction – the learner may read ahead of the presenter, therefore not listening to the presentation or becoming bored knowing what will be discussed next.

- Not interactive or easily changed once the presentation begins.

GUIDELINES FOR PREPARING/USING HANDOUTS

The handouts a presenter is going to distribute should be decided upon when preparing the presentation. Both go hand-in-hand. Handouts that are well thought-out and prepared will assist in achieving the presentation's goals and impact on the presenter's professional reputation. Some points to consider when preparing handouts:

- Tailor handouts around the presentation's goals and objectives.

- Include only information that supports the presentation.

- Don't force too much information on one page—space it out.

- Leave an ample amount of white space on your handouts, such as wide margins, to allow for notetaking.

- Put the name of the topic and a page number on each page, so that if pages get separated, the correct order can be reestablished. The speaker's name and phone number is optional.

- Use graphics such as pictures, graphs, diagrams, etc. to convey complex material instead of text. Your audience will be more likely to review the graphics than read lengthy text to get the same information.

- Avoid mixing vertical and horizontal formats in the same handout. The audience will quickly tire with having to move the pages back and forth between the formats.

- If possible, use color to catch the reader's eyes.

- Stationery or art supply stores, as well as mail order catalogs, offer a large array of color and design printed paper of various stock and sizes.

- Use language consistent with the learner's reading level. Avoid using slang, jargon, and complicated words.

- Use correct grammar and punctuation, and proofread for typographical errors. If using a computerized spell check, do a final proofreading to catch misplaced words that are spelled correctly.

- Assure that the handout information flows in a logical sequence.

- Avoid using copies of your overhead transparencies or 35mm slides as handouts.

- Make the handout look as professional as possible. You want it to impress the audience since it is representative of you.

- Final copies should be neat, clean, and straight.

- Make sure you have enough handouts for all participants.

- Distribute your handouts in a pre-labeled file folder so that your audience can take the information and file it at home or work for easy reference.

VIDEOTAPES

Videotapes can dramatically illustrate a point better than any other visual aid. Unfortunately, if used incorrectly, a videotape can also overshadow your presentation. Therefore, it is best to use short videotapes as an adjunct to your presentation when words alone are not enough to illustrate a point. They are particularly helpful when demonstrating a procedure.

Videotapes can be purchased from instructional media companies, rented, or produced in-house. Some pharmaceutical and patient care equipment/product companies contracted with your institution have videotapes explaining and/or demonstrating the use of their products for free. In-house video production can be costly and time consuming. There are several skills involved in the creation of a video program, such as writing a script, setting a stage or scene, acting a role, and shooting and editing the video and audio components, not to mention all the expensive equipment that is required. A production company can be hired to create the video but this can be extremely costly as well. In the long run, it is easier and cheaper to purchase or rent a preproduced videotape that can be adapted to your presentation.

When using videotapes, you need to assure that all members of the audience can see. Depending on the size of the audience, a large monitor or several small ones may be required. Video monitors are available in many sizes, ranging up to as large as 60 inches diagonally. However, the larger the size, the heavier it will weigh. When large monitors are not available, videotapes can be projected via an LCD (liquid crystal display) projector onto a large screen. LCD projectors, which are lightweight and portable, can also display computer-generated programs.

ADVANTAGES TO USING VIDEOTAPES:

- Portable.

- Cost-effective to purchase preproduced.

- Consistent delivery of information.

- Full motion synchronized with sound.

- Can substitute for a lengthy presentation.

- Able to show realistic situations.

- Can pause for discussion – interactive.

- Excellent medium for all learning domains.

- Instant replay is available.

- Self-learning medium.

- Can capture expertise of different presenters by videotaping their lectures.

DISADVANTAGES TO USING VIDEOTAPES:

- Requires electrical power.

- Costly and time consuming to self-produce.

- Size of monitor limits size of audience due to visibility.

- Difficult to edit or revise content.

- Cannot legally make multiple copies of purchased videotapes.

GUIDELINES FOR USING VIDEOTAPES

Utilizing videotapes can enhance your presentation by generating discussion and breaking up the content. Practice using videotapes prior to your presentation. A presenter who cannot operate a video projector or fumbles around looking for a specific spot on the videotape looks unprofessional and loses credibility with the audience. Some guidelines for using videotapes include:

- Review the videotape prior to use for visual clarity and audio levels. Adjust picture tracking and volume accordingly.

- Prior to the presentation, cue the program by advancing the tape to a few seconds before the starting point. Use the numerical counter to help you pinpoint specific areas on the videotape.

- Place the monitor in front of the room.

- Practice using all related equipment prior to the presentation. Know how to troubleshoot.

- Don't seat anyone closer than five feet from the monitor or screen.

- Slightly dim the lights in the room to focus the audience's attention to the monitor.

LCD/MULTIMEDIA PROJECTOR PRESENTATIONS

Computer presentation packages have gained an increased popularity over the years due to the emergence of laptop computers, LCD (liquid crystal display) panels and projectors, and graphic presentation software.

The LCD panel is designed to connect to the monitor output cable of a laptop or desktop computer. The panel is then placed on the stage of a high resolution (4000 or > lumens) overhead projector. The emergence of LCD projectors has simplified this process. The laptop or desktop computer is plugged directly into the LCD projector, bypassing the need for the overhead projector. The presentation, which is created on graphic software, such as Microsoft's Powerpoint or Lotus' Freelance (the same way overhead transparencies and 35mm slides are created) is then projected from the computer to a projection screen or monitor via the LCD panel or projector. Color, animation, video, pictures, and sound can be incorporated to add life and variety to the presentation.

ADVANTAGES TO USING LCD PROJECTION:

- Provides stimulating presentations. Can integrate, sound, animation, pictures, and video.
- Can be used for large audiences when projected onto a large screen.
- Editing ease – can edit or change content at no cost.
- Cost-effective to use in the long run–save money by not having to print 35mm slides or transparencies for each presentation.
- Flexibility – screen sequence can be rearranged on some software programs prior to the presentation.

DISADVANTAGES TO USING LCD PROJECTION:

- Requires electrical power.
- Equipment – laptop computer, LCD panel with high-resolution overhead projector, or an LCD projector, is expensive to purchase.
- Cannot view the presentation without a computer.
- Resolution of the computer screen may be less than that of a 35mm slide or transparency. The projected image may not be as clear or smaller text may be unreadable.
- Room lights must be dimmed when projecting.
- Instructor must maintain awareness of screen progression since the screen cannot be visualized immediately before projection.

GUIDELINES FOR PREPARING/USING LCD PROJECTION

- Create the presentation on a user-friendly computer software program according to the same guidelines as 35mm slides discussed earlier.
- Familiarize self with the software's capabilities. Some software packages allow mixing of sound files with test files, resulting in the ability to add narration.
- Create each screen in the sequence to be viewed.

- Add transitional effects such as fades and wipes that can be changed with the mouse or a specific key. Avoid using more than two or three different effects simultaneously.

- Strategically place yourself, the laptop, and the LCD projection equipment in the room to ensure that all members of the audience can see the presentation.

- If unable to use a high-resolution overhead projector with the LCD panel, test the projection to determine if its light is strong enough to project the presentation. Do this before using it in front of an audience.

SUMMARY

As a presenter, you will have many opportunities to utilize visual aids in your presentations. Studies have shown that learner retention is increased when presenters use effective visual aids. Traditional visual aids such as handouts, posters, flipcharts, coupled with computer generated overhead transparences and 35mm slides, gives the presenter more options when creating a presentation. The inappropriate selection, creation, and use of visual aids can make a presenter appear unprepared and distract the audience from learning. Utilizing the tips and techniques discussed in this chapter will help you create visual aids that enhance your presentation, not detract from it.

REFERENCES

Adelman, E. M. & Thornton, S. R. (1993). Say it with pictures. RN, 56(10), 21-22, 24.

Bach, C., McDaniel, R., & Poole, M. (1994). Posters: Innovative and cost-effective tools for staff development. Journal of Nursing Staff Development, 10(2), 71-74.

Budassi-Sheehy, S. (1992). Preparing audiovisual materials: Overhead transparencies. Journal of Emergency Nursing, 18(2), 164-165.

Chang, B. L. & Hirsch, M. (1994). Videotape intervention: Producing videotapes for use in nursing practice and education. The Journal of Continuing Education in Nursing, 25(6), 263-267.

Endicott, J. (1998). An amateur woodworker's top 7 PowerPoint solutions. Presentations, May, 32-34.

Endicott, J. (1998). For better presentations avoid PowerPoint pitfalls. Presentations, June, 36-37.

Gigliotti, E. (1995). Let me entertain. . .er. . .teach you: Gaining attention through the use of slide shows. The Journal of Continuing Education in Nursing, 26(1), 31-33.

Hanke, J. (1998). The psychology of presentation visuals. Presentations, May, 42-51.

Healey, K., & Hoffman, M. (1991). Self-instructional posters: One way to save time and money. Journal of Continuing Education in Nursing, 22(3), 123-125.

Heimes, S. (1997). 10 tips for designing effective presentation visuals. Presentations, September, 26.

Jossi, F. (1996). 50 Windows 95 presentation software tips. Presentations, November, 28-30, 32, 34, 36-37.

Jossi, F. (1996). 10 tips for better presentations. Presentations, November, 31.

Laskowski, L. (1997). 11 tips for using flipcharts more effectively. Presentations, October, 26.

Laskowski, L. (1997). When using overheads, don't forget the basics. Presentations, November, 30.

MacLean, I. (1991). Twelve tips on providing handouts. Medical Teacher, 13(1), 7-12.

Parker, R. (1996). 10 tips for using type. Presentations, November, 39-40, 42, 44.

Schramm, A., & Guido, B. (1992). The traveling poster project. Nursing Management, 23(9), 120, 122.

Sheehy, S. B. (1992). Preparing audiovisual materials: Overhead transparencies. Journal of Emergency Nursing, 18(2), 164-165.

Simons, T. (1999). Handouts that won't get trashed. Presentations, February, 47-50.

Sternberger, C. & Freiburger, O. (1996). Faculty-produced videos. Journal of Nursing Staff Development, 12(4), 173-178.

Torok, G. (1999). Go 10 extra steps when using computer projection. Presentations, January, 30.

Williams, N., Wolgin, F., & Hodge, S. (1998). Creating an educational videotape. Journal for Nurses in Staff Development, 14(6), 261-265.

CHAPTER 9

Administrative Guidelines for the Emergency Nurse Educator

OBJECTIVES

Upon completion of this chapter, the emergency nurse educator will be able to:

1. Identify three characteristics of effective delegation.

2. Articulate the process involved with decision-making.

3. Describe three methods used to provide feedback as part of performance appraisal.

4. Recognize five key elements of a job description.

5. Identify eight types of meetings.

6. Recognize distinguishing characteristics of nine types of meeting participants.

7. Describe characteristics of a successful leader.

8. Identify three organizational budget styles.

9. State three components of the ED expense budget.

10. Define productivity.

CONCEPTS OF MANAGEMENT AND LEADERSHIP

INTRODUCTION

The emergency nurse educator may be charged with a number of managerial or leadership responsibilities, e.g., staff supervision, chairing a committee, running a staff meeting, or contributing to performance appraisals. It is not the purpose of this manual to prepare the emergency nurse educator for the manager role; therefore, a comprehensive discussion of managerial concepts is not presented. It is a certainty that regardless of the administrative structure of an ED the educator is viewed as a leader and should possess qualities indicative of this role. Certain managerial and leadership concepts are germane to the educator role. Delegation, role modeling, decision-making, and performance appraisal are managerial and leadership processes within the domain of the emergency nurse educator.

For additional information on management concepts, the reader should investigate the multitude of management texts currently available.

DELEGATION

Delegation can be defined as getting work done through others or as directing the performance of one or more people to accomplish organizational goals (Marquis & Huston, 1996). Delegation enables the emergency nurse educator to demonstrate trust for another person, nurture development of staff, and accomplish goals with greater efficacy. To delegate, one must understand what constitutes delegation. Giving unpleasant tasks to a subordinate is not delegation. It is dumping and an abuse of power. Delegation is not an option, it is a necessity.

GUIDELINES FOR EFFECTIVE DELEGATION

Marquis and Huston (1996) have identified the following as guidelines for the effective delegation of duties to others.

- Identify the skill or educational level necessary to carry out the task(s).
- Identify the person BEST able to accomplish the task keeping in mind the following:
  - The capabilities of the person.
  - Does the person have the freedom of time to accomplish the task?
  - Is the task considered important by the person to whom it is being delegated?
- Clearly communicate:
  - The purpose for the task.
  - Your trust in the individual.
  - Limitations or qualifications that have been imposed.
  - Expected outcome.
  - Resources, e.g., other leaders, colleagues, managers.
  - Time line for expected completion.
  - Timely feedback.
  - The leader needs to make him/herself available as a resource if needed.
- Avoid excessive supervision.
  - Identify deadlines and checkpoints for your input, then stay away unless a crisis occurs.
  - Balance supervision with freedom to accomplish the task.
- Evaluate the performance of the person completing the delegated task after it has been completed.

COMMON MISTAKES OF DELEGATION

Underdelegating:
This mistake stems from a leader's incorrect notion that delegation is a sign of weakness or that it shows a lack in the individual's ability to be able to get the job done without help. In addition, leaders may underdelegate because they feel compelled to get the job done themselves, often due to a lack of trust in colleagues or subordinates (Marquis, 1996). In time effective leaders come to understand and accept the need for hierarchical responsibilities of delegation.

Overdelegating:

Some leaders overdelgate, unfairly burdening their subordinates and colleagues. Common reasons for overdelegation include disorganization, poor time management, and insecurity on the part of the delegator (Marguis, 1996). Leaders must be careful not to overdelegate as this may overburden and frustrate competent employees resulting in resentment and deterioration of their job performance.

Improper Delegation:

Improper delegation occurs when a leader delegates tasks to an individual who is wrong for such responsibility, or when delegation occurs either at the wrong time or for the wrong reason. This mistake also commonly occurs when the leader delegates tasks and responsibilities that are beyond the capability of the individual to whom they are being delegated or should be done by the leader him/herself (Marguis, 1996). Delegating without the provision of adequate information and dividing a delegated task between individuals often prove to be detrimental to effective problem solving or task accomplishment (Frohman & Johnson, 1993).

DECISION MAKING/PROBLEM SOLVING

Decision making is a complex, cognitive process defined as choosing a particular course or action. Decision making occurs when a choice must be made. Problem solving, a systematic process that focuses on analyzing a difficult situation, is a form of decision making. Critical thinking, another decision-making process, is a term commonly used in nursing care when evaluating and determining plans of care for patients. Of even greater importance to nursing, and the nursing process, is a decision-making model.

THE TRADITIONAL PROBLEM-SOLVING PROCESS

The traditional problem-solving model is widely used and perhaps the most well known of the various models. It is a seven-step process (Marquis, 1996) with decision making occurring at step five.

1. Identify the problem.

2. Gather data to analyze the causes and consequences of the problem.

3. Explore alternative solutions.

4. Evaluate the alternatives.

5. Select the appropriate solution.

6. Implement the solution.

7. Evaluate the results.

Although traditional problem-solving is an effective model, its weakness lies in the amount of time required for proper implementation. This process is therefore not very effective when time constraints are imposed. Another weakness with this model is the lack of a goal-setting step (Marquis, 1996).

MANAGERIAL DECISION-MAKING PROCESS

The managerial decision-making model, a modified traditional model, eliminates one weakness of the traditional model by adding a goal-setting step. The managerial process includes the following steps (Marquis, 1996):

1. Set objectives.

2. Search for alternatives.

3. Evaluate alternatives.

4. Choose.

5. Implement.

6. Follow up and control.

THE NURSING PROCESS

The nursing process provides yet another model for solving problems and making decisions. It has the strength that the previous two models lack, namely its feedback mechanism (Marquis, 1996). Educators have identified the nursing process as an effective decision-making instrument. When the decision point has been identified, initial decision-making occurs and continues throughout the process by using a feedback mechanism. Although the process was designed for nursing practice with regard to patient care and nursing accountability, it can easily be adapted as a theoretical model for solving leadership and management problems (Marquis, 1996).

PERFORMANCE APPRAISAL

Assessment and evaluation are an integral part of the education process. The emergency nurse educator evaluates student performance to determine effectiveness of educational endeavors, evaluates the new nurse's progression through orientation, and evaluates certain aspects of clinical performance to identify specific learning needs. These activities are an ongoing process made up of informal and formal observation and assessment.

Formal appraisal of job performance is ultimately the responsibility of the employee's immediate supervisor; however, the educator may be asked to provide feedback on performance, assist with development of a plan for employee improvement, or serve as an impartial observer during the appraisal conference. Additionally, the educator's professional performance is evaluated through this process. Knowledge of the various components of performance appraisal enables the educator to maximize benefits to the employee, manager, and educator.

In many settings, the educator is responsible for planning and evaluating an individual's orientation to the work environment. In these instances the educator will be constantly evaluating the progression of the nurse and will need to take appropriate action when the orientee is failing to meet the goals of orientation. Such actions may be as simple as verbal recommendations for improvement with the nurse manager or may require more complex actions such as a written evaluation of performance and a plan of action that the orientee needs to follow in order to maintain his/her position. Educators may be required to complete an orientation evaluation for each orientee upon successful completion of orientation.

Performance appraisal refers to evaluation of employee performance against established standards. The performance appraisal process is based on performance standards, job analysis, job evaluation, and job description (Swansburg, 1993). The emergency nurse educator may be asked to review a performance appraisal or comment on issues pertaining to education and clinical practice. Depending on the educator's role (many educators hold leadership positions within the institutional structure), he or she may be heavily involved in the evaluation of employee performance or not be personally involved in any aspect of the performance appraisal; in any case, an understanding of the entire process contributes to overall educator performance.

PERFORMANCE STANDARDS

Performance standards delineate quantitative and qualitative aspects of the job. These standards are the yardstick by which the employee is measured. The standards should be measurable, clearly defined, and job-related (Swansburg, 1993).

JOB ANALYSIS

Job analysis refers to a collection of information related to duties, tasks, and responsibilities performed by the incumbent in a given job (Ignatavicius and Griffith, 1982). Identification, organization, and display of this information reveals job overlap. This activity allows job modification and revision, a process essential for continued effectiveness of the individual job description (Swansburg, 1993).

JOB EVALUATION

Job evaluation measures the basic elements found in the job, i.e., knowledge, experience, and responsibility under similar working conditions (Swansburg, 1993). This process assures equitable pay for comparable work for women and minorities (Waintroob, 1985).

JOB DESCRIPTIONS

The job description describes the job rather than the person currently in the job (Swansburg, 1993). It provides a map for a specific position in an organization. The job description is a competency-based document that delineates job responsibilities and provides a mechanism for evaluation of responsibilities. A numerical rating system is used to measure performance and determine attribution and size of any merit increase.

To fulfill position responsibilities and meet organizational expectations, the emergency nurse educator must understand the language and style of job descriptions. Appendix B provides an example of an emergency nurse educator job description.

- Format.
  - Standard format and numerical rating scale employed by most organizations.
  - Length may be limited to two or three pages.
  - Style is terse and direct, unnecessary words are omitted.
  - Text is present tense, verbs are active.
- Content.
  - Purpose and responsibilities related to behavior, results, and domain are specifically stated or strongly implied.
  - Qualitative or quantitative standards of evaluation are included for each duty.
  - Education, training, and licensure requirements are outlined.
  - Comprehensive list of clinical skills and expectations is provided as a separate inventory.
- Title.
  - Refers to a group of positions identical with regard to significant duties and responsibilities.
  - Titles can be deceptive between organizations and between departments.
  - Position responsibilities are more descriptive of purpose than the job title.

- Position description.

    - Provides narrative of duties and responsibilities for a position within a specific department.

    - For example, the job description for a registered nurse will be different in the neonatal intensive care unit, the ED, and the orthopedic unit.

- Department/division.

    - Identifies the location of the position.

    - Provides essential information about chain of command.

- Effective date.

    - Date the position was created or activated.

    - Assures current, timely job descriptions.

- Job summary.

    - Abstract providing a brief overview of the position.

    - Used to post or announce available positions.

- Organizational chain of command.

    - Clarifies reporting lines for the position.

    - Dual reporting requirements should be clearly stated.

    - It is helpful to have a clear understanding of the organizational chart when evaluating chain of command.

- Organizational values.

    - Reflect the organization's philosophy.

    - Employees are often evaluated on demonstration of organizational values.

- Job requirements.

    - Identify minimum requirements for experience, education, training, licensure, knowledge, skills, and abilities.

    - Professional certifications and other required credentials are listed here.

- Job context.

    - Addresses environmental and structural conditions under which the job must be performed.

        - Is the work performed indoors or outdoors?

        - Is the job performed without benefit of heating or air conditioning?

        - Does the job require travel by private car?

        - How much lifting, sitting, and standing are required?

        - Is there exposure to hazardous materials such as chemicals or body fluids?

- Work performed.

    - Describes duties and underlying tasks.

    - Limited to those duties that are significant and recur over time.

- **I** Trivial requirements or rarely encountered duties should not be included.

- **I** Nursing job descriptions generally categorize duties and tasks according to the nursing process.

- Additional comments.

- **I** Allows discussion of specific issues by the evaluator and the employee

FEEDBACK

Feedback may be provided through counseling, coaching, or interviewing (Swansburg, 1993). It should be positive, constructive, and individualized for each employee. Matching feedback to the person often determines success of the encounter and significantly enhances staff morale and motivation (Ringer, Balkin, & Boss, 1993). Many organizations utilize peer review and self-assessment to evaluate ability and performance (Swansburg, 1993; Boud, 1988).

COUNSELING

Counseling involves direct interaction between the manager and the employee, a personal, face-to-face encounter. Swansburg (1993) suggests a counseling interview for the following purposes:

- Explore resource options and courses of action.

- Develop a realistic picture of employee's abilities, potential, and deficiencies.

- Reconcile personal limitations to job performance.

- Make choices and improve abilities.

COACHING

Coaching refers to continuous reinforcement of tasks well done (Swansburg, 1993). This approach eliminates surprises because the employee receives progress reports throughout the year. Coaching tends to be personal, requiring regular interactions between the coach and the employee.

INTERVIEWING

Interviewing refers to the process in which the manager and employee interact fact-to-face. A series of probing questions is used in order to illicit information concerning a particular event.

MEETINGS

INTRODUCTION

Educators are frequently involved in, and will often chair, various hospital committees. As would be expected, they will undoubtedly attend and/or run meetings of varying importance. Understanding meeting types, purpose, and leader/participant responsibilities is the key to successful, productive meetings.

MEETING TYPES

Regardless of name, location, or sponsoring organization, most meetings fall into eight types (Kieffer, 1988). Each type carries its own set of dynamics and rules for success.

GIVE OR EXCHANGE INFORMATION

- Information exchange may occur as oral and written presentations.

- Information gathering should be concentrated in low-level organizational meetings, delegating the process closer to the source.

- Gathering information at high-level meetings is generally unproductive.

- Clarification of information already provided is a more efficient use of time in high-level meetings than the actual presentation of large amounts of information.

- Distribution of pertinent information in written form prior to the meeting increases productivity.

CREATE OR DEVELOP IDEAS

- The best environment for brainstorming is one of openness, providing the freedom to express ideas and make mistakes.

DECIDE ON GOALS OR ISSUES

- The challenge in this type of meeting is to understand where the group stands or is headed in the particular process.

- Preliminary steps should be completed prior to the meeting, rather than during the meeting.

- Information gathering, issue clarification, brainstorming, and persuading should not be on the agenda if the purpose of the meeting is to make a decision.

DELEGATE WORK OR AUTHORITY

- Allows clarification and amplification of specific work or authority.

- At the end of the meeting, there should be a clear understanding of what will happen next and who is responsible for that action.

SHARE WORK OR RESPONSIBILITY

- Creates a forum for work that must be done by several individuals.

- Smaller groups are more effective.

- The danger is that the meeting may be called to avoid rather than share work.

PERSUADE, INVOLVE

- Called to change an individual's point of view.

- Given the inherent difficulty in changing someone's view, proper preparation is critical for successful persuasion meetings.

INSPIRE

- Inspirational meetings are a matter of ceremony or ritual.

- These meetings are held to kindle respect, trust, faith, dedication, or other values.

ESTABLISH OR MAINTAIN RELATIONS

- Clear understanding of purpose and the relations that exist between meeting participants determines the success of this type of meeting.

- If the purpose is to establish a long-term relationship, avoid political or religious debate.

- If the meeting is social, business should not be the primary topic of conversation.

MEETING LEADERS

Meeting leaders may be designated by organizational position, appointed by a superior, or self-appointed. Regardless of selection method, the ability to lead meetings is a skill that requires thought, effective communication skills, flexibility, and perseverance. Without effective leadership, the potential benefits from the meeting become liabilities, wasting time and money, promote stagnation, and interfere with decision making (Swansburg, 1993).

Thought should be directed to the meeting purpose and goals prior to the actual meeting date. Effective communication skills are essential to direct and encourage participants, control aggressive participants, and resolve situations of conflict that may occur. Flexibility and perseverance allow the individual to respond to changing conditions and develop as a leader.

RESPONSIBILITIES

Understanding leader responsibilities facilitates effective, efficient completion of essential tasks. Specific responsibilities include:

- Determine the purpose.
    - Why is the meeting necessary?
    - Can the purpose be achieved by another method such as delegation, written communication, phone call, or conference call?
- Develop the agenda.
    - List agenda items in descending order of importance.
    - Allocate time for each item.
    - Distribute the agenda in advance.
- Identify time limits.
    - Schedule start and stop times.
    - Adhere to these times (even if all of the meeting participants are not on time). Don't stop to bring late-comers up to date with meeting activities.
    - Set meeting and break times in relation to meals, quitting time, and shift times.
    - Are there other time options that will accomplish the meeting's purpose? Can the meeting be held as a stand-up, ten-minute meeting?

- Determine group composition.
  - Identify the participants for the meeting.
  - Invite those individuals essential to achieving the purpose.
  - Congruence and compatibility between the purpose and the participants are essential.
  - Identify natural leaders and followers in the participants.
- Prepare and distribute related material in advance.
  - Tell participants what to bring.
  - Summarize related materials during the meeting.
- Obtain appropriate location.
  - Consider the number of participants and the seating configuration to be utilized.
  - It is better to err on the side of additional seating than not have enough chairs.
  - Confirm environmental support items such as bathroom facilities, lighting, thermostat, electrical outlets, parking, and ease of access.
  - Provide necessary audiovisual supplies.
- Involve all participants.
  - Do not personally dominate the meeting.
  - Lead the discussion.
  - Remain neutral, walk a middle path through controversy.
  - Elicit cooperation from all participants.
  - Bring dissenting parties together.
  - Limit and redirect dominating participants.
  - Speak the language of the participants.
- Avoid digression.
  - Utilize effective speaking skills.
  - Keep the purpose of the meeting foremost in the group's mind.
- Conclude the meeting effectively.
  - Summarize decisions at the end of the meeting.
  - Clarify issues as appropriate.
  - Highlight areas that may require resolution.
  - Recap objectives and specific accomplishments.
  - Clarify follow-up actions and responsible participants.

PARTICIPANTS

Meetings are a microcosm of an organization at work. Professional relationships are on display. The ability to understand these relationships demands recognition of the personalities that may be encountered. McCormack (1989) identified nine personalities that may be encountered during internal organizational meetings.

Participant Types

- Straight shooters.

  - Honest in their opinions—no hidden agenda.

  - These individuals are an asset in any meeting; however, their honesty may lead to self-righteous smugness.

  - The leader must be alert for excessive use of "truth as a defensive tool."

- Martyrs.

  - Good at taking the heat and accepting responsibility when something goes wrong.

  - They may accept blame too quickly, preventing appropriate identification of who or what caused the problem.

- Poker faces.

  - Keep their ideas to themselves or share their ideas with the leader privately after the meeting has ended.

  - Their behavior sends mixed messages about teamwork.

- Cheerleaders.

  - Able to say "You're right. I never considered that."

  - This type of participant provides support to a leader and boosts other participants.

- Orators.

  - These individuals begin softly and build momentum.

  - Emotion and rhetoric take the place of insight.

  - When confronted with these individuals, handle with care.

- Devil's advocates.

  - These individuals consider everything debatable.

  - They often get to the truth; however, they consume a lot of time and energy in the process.

  - If you have a choice, limit the number of devil's advocates to one per meeting.

- Destroyers.

  - These people cannot say no without destroying another person's idea, project, or ego.

  - Identify these people early, preferably before the meeting.

- Recliners.

  - Settle in and get comfortable. These people are in no hurry to resolve the issues at hand.

  - Consider meeting with these individuals in the hall or a room with no chairs.

- Statesmen.

  - These participants advance themselves or the meeting through shrewd application of people skills.

  - Ideally, the leader is a statesman.

PARTICIPANT RESPONSIBILITIES

As with meeting leaders, all participants have responsibilities. Participants should arrive on time, be prepared with pertinent facts, avoid digression, and listen. Communication should be assertive rather than aggressive. Don't attack other participants. Avoid taking pot shots at other participants. Effective speaking skills are essential.

DEVELOPMENTAL PHASES

Swansburg (1993) identified five phases of group development. Understanding and recognition of these phases enhance leader function and strengthen group dynamics.

- **Orientation phase** is characterized by exchange of member information and identification of ground rules.

- **Conflict or storming phase** describes the competition for group position and informal leadership. The formal leader plays a key role in minimizing conflict during this phase.

- **Cohesion phase** is distinguished by establishment of group roles and norms. Members move toward consensus by understanding the problem.

- **Working phase** manifests deeper involvement, greater disclosure, and unity on the part of the members.

- **Termination phase** is a period of closure. Members summarize discussions, express feelings, and make closing statements.

TROUBLESHOOTING

Meetings do not always go well. Regardless of meeting type or participant composition, meetings encounter several common problems (APM, Inc., 1992).

- Floundering.
  - When floundering occurs at the beginning of the meeting, reiterate objectives and group purpose. Add mission statements to the agenda to keep members on track.
  - Floundering may also occur in the middle of a meeting. Use action plans to focus the group on specific processes and requirements. Reiterate the stated purpose or problem.
  - When floundering occurs during the end phase, review specific accomplishments. Utilize consensus building to achieve agreement or identify areas that still require resolution.
- Overbearing participants.
  - Individuals in a position of authority or with an area of expertise.
    - ♦ These experts become detrimental when their authority limits group discussion, prevents group exploration of member suggestions, or discounts other members.
  - Recognize the expert's knowledge without negating input from other members.
  - Data is essential even from the expert.
  - If possible, discuss the problem with the group.
  - Use other experts for a more balanced view.

- Dominating participants.
  - These participants talk too much and consume a disproportionate amount of meeting time.
  - Structure discussion on key issues. Solicit input from quieter participants.
  - Redirect the discussion without belittling the individual. "I appreciate your comments. Why don't we discuss these at a later time so we can concentrate on the current issue?"
- Reluctant participants.
  - May be introverts by nature or simply have a different comfort level with the group process.
  - Develop reflective group processes.
  - Acknowledge different levels of participation.
  - Structure discussion on key issues. Solicit input.
- Acceptance of opinions as facts.
  - Encourage the group to challenge opinions or facts without criticizing the individual.
  - Identify corroborating data.
  - Recognize the primacy of scientific data, i.e., data is essential for group action.
- Rush to accomplishment.
  - May occur when a member becomes inpatient and rushes the group to make a decision.
  - Verify commitment to scientific approach.
  - Utilize constructive feedback to describe the impact of member impatience.
  - Visualize the results of a snap decision with the group.
- Attribution.
  - Motives that may be attributed to members as a result of disagreement or misunderstanding.
  - Comments such as "He's just trying to take the easy way out" lead to resentment and even hostility.
  - Reiterate the need to operate on fact-based information.
  - Ask for validation of specifics, e.g., "How do we know . . . ?"
  - Encourage members to speak from their own experiences.
- Discounts and plops.
  - When someone ignores or ridicules another person's values or perspectives, the person may feel discounted.
  - A plop occurs when a statement is totally ignored.
  - Unchecked, these behaviors lead to resentment and hostility.
  - Encourage active listening and other constructive behaviors by all members.
  - Support the discounted person by recognizing the specific statement or perspective.
  - Speak privately with individuals who frequently discount the opinions of others.
- Digression and tangents.
  - Discussions without focus waste valuable time and energy.
  - Clearly state objectives at the beginning of the meeting.

- ❙ Refer to agenda when discussion strays.

- ❙ Keep perspective on the digression. Consider the benefit of the digression, i.e., letting off steam, building rapport, etc.

- • Feuding members.

  - ❙ Pay attention to symptoms such as increased volume and pointedness of language used.

  - ❙ If confrontation occurs during the meeting, ask adversaries to discuss the issues outside the meeting.

  - ❙ Address the problem with the individuals if the conflict is long-standing.

  - ❙ Encourage feuding parties to establish a contract about their behavior.

FISCAL CONCEPTS FOR THE EMERGENCY NURSE EDUCATOR

INTRODUCTION

While the primary responsibility of the emergency nurse educator is education, the ability to understand the language of finance is vital in today's health care environment. This section will provide an introduction to budget and productivity issues faced in the ED. Preparing a budget for a continuing education program was covered previously in Chapter 7 (Appendix D).

BUDGET

The term budget is derived from the term "bougette," a small leather bag used to carry items of value (Buschiazzo, 1987). The term now refers to a collection of items essential for business. A variety of budget styles are utilized by health care organizations.

STYLES/TYPES

Fixed or Static Budget

The fixed budget is developed from a single estimate of annual volume or activity. Annual volume is divided into 12 increments of time with expenses and revenue allocated proportionately. A fixed budget does not allow for variations in volume.

Flexible or Variable Budget

The flexible budget assumes variation in volume will occur. It utilizes *fixed costs, variable costs,* and *semivariable costs.*

- • *Fixed costs* refer to those costs not related to volume that are constant over time, e.g., the nurse manager's salary.

- • *Variable costs* fluctuate with changes in volume, e.g., supplies.

- • *Semivariable* costs also fluctuate with volume; however, the variation is not as predictable. Personnel and equipment are an example of semivariable costs.

Zero-base Budget

The zero-base budget requires justification for all expenditures. No monies are automatically allocated. Zero-base budgeting compares cost-benefit relationships. Established programs compete with new programs for available funding.

EXPENSE BUDGET

The expense budget for the ED includes personnel, operating expenses, and capital expenditures (ENA, 1994).

PERSONNEL

- Personnel expenses include salaries and wages paid to all employees for the pay period.

- Projected personnel expenses are based on the number of employees required for the workload projected for the next year.

- Employee expenditures and requirements are measured as full-time equivalents (FTEs).

- One FTE equals 80 hours per pay period or 2,080 hours per year.

OPERATING

- Includes supplies and equipment.

- Divided into subaccounts, such as medical supplies, office supplies, printing, and telephone.

- Operating expenses are based on previous costs as well as volume projections for the next year.

CAPITAL EXPENDITURES

- Expenses greater than $300 to $500, depending on the organization.

- Equipment that falls into this category requires formal application and justification of need.

REVENUE

Monies earned from reimbursement for direct patient care are called revenue. Reimbursement for patient charges are based on acuity, procedures, and supplies. Factors that directly or indirectly affect revenue include:

- Fixed reimbursement amount from insurance or other third-party payors.

- Discounted care contracts with third-party payors.

- Indigent care without reimbursement.

PRODUCTIVITY

Productivity refers to resource utilization. In essence, productivity is the ratio of services provided to resources used (Buschiazzo, 1987). Measurement of productivity enables the organization to:

- Determine pricing, long-range goals, and resource allocation.

- Quantify outcomes.

- Evaluate impact of new services, policies, and procedures.

- Monitor attainment of departmental goals.

- Reflect manpower utilization.

PRODUCTIVITY CALCULATION

Productivity is calculated by dividing input into output. The definition of input and output vary from department to department, and institution to institution. In general, input for an ED refers to patient volume, output refers to the number of FTEs used for a given period of time. Input may be specifically defined as the number of patients for each level of acuity. This definition refers to weighted visits; it provides a more realistic assessment of workload.

An institution may utilize multiple calculations to identify, monitor, and evaluate productivity. Generic parameters for productivity measurement are described below. To identify the specific methodology for your respective institution, consult the management engineering department or the nurse manager.

Formula

- Total earned hours divided by total productive hours equals productivity.

  ▌ Total earned hours.

    ♦ ED patient volume, worked hours, and patient acuity for a given pay period are used to calculate total earned hours.

    ♦ Total earned hours may also be called weighted visits.

    ♦ To determine total earned hours or weighted visits, a relative value unit (RVU) is calculated for each patient acuity level.

      ▸ The RVU is a reflection of direct nursing care provided.

  ▌ Documentation, medication preparation, and other indirect patient care activities are not included.

    ♦ Total productive hours.

    ♦ Includes regular hours, overtime hours, and other worked hours, such as time on call.

    ♦ Vacation and sick leave are not included.

    ♦ May also be called total worked hours or weighted FTEs (ENA, 1994).

PRODUCTIVITY ANALYSIS

Regardless of the institution's definition for input and output, productivity is usually plotted on a line graph. The line graph depicts current productivity as it relates to established productivity baseline and variance values. Variance defines the parameters for acceptable productivity deviations above or below baseline. Comparison graphs for volume and FTEs may be used to facilitate productivity analysis. When looking at a productivity graph, the emergency nurse educator should consider the following questions or issues:

- Does the graph reflect weighted or unweighted visits?
  - Weighted visits reflect workload for different levels of patient acuity.
- What is the accepted value for baseline and variance?
  - These values may be analyzed and revised annually.
- Does the graph depict productivity by week, month, pay period, quarter, or year?
  - Productivity graphs usually present calculations by pay period.
- Decreased volume without a decrease in FTEs causes a drop in productivity.
  - Analysis of trends over several years may identify consistent decreases for a specific time of year.
  - The nurse manager can reduce staff during these times and enhance departmental efficiency.
- Increased volume without increased FTEs indicates increased workload for the staff.
  - Consistent productivity values that demonstrate increased workload for the staff demonstrate the need for additional FTEs.
  - The nurse manager is able to document the impact of volume and/or acuity and justify requests for additional staff.
- Are additional graphs used to compare FTEs used and patient visits during the same time frame?
  - A line graph that provides productivity, FTEs, and patient visits is an excellent tool for the nurse manager to easily evaluate department performance.

SUMMARY

The brief review of budget and productivity provided in this chapter is meant to introduce the emergency nurse educator to these processes. For more comprehensive information on these issues, emergency nurse educators should consult resources in their respective institution and explore current literature on the subject. Emergency nurse educators who have been delegated any degree of budget authority are encouraged to seek a mentor with experience in these areas.

REFERENCES

APM, Inc. (1992). <u>Guidelines for meeting management</u>. New York: Author.

Baillie, V., Trygstad, L., & Cordoni, T. (1989). <u>Effective nursing leadership</u>. Rockville, MD: Aspen.

Boud, D. (1982). How to facilitate self-assessment. In K. Cox & CE Ewan (Eds.), <u>The medical teacher</u> (pp. 193-196). Edinburgh, Scotland: Churchill Livingstone.

Buschiazzo, L. (1987). <u>The handbook of emergency nursing management</u>. Rockville, MD: Aspen.Calano, J., & Salzman, J. (1988, May). The careful manager's guide to snap decisions. <u>Working Woman</u>, pp. 86-87.

Emergency Nurses Association. (1994). <u>Emergency nursing core curriculum</u> (4th ed.). Philadelphia: Saunders.

Hansten, R., & Washburn, M. (1992a). Tips for delegating to the right person. <u>American Journal of Nursing</u>, <u>92</u>(6), 64-65.

Hansten, R., & Washburn, M. (1992b). What do you say when you delegate work to others? <u>American Journal of Nursing</u>, <u>92</u>(7), 48-49.

Ignatavicius, D., & Griffith, J. (1982). Job analysis: The basis for effective appraisal. <u>Journal of Nursing Administration</u>, <u>12</u>(7/8), 37-41.

Kieffer, G. (1988). <u>The strategy of meetings</u>. New York: Simon & Schuster.

Manthey, M. (1990). Trust: Essential for delegation. <u>Nursing Management</u>, <u>21</u>(11), 28-29.

Martin, D.C., & Bardol, K.M. (1986, Summer). Training the raters: A key to effective performance appraisal. <u>Public Personnel Management</u>, pp. 101-109.

McConnell, E. (1987). Learn the fine art of delegating. <u>Nursing 87</u>, February, 8DD-8FF.

McCormack, M. (1989). <u>What they still don't teach you at Harvard Business School</u>. New York: Bantam.

Ringer, R.C., Balkin, D.B., & Boss, R.W. (1993, November/December). Matching the feedback to the person. <u>Executive Female</u>, pp. 11-13.

Rubin, T. (1985). <u>Overcoming indecisiveness: The eight stages of effective decision-making</u>. New York: Avon.

Swansburg, R.C. (1993). <u>Introductory management and leadership for clinical nurses: A text workbook</u>. Boston: Jones and Bartlett.

Waintroob, A. (1985, July/August). Comparable worth issue: The employer's side. <u>Hospital Manager</u>, pp. 6-7.

RECOMMENDED READINGS

Bernstein, A., & Rozen, S. (1992). <u>Dinosaur brains</u>. New York: John Wiley & Sons.

Bernstein, A., & Rozen, S. (1992). <u>Neanderthals at work</u>. New York: John Wiley & Sons.

Brightman, H.J., & Verhoeven, P. (1986, April/June). Running successful problem solving groups. <u>Business</u>, pp. 15-23.

Budd, M., & Propotnik, T. (1989). A computerized system for staffing, billing, and productivity measurement. <u>Journal of Nursing Administration</u>, <u>19</u>(7), 17-23.

Bunning, R.L. (1991, August). Smooth steps to transition meetings. <u>Human Resources Magazine</u>, pp. 59-63.

Coeling, H., & Wilcox, J.R. (1988). Understanding organizational culture: A key to management decision-making. <u>Journal of Nursing Administration</u>, <u>18</u>(11), 16-23.

Cromwell, T. (1993). Productivity presented graphically. <u>Nursing Management</u>, <u>24</u>(4), 73-78.

Edwards, M.R. (1991, June). Accurate performance measurement tools. <u>Human Resources Magazine</u>, pp. 95-98.

Faubert, R. (1993). Budgeting for hospital in-service education-A missing standard. <u>Journal of Health care Education and Training</u>, 8(1), 5-7.

Finkler, S. (1992). <u>Budgeting concepts for nurse managers and executives</u> (2nd ed.). Philadelphia: Saunders.

Garre, P.P. (1992). Multi attribute utility theory in decision-making. <u>Nursing Management</u>, 23(5), 33-35.

Goodale, J.G. (1993, May). Seven ways to improve performance appraisals. <u>Human Resources Magazine</u>, pp. 77-80.

Hambrick, R. (1991). <u>The management skills builder</u>. New York: Praeger.

Hirsch, M. (1993, December). New ways to negotiate. <u>Working Woman</u>, pp. 25-26.

Joint Commission on Accreditation of Healthcare Organizations. (1999). <u>2000 Comprehensive manual for hospitals</u>. Chicago: Author.

Keely, B., & Davis, K. (1994). Productivity in education: Facing critical options. <u>Journal of Continuing Education in Nursing</u>, 21(4), 150-153.

Kirk, R. (1990). Using workload analysis and acuity systems to facilitate quality and productivity. <u>Journal of Nursing Administration</u>, 20(3), 21-30.31.

Kouzes, J., & Posner, B. (1990). <u>The leadership challenge</u>. San Francisco: Jossey-Bass.

Mundel, M.E. (1978). <u>Motion and time study</u> (5th ed.). Englewood Cliffs, NJ: Prentice-Hall.

O'Brien-Pallas, L., Cockerill, R., & Leatt, P. (1992). Different systems, different costs? An examination of the comparability of workload measurement systems. <u>Journal of Nursing Administration</u>, 22(12), 17-22.

Quick, T. (1987). <u>Quick solutions: 500 people problems managers face and how to solve them</u>. New York: John Wiley & Sons.

Salluzzo, R. F., Mayer, T. A., Strauss, R. W., et al. (1997). Emergency department managment: Principles and applications. St. Louis: Mosby.

Shott, Susan. (1990). <u>Statistics for health professionals</u>. Philadelphia: Saunders.

Silva, N., & Aderholdt, B. (1989). Computerizing assessment of workload and productivity. <u>Nursing Management</u>, 20(11), 49-55.

Wurman, R. (1992). <u>Follow the yellow brick road: Learning to give, take, and use Instructions</u>. New York: Bantam.

APPENDIX A
ORIENTATION SUMMARY EVALUATION

NEW YORK PRESBYTERIAN HOSPITAL
NEW YORK WEILL CORNELL MEDICAL CENTER
Department of Nursing Education

<u>ORIENTATION NARRATIVE SUMMARY</u>

Nancy Nurse , RN	Steve Weinman , RN
(Orientee)	(Instructor)

12/12/2000	Emergency Department	11.5 hours
(Date of Summary)	(Unit)	(Shift)

Nancy has successfully completed her orientation to the Emergency Department at New York Weill Cornell Medical Center. Nancy began full-time employment on 9/13/2000 and attended HR & Nursing Orientation from 9/13 – 9/27. She completed Emergency Nursing Specialty Orientation (9/21, 22, & 23). She was exempted from the Dysrhythmia (ACLS verification) & sucessfully challenged the Emergency Nursing Exemption Examination (90% prehire). In addition she attended Pediatric Day on 9/28, Geriatric Course on 9/30, and the Trauma Course on 10/4-5. Her 10 week orientation was from 9/13/99 through 11/20/99 and was comprised of 7.5 hours shifts during weeks 1-4 progressing to 11.5 hour shifts from week 5–10.

Nancy completed her orientation to the Adult Emergency Department with sub-specialty rotation to Triage, Pediatric, & Psychiatric Emergency Departments. At Triage she demonstrated good assessment & prioritization of patients. In the Pediatric Emergency Department Nancy practiced appropriate age specific assessments and interventions for infants, children, and adolescents. In the Psychiatric Emergency Department Nancy performed appropriate intake assessment and interventions on patients with established mental illness as well as those experiencing situational crisis. In the adult emergency department Nancy was introduced to trauma, acute and non-acute care as well as OB/GYN. Nancy showed progressive ability to handle multiple patient workloads with varying complexities. Nancy also demonstrated appropriate assessment and interventions for adult & geriatric patient populations.

Throughout her orientation Nancy has demonstrated good progressive in her organizational and prioritization skills. She recognizes that continuing education is very important in emergency nursing and will attend future CE offerings in the department & institution.

Nancy's orientation checklists have been reviewed and are attached to ther summary. While every effort is made to aquaint orientees to the diverse patients and equipment of the ED, Nancy did not encounter the following clinical experiences during her orientation: Haz-Mat decontamination, application of spinal immobilization in a non-simulated patient encounter, radiant warmer in a non-simulation resuscitation, cardioversion/defibrillation, pacemaker (transvenous/cutaneous) application in an unstable cardiac patient, invasive line application (ie arterial line, ventriculosotomy), chest tube/autotransfusion, GL/DPL, & Morgan lens irrigation. Nancy demonstrated these skills in simulated clinical encounteres with the ED Instructor. She is able to verbally recall as well as demonstrate the aforementioned skills/procedures and their use in simulated instances. Nancy actively seeks out resources as needed.

Future goals for Nancy include continuing education and I would also like to see her participate on a ED committee. Nancy has made excellent progress during her orientation, and she has been encouraged to continue doing so now that orientation has concluded.

_____

(Orientee Signature)

_____

(ED Instructor)

_____

(ED Director of Nursing)

G:\FORMS\SUM 12/00

APPENDIX B
EMERGENCY NURSE EDUCATOR JOB DESCRIPTION

JOHN PETER SMITH HOSPITAL

JOB DESCRIPTION

JOB TITLE		JOB CODE
EDUCATION COORDINATOR		6890
DEPARTMENT	DEPARTMENT NO.	EFFECTIVE DATE
EMERGENCY MEDICINE	678	01/08/93

SUMMARY:

Under the direction of the Director, performs duties and manages responsibilities related to education and training of all personnel. Duties and responsibilities also include those associated with affiliating students from professional nursing schools or vocational training experiences. This position will coordinate activities with the Education and Training Department and will maintain official documentation files required for validation of orientation, in-service training, and skills validations.

TYPICAL DUTIES

- Outlines individual orientation program for new staff. This includes assigning preceptors and arranging work schedule.

- Evaluates content and processes associated with departmental orientation; maintains necessary records.

- Develops, implements, and evaluates initial and recurring skills validation components for personnel; maintains necessary records.

- Develops, implements, and evaluates education and training programs based on expressed and implied needs of personnel.

- Maintains a database of personnel with special training capabilities such as CPR instructors, ACLS instructors, TNCC instructors, etc.

- Plans and evaluates training exercises such as "mock codes" or disaster responses on a regularly scheduled basis and plans programs to correct documented deficiencies.

- Meets with Nurse Managers to consider staffing needs related to education and training.

- Provides staff with articles of interest or bibliography relating to Emergency Medicine.

- Develops and maintains unit reference works and library resources.

- Develops and updates educational notices including opportunities for in-house, community, and other offerings.
- Serves as liaison to professional and vocational nursing programs and assists with coordination of educational experiences in the Department.
- Attends operations and management team meetings to address education/training concerns. Available to attend team and QI meetings as requested.
- Coordinates trauma nurse education components with the Trauma Nurse Coordinator.
- Plans Grand Rounds when assigned by the Director.
- Assists with other educational endeavors as assigned by Director.

NOTE: *Any qualifications to be considered as substitutions for stated minimums must be approved by the Manager of Personnel Services.*

EDUCATION AND EXPERIENCE

Graduate of an accredited school of professional nursing required. Bachelor of Science degree in nursing strongly recommended. Three years clinical experience in Emergency Medicine required. Demonstrated knowledge of principles of adult learning and teaching.

- Color vision required to distinguish shades.
- Talking/hearing, speaking required to communicate with staff and other hospital personnel.
- Hearing/speaking required to use telephone.
- Able to enunciate and project voice to speak to groups.
- Work is light on a usual basis; may be required to lift 50 pounds.
- Frequent sitting, walking, and standing.
- Manual dexterity required for writing, use of computer, and calculator.

WORKING CONDITIONS

- Work is inside but may walk outside occasionally.
- Surroundings can be very distracting and noisy.
- Skin/eye/mucous membrane irritants.
- Subject to stressful work, pressures, and deadlines.
- May require local or overnight travel.
- May be exposed to communicable diseases including blood borne pathogen, i.e., HIV and Hepatitis B, airborne pathogens, i.e., tuberculosis, and fetid odors.
- Minimal exposure to low dose radiation, i.e., tandem and avoid placement, portable x-ray, etc.
- Occasionally has to deal with irate, agitated, and uncooperative patients.

SPECIALIZED TRAINING OR CERTIFICATION

Recommended:

- CEN, TNCC provider and instructor, ACLS provider and instructor, CPR provider and instructor.

Required:

- Current RN licensure by State of Texas Board of Nurse Examiners or eligibility for reciprocity.

EQUIPMENT, TOOLS, AND MATERIALS USED

Computer, various audiovisual equipment, educational materials, medical supplies, and equipment.

SUPERVISION GIVEN

Supervises staff in learning situations.

SUPERVISION RECEIVED

Receives direct supervision from the Director.

ATTITUDES

- Ability to provide leadership, promote teamwork, work with groups, and facilitate problem-solving task forces.
- Ability to analyze data, draw conclusions, and make decisions required to adjust standard procedures, assess needs, plan, implement, and evaluate Emergency Medicine activities.
- Verbal aptitude, oral expression, and ability to meet and deal with people required to communicate effectively with all levels of people.
- Clerical aptitude is required to maintain accurate records.
- Arithmetic computation required to monitor fiscal reports.
- Concentration amidst distraction and ability to work rapidly required to perform varied job functions in busy surroundings.
- Ability to develop employee schedules.
- Able to rotate shifts and be available to staff.
- Memory for oral direction required to carry out verbal instructions.
- Ability to read and write English.
- Ability to verbally communicate effectively with customers.
- Ability to communicate effectively through written memos and reports.

PHYSICAL DEMANDS:

- Able to meet the physical demands of the job with assistive or adaptive devices or reasonable accommodation.

- Able to meet the standards of health established by law, regulation, or policy.

- Able to sustain physical activity level necessary to perform essential job elements for full work shift.

- Visual acuity needed to read printed materials.

This description is intended to indicate the kinds of tasks and levels of work difficulty that will be required of positions that will be given this title and shall not be construed as declaring what the specific duties and responsibilities of any particular position shall be. It is not intended to limit or in any way modify the right of any supervisor to assign, direct, and control the work of employees under his or her supervision. The use of a particular expression or illustration describing duties shall not be held to exclude other duties not mentioned that are of similar kind or level of difficulty.

JOB ANALYST: _____   DATE: _____

REVIEWED BY: _____   DATE: _____

APPROVED BY: _____   DATE: _____

John Peter Smith Hospital

ADA ESSENTIAL ELEMENTS

Job Code: 6890

Job Title: Education Coordinator

Dept. No.: 678

Department: Emergency Medicine

ESSENTIAL ELEMENTS:

- Outlines individual orientation program for new staff. This includes assigning preceptors and arranging work schedule.

- Evaluates content and processes associated with Departmental orientation; maintains necessary records.

- Develops, implements, and evaluates initial and recurring skills validation components for personnel; maintains necessary records.

- Develops, implements, and evaluates education and training programs based on expressed and implied needs of personnel.

- Maintains a database of personnel with special training capabilities such as CPR instructors, ACLS instructors, TNCC instructors, etc.

- Plans and evaluates training exercises such as "mock codes" or disaster responses on a regularly scheduled basis and plans programs to correct documented deficiencies.

- Meets with Nurse Managers to consider staffing needs related to education and training.

- Provides staff with articles of interest or bibliography relating to Emergency Medicine.

- Develops and maintains unit reference works and library resources.

- Develops and updates educational notices including opportunities for in-house, community, and other offerings.

- Serves as liaison to professional and vocational nursing programs and assists with coordination of educational experiences in the Department.

- Attends operations and management team meetings to address education/training concerns. Available to attend team and QI meetings as requested.

- Coordinates trauma nurse education components with the Trauma Nurse Coordinator.

- Plans Grand Rounds when assigned by the Director.

- Assists with other educational endeavors as assigned by Director.

Essential elements are those duties that must be performed to accomplish the job. The following statements are descriptors of essential elements:

A. The position exists to perform the function.

B. Only a limited number of employees are available who can perform the function.

C. The function is highly specialized, and the person in the position is hired for special expertise or ability to perform it.

D. There are serious consequences if this function is not performed.

JOB ANALYST: _____ DATE: _____

REVIEWED BY: _____ DATE: _____

APPROVED BY: _____ DATE: _____

Used with permission from John Peter Smith Hosptial, Fort Worth, Texas.

CHAPTER 10

Continuous Quality Improvement

OBJECTIVES:

At the conclusion of this chapter, the emergency nurse educator will be able to:

1. Identify three roles related to continuous quality improvement (CQI).

2. Describe the relationship between CQI and educational planning.

INTRODUCTION

Changes in health care have impressed health care providers with the need to render quality care in a more cost-effective manner. With this impetus, many institutions have committed to continuous quality improvement (CQI), a structured process for improvement that involves all organizational levels.

A major component of CQI is employee participation. Each employee is encouraged to identify areas for improvement. Once a process has been identified, a project statement is developed and submitted to a quality council. The council is responsible for the review of project statements and designation of a project team for the identified process. A multidisciplinary approach to CQI ensures all organizational levels and appropriate health care providers are represented.

Various roles and responsibilities the educator may assume within the constructs of CQI are summarized below. This chapter will provide the basics about CQI. Emergency nurse educators working in an institution where CQI is in its infancy should benefit from the following insights into the process of quality assessment; however, development of a comprehensive knowledge base of CQI will require more information.

CQI PRINCIPLES

Successful CQI programs begin with an understanding of essential CQI principles.

- Every process can be improved.

- CQI strives to achieve the organization's and ED's mission.

- Quality efforts should exceed expectations of internal and external customers.

- Senior management must be committed to quality improvement.

- Sufficient resources should be allocated to enable the process.

- Employees are an organization's greatest asset. Each employee is encouraged to participate through:

   I Decision-making.

   I Goal setting.

   I Problem-solving.

I Participation in the change process (Wilson, 1992).

• Multidisciplinary collaboration encourages shared decision making and promotes the quality improvement process.

• Quality improvement focuses on processes.

• The scientific method is utilized to achieve quality. The acronym "PDCA" can be used to clarify the scientific method:

I **P**lan.

I **D**o.

I **C**heck.

I **A**ct (Schroeder, 1994).

CQI PERSPECTIVES

Historically, nurse educators have taken an active role in assuring quality care. With quality assurance (QA), educator responsibilities included departmental QA activities and staff education on changes implemented as a result of a QA study. With CQI, the educator is involved from four different perspectives:

• Initial CQI implementation.

• Orientation to CQI.

• CQI processes/components.

• CQI education processes.

INITIAL IMPLEMENTATION OF CQI

Initial CQI implementation requires staff orientation and education. Institutions may utilize in-house staff for all or part of the implementation process. The implementation process usually begins with orientation for senior management, often provided by outside consultants (Schroeder, 1994). Regardless of implementation strategy, the nurse educator assumes an important role in the implementation of CQI. Initial involvement of the emergency nurse educator may be limited to familiarizing staff with the tenets of CQI. As the CQI program expands, the emergency nurse educator is often given additional responsibilities, such as team leading or group facilitation.

ORIENTATION TO CQI

Introduction to the hospital CQI program is mandated by the Joint Commission on Accreditation of Healthcare Organizations (JCAHO) and should be an integral part of new employee orientation. The CQI program may be introduced during general hospital orientation or presented during department orientation. If a competency-based orientation or modular orientation program is utilized, a module on CQI should be included. CQI orientation should include:

• Overview of QI.

I History of QA/QI.

I Reasons for CQI.

I Differences between QA and CQI.

- **❙** Definitions.
- ● Basic principles of quality management.
- ● Organizational structure for CQI.
    - **❙** Vision statement.
    - **❙** Project teams.
- ● Effects on job performance.

CQI PROCESSES/COMPONENTS

Once CQI has been initiated, it is almost inevitable that the emergency nurse educator will become involved in a quality project. Specific responsibilities include:

- ● Problem identification.
    - **❙** Project statement.
- ● Project team membership.
    - **❙** Facilitator.
    - **❙** Team leader.
    - **❙** Committee member.
- ● Change.
    - **❙** Agent.
    - **❙** Education.

PROJECT STATEMENT

Nurses and educators are generally insightful regarding department strengths and weaknesses; therefore, the nurse educator is in an excellent position to identify processes that need improvement. When the educator does identify a potential process, the educator should draft a project statement succinctly defining the problem.

Individual organizations may have specific guidelines for project statements; however, the following general guidelines usually apply.

- ● Define the problem in measurable terms.
- ● Use performance criteria to outline the problem.
- ● Avoid assumptions regarding the cause of the problem.
- ● Resist solving the problem in the project statement (ENA, 1994).

PROJECT TEAM MEMBERSHIP

A project team consists of the team leader, a process facilitator, and team members. Team responsibilities include:

- ● Process clarification.
- ● Development of plan for process improvement.

- Selection of improvement techniques.
- Data gathering and analysis.
- Maintenance of improvements.

FACILITATOR

The group facilitator need not be an expert on the process being studied; however, the facilitator must demonstrate expertise in CQI principles/tools and group dynamics. The facilitator is not considered a member of the project team (ENA, 1994). Ideally, the facilitator interacts with the project team, but maintains a neutral role. Specific responsibilities include:

- Assist team leader with future meetings.
- Facilitate team progress through group dynamics:
  - Orientation.
  - Interpersonal group conflict.
  - Cohesion building.
  - Interdependence/loyalty.
- Act as resource for CQI processes and tools (Schroeder, 1994).

TEAM LEADER

The team leader plays a pivotal role in the success of the project team. The most effective team leader has a vested interest in the process under consideration. Involvement of the leader and the members in the process enhances the motivation necessary to improve the process (ENA, 1994). Team leader responsibilities include:

- Schedule meetings.
- Develop agendas.
- Keep meeting productive and appropriate (ENA, 1994).

CHANGE

Change is inherent to CQI; it is the basis for all improvement. Forces that may work against change can be dealt with more effectively when involved parties are aware of their existence. When restraining forces are identified and the appropriate people are involved in overcoming these forces, the transition from one process to another causes minimal disruption. To ensure this smooth transition, recommended changes must have staff support and involvement at various levels of the project. Team actions, such as surveys, process evaluations, and force field analyses, enhance staff support for recommended changes.

CQI WITHIN THE EDUCATOR ROLE

In addition to the educator's role in CQI implementation and subsequent CQI processes, the educator must also monitor specific education processes for improvement. Education processes that may benefit from CQI include staff orientation and continuing education.

CQI as a Component of Orientation

Orientation is essential for quality attainment. Continuous monitoring and evaluation of the orientation process assures desired outcomes. Monitoring and evaluation should address orientation as well as the customers of the process. These customers include:

- Department manager.
- Orientee.
- Peers of the orientee.
- Patient.

Input from the nurse manager is a critical component in evaluation of the education process. First, it provides the nurse manager an opportunity to clarify specific expectations of the orientation process. Subsequent to this communication, the educator can educate the nurse manager about the orientation process. With better understanding of the orientation process, the manager has a more realistic perception of time required to produce a quality employee (Schroeder, 1994).

Feedback from past orientees is beneficial in improving current and future orientations. Mechanisms to obtain this feedback must consider the orientee's expectations of the program. Nurses with prior experience want an orientation that is concise, to the point, limited to essential policies, and procedures. Less experienced nurses want an orientation that progresses slowly until the orientee feels competent.

Patient feedback is often overlooked in evaluation of the orientation program. This type of feedback enables the educator to evaluate orientee function after the orientation program is complete. Surveys, questionnaires, follow-up phone calls, and complaint records may be used to obtain patient feedback.

Continuing Education Programs

The CQI monitoring process focuses on high-volume, high-risk, high-cost, and problem-prone areas. It is an excellent method for identification of specific topics for continuing education. Evaluation of CQI outcomes is also beneficial in identification of pertinent topics for continuing education programs. When outcomes are undesirable, education can be developed to improve outcomes.

SUMMARY

Documentation of value to the organization is essential for the educator. Despite the importance of education to quality patient care, the educator is often an early victim of staffing redesign or cutbacks. Quality improvement methods enable the educator to demonstrate professional value by quantifying the educator's effect on patient care.

REFERENCES

Emergency Nurses Association. (1994). CQI: Building the foundation. Park Ridge, IL: Author.

Schroeder, P. (1994). Improving quality and performance: Concepts, programs, and techniques. St. Louis: Mosby.

Wilson, C.K. (1992). Building new nursing organizations: Vision and realities. Gaithersburg, MD: Aspen.

RECOMMENDED READINGS

Arikian, V.L. (1991). Total quality management: Applications to nursing service. Journal of Nursing Administration, 21(6), 46-50.

Berwick, D.M., Godfrey, B.A., & Goessner, J. (1990). Curing health care: New strategies for quality improvement. San Francisco: Jossey-Bass.

Blake, C. (1994). Value leadership in total quality management. Nursing Management, 25(7), 88-89.

D'Aquila, N.W., Habegger, D., & Willwerth, E.J. (1994). Converting a QA program to CQI. Nursing Management, 25(10), 68-71.

Hames, D.S. (1991). Productivity-enhancing work innovations: Remedies for what ails hospitals. Hospital & Health Services Administration, 36(4), 545-558.

Harachleroad, F.P., Martin, M.L., Kremen, R.M., & Murray K.W. (1988). Emergency department daily record review: A quality assurance system in a teaching hospital. Quality Review Bulletin, 14(2), 45-49.

Joint Commission on Accreditation of Healthcare Organizations. (1993, November/December). A framework for improving the performance of health care organizations. Joint Commission Perspectives Insert, pp. A1-A6.

Joint Commission on Accreditation of Healthcare Organizations. (1999). 2000 Comprehensive manual for hospitals. Chicago: Author.

Keeler, E., Rubenstein, L.V., Kahn, K.L., Draper, D., Harrison, E.R., McGinty, M.J., Rogers, W.H., & Brook, R.H. (1992). Hospital characteristics and quality of care. Journal of the American Medical Association, 268(13), 1709-1714.

Kennedy, M. (1992). Combining the best of QA and TQM. Quality Management Update, 2(1), 1, 10-14.

Kirk, R. (1992). The big picture: Total quality management and continuous quality improvement. Journal of Nursing Administration, 22(4), 24-31,

Miles, C.A., & McCloskey, J.M. (1993, February). People: The key to productivity. Human Resources Magazine pp. 40-45.

Reilly, P., Seibert, C.P., Miller, N.E., Canney, K.C., & McHugh, M. (1994). Implementation of a collaborative quality assessment program. Journal of Nursing Administration, 24(5), 65-71.

Salluzzo, R. F., Mayer, T. A., Strauss, R. W., et al. (1997). Emergency department managment: Principles and applicaitons. St. Louis: Mosby.

Sherman, J.J., & Malkmus, M.A. (1994). Integrating quality assurance and total quality management/quality improvement. Journal of Nursing Administration, 24(3), 37-41.

Simpson, R.L. (1994). How technology enhances total quality improvement. Nursing Management, 25(6), 40-41.

Stiles, R.A. (1994). Classifying quality initiatives: A conceptual paradigm for literature review and policy analysis. Hospital & Health Services Administration, 39(3), 309-326.

Swor, R.A. (1992). Quality assurance in EMS systems. Emergency Clinics of North America, 10(3), 597-610.

CHAPTER 11

A Treasure Chest of Resources for the Emergency Nurse Educator

OBJECTIVES

Upon completion of this chapter, the emergency nurse educator will be able to:

1. List the common internal reference sources for the educator.

2. List the common external reference sources for the educator.

3. Briefly describe the Internet.

4. Distinguish three forms of Internet communication with potential value to emergency nursing educators.

5. Discuss the potential impact of the Internet upon emergency nursing education.

6. Name examples of Internet sites that are useful to emergency nursing.

7. Envision ways that Internet usage may be incorporated within and enhance emergency nursing education and be desirous of doing so.

INTRODUCTION

Resources are people, products, and services. Type, quality, and quantity of resources vary from institution to institution and from community to community. Resources available in a large teaching hospital are dramatically different than those available to a small, rural hospital. The primary determinant of resource utilization is often knowledge of where to look in the organization, the community, and now thanks to technology, worldwide via the Internet. This chapter provides a generic list of services and products that may be found in various departments, organizations, communities, and on the Internet.

INTERNAL RESOURCES

Internal resources may be found in a variety of hospital departments. This section provides a list of generically identified hospital departments further broken down into the assistance, advice, instruction, support, consultants, and products that each department may have available. This list is by no means complete. The educator should seek additional sources of support and assistance within their respective institution.

- Admissions.
  - Patient valuables management.
  - Admission trends.

- Anesthesia.
  - Conscious sedation procedures.
  - Pain management.
  - Airway management.
  - Invasive monitoring.
- Critical care nursing.
  - Pain management.
  - Invasive monitoring.
- Education/staff development.
  - Other educators/experts.
- Multimedia equipment and support.
  - Slide bank and slide production.
  - Ccontact hour/CME approval.
  - Basic life support/advanced life support training equipment.
  - Database for attendance records.
  - Computer assistance.
  - Computer-assisted instruction.
  - Graphics production.
  - Photography.
- Emergency medicine.
  - Airway management.
  - Clinical practice issues.
  - Assistance with ED education.
  - Research.
  - Collaborative efforts.
- Endoscopy lab.
  - Conscious sedation procedures.
  - Video monitoring.
- Engineering/maintenance.
  - Cost estimates for construction.
  - JCAHO regulations related to structures, airflow, and environment.
  - Electrical safety.
  - Fire codes and regulations.

- Information systems.
  - Computer support.
  - Data analysis.
- Intravenous therapy.
  - Venous access devices.
  - Peripherally inserted central catheters.
  - Patient-controlled analgesia pumps.
- Management engineering.
  - Productivity analysis.
  - Computer support.
  - Time and motion studies.
  - Acuity analysis and validation.
- Marketing/public relations.
  - Market surveys and results analysis.
  - Media support.
  - Demographic statistics for service area.
  - Photography.
- Medical library.
  - In-house librarian.
  - Computer search capability.
- Medical records.
  - ICD-9 coding for diagnoses, procedures, and etiology of injury.
- Nutrition and food services.
  - Catering.
  - Nutrition references/consultants.
  - Food/drug interactions
- Oncology.
  - Hospice.
  - Bereavement support groups.
  - Venous access devices.
  - Radiation safety.
  - Chemotherapy.
- Pastoral care service.
  - Employee counseling.
  - Grief counseling.

- Religious and cultural issues.
- Spiritual assessment.
- Personnel.
  - Job descriptions.
  - Performance appraisals.
  - Labor laws.
  - Employee benefits.
- Pharmacy.
  - Formulary.
  - Medication database.
  - Food/drug interactions.
- Quality management/utilization review.
  - Statistical data on patient diagnoses.
  - Reimbursement parameters for insurance carriers, Medicare, and Medicaid.
  - Case management.
- Radiology.
  - Radiation safety.
- Risk management.
  - Case law/state law/federal law.
  - Legal issues.
  - OSHA regulations.
  - Impaired nurse procedures.
- Security.
  - Personal safety.
  - Fire safety.
  - Electrical safety.
  - Patient restraint.
  - Emergency department violence monitoring and prevention.
  - Patient valuables management.
- Telecommunications.
  - Language lines.
  - Phone services for the hearing-impaired.
- Volunteers.
  - Emergency photocopying.
  - Collation/distribution of materials.

- Miscellaneous.
  - In-house printer.

EXTERNAL RESOURCES

External resources are available from professional, private, and community organizations. Networking with various professional and community groups is an effective method for identifying potential resources, soliciting feedback on new ideas, and enhancing existing support. A brief list of professional and community agencies is provided. Agencies and services vary with location, therefore the educator should explore additional sources of information and support within their community.

PROFESSIONAL RESOURCES

Look for professional networking opportunities at professional meetings and educational offerings. Expand networking to include contacts with EMS providers, police, fire, and local military organizations. Remember that networking is a two-way street. Exchange of services and information strengthens the networking relationship and increases benefit for both parties.

- Consultants.
- Emergency nursing consultants.
- Triage.
- Disaster management.
- Speakers for continuing education.
- Coroner/medical examiner.
  - Death investigations.
  - Mortality demographics.
  - Injury patterns.
- EMS agencies.
  - Loaner equipment.
  - Disaster triage.
- Trauma resources
- Verification courses such as ACLS, ATLS, BLS, PHTLS
- Fire departments.
  - Hazardous materials management.
  - Fire safety.
  - Trench rescue.
- Health department.
  - Statistical data on diseases.
  - OSHA regulations.
  - HIV counseling.

- Suicide prevention programs.
- Immunizations.
- Rabies prophylaxis.
- Trauma resources
- Medical associations.
  - Publications/reference materials.
  - Speakers/consultants.
  - CE credits.
- Military bases/organizations.
  - Terrorist demographics/activities.
  - Aircraft safety.
  - Explosives.
  - Mass casualty management.
- Nursing organizations.
  - Publications/reference materials.
  - Speakers/consultants.
  - Contact hour credits.
  - Professional certifications.
  - Continuing education courses
- Poison control centers.
  - Poison database.
  - Speakers
  - Continuing education for staff
  - Reference materials.
- Police departments.
  - Violence demographics.
  - Gang activity.
  - Personal safety.
  - Evidence collection and preservation.
- Universities/colleges (nursing, medicine, and health-related professions).
  - Speakers.
  - References.
  - CME/Contact hour approval.
  - Mentors.

- Utility company.
  - Electrical safety.
  - Trench rescue.

COMMUNITY RESOURCES

Community resources include civic groups, social clubs, and special interest groups. The yellow pages, local chamber of commerce, and the newspaper classified section are all excellent sources of information on available services, products, and personnel. Examples include:

- Local services for the blind, hearing-impaired, physically disadvantaged, and others.
- Rape crisis.
- Battered women shelters.
- Homeless shelters.
- Alcoholics Anonymous, Narcotics Anonymous, Cocaine Anonymous, and other 12-step programs.
- Agencies for help and support of special patient populations, e.g., AIDS, Cystic Fibrosis.

USING THE INTERNET AS AN EDUCATIONAL RESOURCE

Introduction

The Internet presents an unrivaled scope of opportunities for the educator. It provides accessibility and ease of communication for a plethora of emergency nursing related content. A classroom exists whenever a willing learner interacts with content or communicates with its provider. Images and sounds, still or moving, recorded or real-time, provide a basis for clinical study and simulation of clinical situations. Using the Internet allows the educator to transcend textbooks, time, and distance.

Historic Background

During the 1960s, the United States Department of Defense sought a means of communication between larger and smaller, remote installations that would be highly resistant to collapse from nuclear catastrophe. What evolved was a network of computers (originally, governmental and military, then extended to academic and industrial sites). Each computer was a conduit for the acquisition and transmission of data. The convenience and capabilities fostered vast growth in the number of users as access increased. Today, the Internet has grown far beyond the vision of the original network.

How the Internet Works

Any computer which has a modem and is connected via a communication line to an Internet Service Provider (or with large institutions, to a "backbone" connection to the Internet) is able to exchange its signals with other computers. Communication is sent out in the form of digital bits that rapidly scan the Internet until the sought-after file is accessed and returned at the speed of electrons to be displayed and acted upon. Exchange of electronic mail (E-mail), files of data or text, images, sounds, even video conferencing, are the products of this process.

Components of the Internet

- E-mail: The exchange of messages directed to an individual or to named entities. Digital files can be attached.

- Telnet: A means by which outside users can be permitted to "operate" a remote computer and give it commands. Remote access to mail servers and use of online databases, e.g., library catalogues, are examples.

- Gopher: An early means in which data on a remote computer can be found and retrieved.

- Usernet: A hierarchical structure of subject-related distributed postings to news groups to which one can subscribe. The administrator of one's system can regulate which news groups can be subscribed. All, or most, generally are available; this is a relatively public way of making views known to all who "go there." Archives are usually kept of past messages.

- Mailing Lists: Membership-based software programs that redistribute one's message to all others on the list by E-mail. The operators of such lists may define the affinity group and may permit easy subscription and access or may regulate it through moderators and editors or close it entirely to outsiders. Successful software programs for servers to run E-mail lists include Listserv®, MajorDomo®, Listproc®, and others. An individual and private relationship is had with the list by the subscriber; as contrasted with Usernet, wherein all persons with Internet access through the same administrator can download the subscribed groups.

- World Wide Web (WWW) "the Web": Originally, a way of obtaining documents posted on the web which are typically "hyperlinked" to others (whether on the same site or to another location on the web). It has grown into a highly graphical and multimedia means of providing information and even interaction between users and servers.

- WWW Discussion Forums: Some websites use software that lets readers post messages for public viewing at the website. The advantage is that only a browser is needed (from a public computer or at work, for example), but one must choose to go to that site rather than have messages arrive in mail or download from the newsgroup (Usernet) server. Likewise, anyone going to the site can view the messages; doing so then is somewhat more public.

- Chat Rooms: Chat rooms are locations where a number of computer users can be online together simultaneously for nearly real-time discussions. Whether spontaneous or pre-arranged, regardless of one's own time zone, all must be online at the same time.

Searching and Finding Things on the Internet

Virtually all Internet providers, i.e., America On-Line, Compuserve, Microsoft Network, provide some form of a search process. The following are search components that typically provide a very comprehensive search of the Internet.

Directory: Yahoo (http://www.yahoo.com) is the best known example of a directory service. It is like using a library card catalogue or telephone "yellow pages" business directory. One selects preassigned categories and subcategories (assigned by a human being) of increasing specialization and precision to find all listed sites of a category.

Search Engine: Search engines are computers which on a periodic basis access as many www sites as possible to compile a database of addresses and their attributes, e.g., title, type of file, content as determined by meta tags in the ordinarily unviewed "head" of the document, or by reading the document itself. This database can then be queried to find files by name or by keywords. An analogy would be finding an unknown telephone number from an information operator with a series of questions, i.e., city, surname, first name or initial, street or type of business, etc.

Meta-Engine: Since each search engine has operating instructions that differ from others, or may have different success in scavenging the entire web, a meta-engine attempts to harness the power of many by constructing from one query a set of search terms that can interrogate multiple search engines and return their results. This may cast a wider net and retrieve more findings. Additional time will be needed and some duplicate results may obtain.

Effectively Using the Web as a Teaching Instrument:

Make friends with your Web Administrator: Networking with your institution's web administrator can provide powerful consultancy, allocation of resources, troubleshooting capability, and facilitating realization of your goals for your program.

Use and Cruise the Web: Being a frequent user of the web makes you familiar with available resources and of trends in website development. Resources are constantly changing/evolving.

Searching: Understand the methods of searching. Learn the characteristics of each search engine used. Make your own documents easier to be searched by ensuring good titles and good meta tags indicating description, keywords, authorship, copyright.

Keywords: These meta tags indicate appropriate searchable terms to allow easier finding. Thus, "difficult airway, resuscitation, endotracheal intubation, failed intubation, cricothyrotomy, tracheostomy, laryngeal mask airway," will produce specific useful findings rather than anesthesia, anesthesiology, or even anaesthesiology, which will bring up too many results to be practical.

Save what you find: (-bookmarks, -locally, -printed out) If you wish to return to a webpage again, save it as a "bookmark" or "favorite." However, if you really wish to have it available when you need it, save it on your hard drive, storage media (floppy disc, ZIP drive, tape), or even print it out to paper. You may otherwise find when you really must have it, that the URL is changed, defective, the server is down, your Internet connection is down, or the document has been edited, revised, deleted, or made inaccessible to those outside the "firewall" of the source server.

Click on through (hints for retrieving web documents):

When surfing for useful web material, check the list of links given by a webpage and follow the links provided as you may find better material in such lists or supporting references.

How the destination is named in the link which is provided might not be indicative of the true title of that URL, as in "click here" or editorial renaming by the provider of the link ("check this out!"). Most browsers provide a line that indicates the hypertext address that will be activated if clicked when the cursor or pointing device is over it. Thus, you will have a clue as to the destination without actually going there. You may then recall if it is a link that you have otherwise visited.

If you wish to continue on the page that you are visiting during the contact and download time for the link that you have selected, it is useful to "right-click" the mouse button or otherwise choose "open link in new window." You can then return to your original task. Individual frames of a site can be opened in this manner to which will allow either full-size viewing of the frame, or if an external link to view the new site without being trapped in the frames of the original site. The number of windows that you may have open at one time is limited only by the processing power of your computer and the speed of your Internet connection as the amount of work being done by your computer slows down other tasks. If, however, you lose your connection, or your computer "crashes," you will lose all unsaved work on documents and any unsaved bookmarks/favorites that you might have wished to save.

You may wish to "right-click" or choose "add bookmark" to directly save a desired URL as a bookmark, or "save location as..." to save the file as an html file on your hard drive. Generally, only the text of the page will be saved unless you "open" that page in an html editor before saving or you separately save the images on your hard drive also.

When saving hypertext links as bookmarks, the bookmark will display the text of the link (if you are saving from a link), or if bookmarking from the page itself the default caption will be the title, if any, provided by the page's creator. This may be nondescript ("My Home Page" or "links") and require editing in your bookmark file to be useful to you. You may create folders to organize like-minded sites or use keywords in the listing to allow easier searching.

If you receive an error message, typically "404: file not found," the site may have been restructured, the file deleted, or the person who previously placed the document may no longer have an account on that server. Try again after "truncating" the URL display in your browser's location line beginning with the final element, each time shortening the URL by an element following a forward slash (/). If one cannot find directions to your goal by the time you reach the domain name, then your effort is fruitless at that server. Next, try a search engine strategy of seeking the name of the site or any information known about its originator, or for applicable keywords to attempt finding a more recent URL.

Permissions and Copyrights: Place copyright statements on all web documents. You may do so and still specifically permit fair use with attribution. You may provide a link for requesting copyright license when desirable. However, you may reasonably expect that others may copy your material without notifying you just as videotaping is freely practiced. Responsible users of the material will do so with attributions included.

Citation of Web Sources: Several citation formats have been offered. Certainly, in addition to a traditional listing of title and author, always include the URL from which obtained and the date upon which it was accessed as a subsequent reader may find considerable difference from the work that you consulted.

For example...

Consult:

> Columbia University Press: Columbia Guide to Online Style
> http://www.columbia.edu/cu/cup/cgos/idx_basic.html

Or

> Electronic Sources: APA Style of Citation *[from University of Vermont]*
> http://www.uvm.edu/~xli/reference/apa.html

Criteria for determining reliability of a site as a source for medical and nursing subjects:

How do you determine the reliability of information offered on the web?

- HON Code. Health on the Net Code of Conduct tells if the site contains authoritative and reliable medical information.

- Affiliation with respected institution.

- Author identifies self, provides link and contact information.

- References are provided for material or opinions wherever possible with weblinks if available.

- Reviewer recommendation.

- Commonly provided as link by other reputable sites.

Search resources of allied disciplines: If searching for subject content, remember to check web resources for other professions or specialties which may be interested in the topic, rather than merely for nursing resources, or to search upon relevant keywords rather than nursing topics and titles. For example, airway management resources may be found in sources devoted to emergency medicine, critical care, anesthesia, otorhinolaryngology, trauma surgery, respiratory therapy, emergency medical services, and subcomponents for emergency medical technicians and paramedics. While MEDLINE searches will draw from many respected national and international journals, it will not do so for some of these fields, nor will they point to Internet resources or to texts.

Safety and Privacy: Do not place on the Internet personal information that you do not wish to be seen. Encryption of data by secure sites is quite good; however, before purchasing something you may wish to telephone the seller and exchange credit information by telephone. Do not publish information about someone or their likeness without permission or meeting "fair use" journalistic standards of reporting.

Distance Learning and Testing: An advantage of the Internet is the easy exchange of files that can be rendered digitally. An educator can send messages, receive reports or assignments with supporting attachments and hyperlinks to sources, and control access to server files with passwords or cookies. Testing can be done by submitting forms or by interactive means.

Re-verify links frequently: Although ease of revision is an advantage of electronic publishing of documents, it is also true that the document retrieved later:

- may not be the one originally found,

- may not be found again if the site is drastically reorganized,

- may have changed servers (without a forwarding address),

- or may have been withdrawn from the web.

Web Authoring and WYSIWYG programs

Writing web documents can be done with:

- simple text programs such as Notepad,

- a word processing program which has a conversion utility to "save as html,"

- an html editing program with "what you see is what you get (WYSIWYG)" features (create the document; the program writes the html for the formatting).

Some very good weblinks for Emergency Nursing:

(This list is not intended to be exhaustive or comprehensive. These are stable sites from which one can begin to explore.)

EMERGENCY NURSING PROFESSIONAL BODIES

ENA–Emergency Nurses Association	http://www.ena.org
Queensland Emergency Nurses Association, Inc.	http://www.kmtech.com.au/~qena/
Association Francophone des Infirmier(e)s d'Urgence	http://users.skynet.be/chritoum/
NENA–National Emergency Nurses Affiliation, Inc.	http://www.nena.ca/infonena/index.htm
Irish Emergency Nurses Association	http://eire.org/iena/
Cives–Infirmieri per l'emergenza–Italian	http://www.cives.it/
SNA–Emergency Nurses Chapter Homepage [Singapore]	http://members.tripod.com/~somchai/index.html
Swedish Association of Trauma Nurses (English language version)	http://www.TRAUMA.C.SE/english/index.html
Swedish Association of Nurses in Accident & Emergency Care	http://home6.swipnet.se/~w-60591/
Trauma Nurse.org	http://www.trauma nurse.org/
ENA State Council	http://www.ena.org/about/chapters

Emergency Nursing "content" sites

"Emergency Nursing World!"	http://ENW.org
Emergency-Nurse.com (UK)	http://Emergency-Nurse.com
Willy's Emergency Nursing Web	http://virtualnurse.com/er/er.html
OZ Nurse World–A page for Australian Emergency Nurses	htt://www.quaydesign.com/oznurse
	Default.asp#OZ Nurse World
Homepage for CODERN2	http://home.earthlink.net/~codern2/

Trauma

Trauma.org (United Kingdom)	http://www.trauma.org/
TraumaNET (Orlando, Florida)	http://www.trauma.orhs.org/htmls/homepage2.html
UTHSCSA Trauma (Dr. Ron Stewart, Univ. of Texas Health Science Center at San Antonio	http://rmstewart.uthscsa.edu/
Liverpool Trauma Home Page (Australia)	http://www.swsahs.nsw.gov.au/livtrauma
American Association for the Surgery of Trauma	http://www.aast.org/
Eastern Association for the Surgery of Trauma	http://www.east.org/
LAC+USC Medical Center Trauma Management/SICU Protocols	http://www.usc.edu/hsc/medicine/surgery/ trauma/0toc.html

Emergency Medicine Professional Associations

American Academy of Emergency Medicine	http://www.aaem.org/
ACEP ONLINE–American College of Emergency Physicians	http://www.acep.org/
SAEM–Society for Academic Emergency Medicine	http://www.saem.org/
American College of Osteopathic Emergency Physicians	http://www.acoep.org/
American Trauma Society	http://www.amtrauma.org/
The Emergency Medicine Resident's Association	http://www.emra.org
Society of Emergency Medicine Physician Assistants	http://www.sempa.org/
Australasian College of Emergency Medicine	http://www.acem.org.au/open/documents/home.htm
British Association For Accident and Emergency Medicine	http://www.baem.org.uk/
Canadian Association of Emergency Physicians	http://www.caep.ca/

Other Nursing Specialties

American Association of Critical Care Nurses	http://www.aacn.org
Association of Operating Room Nurses, Inc.	http://www.aorn.org/
American Association of Neuroscience Nurses	http://www.aann.org/
American Association of Nurse Anesthetists	http://www.aana.com/
American Nurses Association	http://www.ana.org/

Medical Professional Organizations

American Medical Association	http://www.ama-assn.org/
American College of Surgeons	http://www.facs.org/

Emergency Medicine Web sites

EMBBS Emergency Medicine and Primary Care Home Page	http://www.embbs.com/
emedicine Online Text–Emergency Medicine	http://www.emedicine.com/emerg/index.shtml
Weekly Web Review in Emergency Medicine	http://www.wwrem.com/
Rehoboth McKinley Christian Hospital ED	http://www.rmch.org/erlinks.htm#emergency
ER World	http://www.erworld.com/
The Center for Pediatric Emergency Medicine (CPEM)	http://www.cpem.org/
Vanderbilt University Medical Center Dept. of Emergency Medicine Teaching Files	http://www.mc.vanderbilt.edu/vumcdept/ emergency/cases.html

Policy and Regulatory Bodies

Joint Commission on Accreditation of Healthcare Organizations	http://www.jcaho.org/
Food & Drug Administration	http://www.fda.gov/
Health Care Financing Administration	http://www.hcfa.gov/

Emergency "Content" from the Medical Specialties

Neurological Emergencies *from* Neurosurgical Web Page *by* SUNY–HSC Syracuse, New York	http://139.127.99.12/teachfile/emerg/emerg.html
Emergencies in Otolaryngology–Head & Neck Surgery *from* Baylor College of Medicine. Department of Otorhinolaryngology	http://www.bcm.tmc.edu/oto/studs/emerg.html
Vanderbilt Pediatric Interactive Digital Library	http://www.mc.Vanderbilt.Edu/peds/pidl/index.htm
John's Airway/Respiratory InfoCenter	http://doyle.ibme.utoronto.ca/awric/index.htm
Society for Airway Management	http://samhq.org

Outstanding Interactive Educational Examples Using the Internet

Triage: Life In The ER	http://parsons.umaryland.edu/triage/
Critical Care Nurse Snapshots Welcome to Critical Thinking in Critical Care	http://www.nursing.ab.umd.edu/students/~jkohl/scenario/opening.htm
Trauma Moulage *from* Trauma.org	http://www.trauma.org/resus/moulage/moulage.html
Interactive Triage Cases *from* Disaster Management Central Resource	http://206.39.77.2/DMCR/triage/cases.html
Sudden Death Trauma Scenarios *from* Liverpool Trauma Home Page, Sydney, Australia	http://www.swsahs.nsw.gov.au/livtrauma/education/sudden.asp
"Fly with HEMS" Helicopter Emergency Medical System, London UK	http://hems-london.virgin.net/
Virtual Phlebotomy: A Computer Aided Course of Instruction	http://parsons.ab.umd.edu/~vguy/phleb.htm
The Interactive Patient	http://medicus.marshall.edu/medicus.htm

Nursing Educator's Topics on the Web

Electronic Learning In A Digital World	http://www.edgorg.com/
How to Offer a Course Over the Internet	http://www.edgorg.com/course.htm
Evaluating Web Sites and other Electronic Resources *from* Virtual Nursing College	http://www.langara.bc.ca/vnc/eval.htm

EMS and Other Emergency Organizations

Paramedic & EMT–Intermediate: National Standard Curricula Revision Project	http://www.pitt.edu/~paramed/
National Association of EMS Educators	http://www.naemse.org/
National Association of Emergency Medical Technicians	http://www.naemt.org/default.htm
National Highway Traffic Safety Administration EMS Division	http://www.nhtsa.dot.gov/people/injury/ems/

Research

MEDLINE	http://www.nlm.nih.gov/databases/freemedl.html	Search abstracts of indexed journals
Deja' News	http://www.dejanews.com/home_ps.shtml	Search archives of usernet groups
Library of Congress	http://www.loc.gov/	
MMWR–Morbidity & Mortality Weekly Report 1	http://www.cdc.gov/epo/mmwr/mmwr.htm	
Center for Disease Control	http://cdc.gov	
National Library of Medicine	http://www.nlm.nih.gov/	
National Center for Health Statistics	http://www.cdc.gov/nchswww/	

Internet Mailing Lists of Interest to Emergency Nursing

Acronym	*List Title*	*Subscribing Address*
Em-Nsg-L	The Emergency Nursing List	LISTSERV@ITSSRV1.UCSF.EDU
ENA Listserv-Managers		managers@ena.org
ENA Listserv-Trauma		trauma@ena.org
ENA Listserv-Pediatrics		pediatrics@ena.org
ENA Listserv-Telephone Triage		teletriage@ena.org
ENA Listserv-Journal		journal@ena.org
ENA Listserv-Government Affairs		government@ena.org
ENA Listserv-Research		research@ena.org

ENA Listserv-Injury Prevention		injuryprev@ena.org
ENA Listserv-EMS		ems@ena.org
ENA Listserv-Forensics		forensics@ena.org
EMED-L	List for Hospital Based Emergency Medicine Practitioners	LISTSERV@ITSSRV1.UCSF.EDU
PED-EM-L	Pediatric Emergency Medicine Discussion List	ped-em-l@brownvm.brown.edu *or* http//www.brown.edu/Administration Emergency_Medicine/ped-em-l.html
Trauma-List	Trauma mailing list from Trauma.org	majordomo@ftech.net
TRAUMA-L	Trauma	join-trauma-l@lists.aast.org
TRAUMA NURSE	Trauma Nurse List (Illinois-based)	trauma nurse@trauma nurse.org
Aenurses (Accident & Emergency UK)	Accident & Emergency Nurses (UK)	contact aenurses-owner@onelist.com
Flightmed	Flight Medicine/Helicopter Transport	LISTSERV@rotor.com
EMED-INFORMATICS	Emergency Medicine Informatics	majordomo@smi.bidmc.harvard.edu
EMS-L	Emergency Medical Services List	listserv@listserv.acns.nwu.edu
CCM-L	Critical Care Medicine List	Majordomo@list.pitt.edu
INJURY-L	Injury Surveillance, Control, & Intervention	LISTSERV@WVNVM.WVNET.EDU
SAR-L	Search & Rescue Discussion List	SAR-L-request@islandnet.com
Question-A-Day [QAD-EMED]	Emergency Medicine Question-A-Day	majordomo@colossus.net *or* http://ncemi.org
WEMS	Wilderness Emergency Medicine	Majordomo@list.pitt.edu

Academic Nursing Exceptional Websites

Where	*Why*	*URL*
University of Vermont School of Nursing	Web Based Courses-"Virtual Classrooms"	http://www.uvm.edu/~nursing/
Virtual Nursing College	Educator's & student's resources for "virtual" nursing education	http://www.langara.bc.ca/vnc/
Nursing Theory Page	Examining the higher plane of nursing theory and theorists	http://www.ualberta.ca/~jrnorris/nt/ theory.html
Susan Newbold's Nursing Informatics Page	Excellent resource and exposition of computerized information management in nursing	http://134.192.4.195/students/ ~snewbol/

An Educator's Strategies for Using the Internet:

- Exchange materials and communication with other instructors and institutions.

- Make material more widely available.

- Provide active hypertext links to references.

- Students' coursework submissions by E-mail with exchange of comments and revisions.

- Post students' papers and projects on web.

- Post quizzes that are answered by form from the website.

- Modular learning units can be placed on the website for self-paced learners to advance through material.

- Rare materials previously kept "on reserve" in libraries can (if no copyright problems exist) be scanned and made accessible to all for own use regardless of library "hours," concurrent usage by others, or distance.

- Have students participate in discussions from selected mailing lists, e.g., Em-Nsg-L, EMED-L, PED-EM-L, Trauma-L, etc.

- Assign an Internet-based review of literature.

- Assign a MEDLINE search to gather evidence to resolve classroom questions.

- Use the sites of manufacturers or resellers to obtain information or images of equipment and supplies.

- Provide feedback on products via manufacturer's websites.

- Provide distance education and rural outreach programs.

Hints for Web Pages:

- Always place a title in the head of the html page.

- Always have a "short title" for the site preceding the title of the page.

- Always have an E-mail link to the webmaster or person responsible for communicating for the site.

- Always state the organization "backing" the site.

- Always provide a date of last revision.

- Always provide a "text" version of the site's URL so that copies printed out will have a reference to the page.

- Always provide "navigation" features (links to other portions of the site).

- Always provide a table of contents or site map so that contents can be previewed.

SUMMARY

The effectiveness of a resource lies not just in its existence, but in the educator's ability to locate it. It is impossible to provide a list of resources available to each educator; however, the references and recommended reading sections in this chapter should help the emergency nurse educator in establishing a resource network.

RECOMMENDED READINGS

Aquilera, D.C. (1990). Crisis intervention: Theory and methodology. St. Louis: Mosby.

Bartlett, J. (1992). Familiar quotations (16th ed.). Boston: Little, Brown.

Bennett, W.J. (1994). The index of leading cultural indicators: Facts and figures of the state of American society. New York: Simon & Schuster.

Buenker, J.D., & Ratner, L.A. (Eds.). (1992). Multiculturalism in the United States. New York: Greenwood Press.

Curtin, L.L. (1990). Attitude: The new posture for the nineties. Nursing Management, 20(11), 7-8.

Donker, R.B., & Ogilvy, J.A. (1993, November/December). The iron triangle and the chrome pentagon. Health care Forum Journal, pp. 72-77.

Friedman, E. (1993). Managed care and managed ethics. Health care Forum Journal, 36(4), 9-15.

Godfrey, C. (1994). Downsizing: Coping with personal pain. Nursing Management, 25(10), 90-93.

Gonens, A. (Ed.). (1993). The encyclopedia of the people of the world. New York: Henry Holt.

Goodwin, D. (1994). Nursing case management activities: How they differ between employment settings. Journal of Nursing Administration, 24(2), 29-34.

Guild, S.D., Ledwin, R.W., Sanford, D.M., & Winter, T. (1994). Development of an innovative nursing care delivery system. Journal of Nursing Administration, 24(3), 23-29.

Hammerschmidt, R., & Meador, C.K. (1993). A little book of nurses' rules. Philadelphia: Hanley & Belfus.

Hill, B. (1998). Internet searching for dummies. Foster City, CA: IDG Books.

Hulbert, J. (1992). Dictionary of symbolism (H. Biederman, Trans.). New York: Facts on File. (Original work published 1989).

Jablonski, S. (1993). Dictionary of medical acronyms and abbreviations (2nd. ed.). Philadelphia: Hanley & Belfus.

Levine, J. R., Baroudi, C., & Levine-Young. (2000). Internet for dummies (7th ed). Foster City, CA: IDG Books.

Mount, E., & List, B.A. (1987). Milestones in sciences and technology. Phoenix: Oryx Press.

Rheaume, A., Firsch, S., Smith, A., & Kennedy, C. (1994). Case management and nursing practice. Journal of Nursing Administration, 24(3), 30-36.

Shott, S. (1990). Statistics for health professionals. Philadelphia: Saunders.

Simpson, R. (1991). Nursing and business: The new frontier. Journal of Continuing Education in Nursing, 22(5), 203-204.

Styles, M.M. (1993). Macrotrends in nursing practice: What's in the pipeline. Journal of Continuing Education in Nursing, 24(1), 7-11.

Taleja, T. (1987). Curious customs: The stories behind 296 popular American rituals. New York: Stonehenge Press/Harmony.

Westman, N., Eger, P. Combro, M., & Belar, E. (1993). Shared resources: Joint hospital sponsorship of continuing education. Journal of Health care Education and Training, 7(2), 6-7.

White, J. (1993, March). Cutting through the confusion of managed competition. Health Progress, pp. 10-13.

Wing, K., Whitehead, P., & Maran, R. (1999). Internet and world wide web simplified (3rd ed). Foster City, CA: IDG Books.

Winter, K. (1991). Educating nurses in political process: A growing need. Journal of Continuing Education in Nursing, 22(4), 143.

GLOSSARY

35 mm Slide: transparent, instructional visual produced on a 35 mm format camera.

Affective: states of feeling and/or valuing.

Bicultural Training: a program initiated near the end of orientation to assist the new graduate in handling the reality shock thought to be experienced by the graduate nurse.

Buddy: a seasoned, competent nurse assigned the responsibility of orienting a new staff member to the unit.

Checklist: a list of skills or content information provided to individuals to determine learning needs through the process of self-appraisal.

Cognitive: intellectual ability.

Competency: ability to perform required skills in safe and proficient manner.

Competency-based Orientation: a method of orientation that focuses on the ability of the orientee to achieve expected performance outcomes.

Conference: see Program.

Content Evaluation: Evaluation of cognitive, psychomotor and/or affective learning that has occurred.

Continuing Education: "planned learning experiences beyond a basic nursing educational program. These experiences are designed to promote the development of knowledge, skills, and attitudes for the enhancement of nursing practice, thus improving health care to the public" (ANA, 1984, p. 15).

Core Educational Program: sequenced educational experiences for professional development of a target population.

Course: see Program.

Course Handouts: printed materials distributed before, during, or after an educational event.

Delphi Technique: an assessment strategy that uses a series of questionnaires to achieve consensus and prioritization of learning needs.

Dry Marker Boards: white, smooth-surfaced writing boards that utilize specialized dry markers and are used in the fashion of a chalkboard. Also called dry erase board.

Educational Event: an in-service or continuing education offering or program.

Felt Need: a perceived need regarded as necessary by the involved individual.

Flyer: advertising circular intended for posting and distribution.

Focused Group Discussion: a meeting designed to provide for collective exchange of ideas among participants and an opportunity to validate and record group data in a relatively short period of time.

Impact Evaluation: the final level of education programs, explores the operational result of educational programming on the institution, such as increased quality of care and/or reduction in cost.

Independent Study Offering: "a self-paced learning activity developed by an organization for use by an individual learner" (American Nurses Credentialing Center, 1991, p. 59).

In-service Education: "learning experiences provided in the work setting for the purpose of assisting staff in performing their assigned functions in that particular agency" (ANA, 1992, p. 5).

Instructional Materials: adjunctive audio, visual, or printed materials designed to support teaching and facilitate learning.

Instructional Media: formats utilized to disseminate ideas in the arena of education.

Interactive Instructional Materials: computer-generated video or computer educational activities or programs designed to elicit input from the learner and provide a response to the input.

Internship: highly structured transition program designed primarily for new graduates. Uses a combination of classroom and clinical instruction over an extended period of time.

Interview: a meeting, scheduled or impromptu, conducted for the purpose of gathering information.

Learning Objective: see Objective.

Liquid Crystal Display (LCD) Panel: piece of instructional equipment that interfaces an overhead projector to a computer for the purpose of projecting computer-generated presentations onto a projection screen.

Needs Assessment: the investigation of learning needs for a defined population of individuals using any number of strategies designed for obtaining information.

Nominal Group Technique: a structured meeting that "allows individual judgments to be effectively pooled and used in situations in which uncertainty or disagreement exists about the nature of the problem and possible solutions" (Moore, 1987, p. 24).

Normative Need: the deficit that exists between a desirable standard and the standard that actually exists.

Objective: defined expectations (outcomes) of an educational experience that delineate the expected achievement level, direct learning behaviors, and provide evaluation guidelines for the educational experience.

Offering: "single educational activity that may be presented once or repeated" (American Nurses Credentialing Center, 1991, p. 49).

Outcomes Evaluation: measures a change in behavior that has occurred and persisted after the learning experience.

Overhead Projector: instructional equipment designed to project the image from an 8½ × 11-inch transparency onto a projection screen.

Preceptor: staff nurse assigned the responsibility of orienting the new staff member who has attended a educational program that focuses on adult learning principles.

Presentation: computer-generated series of visuals.

Process Evaluation: addresses the satisfaction of the participants with the structure and coordination of the course, the facilities, and the relevancy of the content and objectives to their personal goals.

Program (conference/course): "a series of offerings that have a common theme and common overall goals. Examples of a 'program' might be a course (critical care) or a conference with multiple educational sessions" (American Nurses Credentialing Center, 1991, p. 53).

Psychomotor: manipulative and motor skills.

Questionnaire: survey of questions used to collect data from large groups in a relatively short period of time.

Real Education Need: a deficiency related to understanding, skills, or attitudes that can be improved by a learning experience to obtain a better condition or outcome.

Reality Shock: the conflict that occurs when the professional ideals stressed in school confront the bureaucratic principles that operate in the hospital. This conflict experienced by the new graduate may result in feeling of moral outrage and rejection.

Real Need: a deficiency that exists but may or may not be recognized by the individual who has the need.

Reliability: consistency with which a test measures what it was designed to measure.

Staff Development: "a process consisting of orientation, in-service education, and continuing education for the purpose of promoting the development of personnel within any employee setting, consistent with the goals and responsibilities of the employer" (ANA, 1990, p. 3).

Syllabus: summary of an educational event.

Target Audience: those who will benefit from an educational opportunity.

Transparency: an 8½ × 11-inch acetate sheet used as the base for design projection onto projection screen with the use of an overhead projector.

Validity: extent to which a test measures what it was intended to measure.